Critical Essays on Samuel Beckett

Critical Essays on Samuel Beckett

Patrick A. McCarthy

G. K. Hall & Co. • Boston, Massachusetts

Library of Congress Cataloging-in-Publication Data
Critical essays on Samuel Beckett.

(Critical essays on modern British literature—
Includes index.
1. Beckett, Samuel, 1906– —Criticism and interpretation. I. McCarthy, Patrick, A., 1945–
II. Series.
PR6003.E282Z622 1986 848'.91409 86-11943

ISBN 0-8161-8760-6 (alk. paper)

This publication is printed on permanent/durable acid-free paper
MANUFACTURED IN THE UNITED STATES OF AMERICA

CRITICAL ESSAYS ON MODERN BRITISH LITERATURE

In his introduction Patrick McCarthy discusses the problems of "translating" or interpreting Beckett's work, which is the natural outcome of the "strangeness" of his text, compounded by the problem of literally translating his English texts into the French language and vice versa. This has led to a tendency to look for or to invent a "system" to make the text fit a critical analysis, which as often as not is the creative inspiration of the critic rather than Beckett himself.

In chronological order McCarthy summarizes and evaluates the major Beckett criticism, beginning with Hugh Kenner's seminal book, which established Beckett in the critical canon, through the most recent critical books. McCarthy's collection includes criticism on each major aspect of Beckett's work: the early fiction, the later prose, and the dramas, with a special section of five essays on his trilogy of novels. Collected for a general audience, as well as for scholars, all essays focus on critical interpretation of Beckett's works rather than on such scholarly issues as biography, etc. The volume, which contains three original contributions and two others previously not available in English, is balanced and comprehensive, a genuine contribution to Beckett criticism.

Zack Bowen, General Editor

University of Delaware

CONTENTS

INTRODUCTION

"The danger," according to the twenty-three-year-old Samuel Beckett, "is in the neatness of identifications."[1] The year was 1929, and Beckett was writing about James Joyce's *Work in Progress*, fragments of what was eventually to become *Finnegans Wake*; yet the statement has often, and accurately, been associated with Beckett's own work, which seems both to attract and to resist overly neat identifications. Despite Beckett's explicit rejection of two sources of critical error—"that the writer is necessarily presenting some experience which he has had, and that he necessarily writes in order to affirm some general truth"[2]—readers often find that the very indeterminacy of the text requires the imposition of a biographical or philosophical meaning on the work. It is difficult indeed to adopt the admirable attitude of Jacques Moran who, meditating on the beautiful but mysterious pattern of the dance of his bees, thinks, "I was more than ever stupefied by the complexity of this innumerable dance, involving doubtless other determinants of which I had not the slightest idea. And I said, with rapture, Here is something I can study all my life, and never understand."[3]

Denis Donoghue's useful distinction between the richness of "mystery" and the simpler and less satisfying nature of a "problem"[4] might well be invoked here. Unlike "problems," which may be rationalized (reduced) into simpler terms with no great loss, a mystery is essentially irreducible and therefore inexhaustible: problems can be paraphrased, mysteries can only be experienced. In part, this mystery in Beckett's works derives from what H. Porter Abbott calls their "radical displacement" of reality, their reflexive cancellation of the simple mimetic displacement of recognizable terms. Abbott argues that while "*Gulliver's Travels* is founded in a confidence of mimesis, its displacement is traditional, and most of its detail functions as dystopic allegory," the typical Beckett work gives us, "in place of translatable material like rope-dancing and the School of Political Projectors . . . detail that refuses to become familiar: 'To be on the right was more than he could bear'; 'One pair of gloves was enough. The free or outer hands hung bare.' These are details that refuse to be translated; they are assertions of strangeness."[5] Although Abbott intends "translated" in the sense of "interpreted," his point might also be illustrated by reference to

Beckett's own process of translating his works from one of his languages to another: the "translation" inevitably introduces not only fresh nuances but actual details into the work. Beckett's inability or unwillingness to produce a faithful translation of his work is partly attributable to the artist's urge to continue the creative process into the translation, but it is also an admission that works so heavily dependent upon the medium of a particular language tend to resist translation much as they resist straightforward interpretation.

The dangers of interpretive "translation," with its overly neat identifications, are often encountered in essays that find a central religious or philosophical meaning in, say, *Waiting for Godot*. A more plausible (but equally dangerous) form of critical reductiveness may be found in the temptation to press the life into service as a gloss on the works. The difficulty of the works leads to the tendency to look for a "system" into which all the details may be fitted, and the system all too often controls the direction of the analysis. The traps that lie in wait for even a very good critic may be illustrated by the following analysis of the two numbers in the threne that Watt hears as he goes toward Mr. Knott's house:

> Human labor is circular and futile, a closed system that encloses nothing but meaninglessness. The porter in the train station spends his time wheeling milk cans back and forth, from one group to another. Watt's experience of life is similar to the porter's. Approaching Knott's house, he hears a threne or mixed choir. The number 52.28571428 is a surd representing the number of weeks in a year; the surd in the second verse, 51.1428571, is more puzzling and seems to be the result of merely dividing 360 by 7, as if to show the infinite nature of a circle (= 360 degrees). As surds, or irrational numbers that repeat their decimals *ad infinitum*, both figures represent an endless, circular continuity.[6]

There are several problems with this analysis, among them the fact that 360 / 7 is not an irrational number—and therefore not a surd—since it is expressed as a ratio of integers. Furthermore, 52.28571428 . . . is 366 / 7, or the number of weeks in a *leap* year, while 51.1428571 . . . is actually 358 / 7 rather than 360 / 7. (This number, it develops, is a printer's error in the Grove Press text of *Watt:* as Rubin Rabinovitz has noted, the number Beckett wrote was 52.1428571 . . . , or 365 / 7, the number of weeks in a non-leap year.[7]) There is in this passage nothing to suggest the number of degrees in a circle—for that matter, there is no reason why a circle should be divided into seven parts—but a predisposition to find references to circles leads here to a line of interpretation that is as flawed as the critic's arithmetic.

Despite the temptation to force interpretations on the texts, criticism of Samuel Beckett has been, for the most part, intelligent and illuminating. Much of the credit goes to the earliest serious studies of Beckett's mature work, which set high standards—and provided good models—for later critics. Beckett's apprentice work of the 1930s, especially *Murphy*, received some critical attention shortly after publication but was unable to sustain the interest of critics or general readers during the war years. In the ten years between 1942 and 1952, Beckett wrote much of the work on which his reputation now rests: *Watt*, the trilogy, and *En attendant Godot*, as well as *Mercier et Camier*, *Premier amour*, and the various pieces that constitute *Nouvelles et textes pour rien*. By the middle and late 1950s critics were writing substantial essays about *Godot* and the trilogy, and the publication in 1961 of Hugh Kenner's *Samuel Beckett: A Critical Study* confirmed Beckett's importance.

Appearing just ten years after the first volumes of the trilogy and a mere four years after the first French publication of *Fin de partie*, Kenner's study was the first book in English devoted entirely to Beckett's work; two and a half decades later, it is still widely acknowledged as the best introduction to the world of Samuel Beckett. Originally written in five chapters (the new edition of 1968 includes an appendix entitled "Progress Report, 1962–1965," with brief commentaries on later works), Kenner's book concerns itself with such characteristic Beckettian themes as the dilemma of artistic expression (useless but unavoidable), the numerical dimensions of rationality, the Cartesian separation of body and mind, and the limited possibilities of life; the last of these themes is also explored in greater detail in Kenner's subsequent study *The Stoic Comedians: Flaubert, Joyce and Beckett* (1962). Kenner's other book devoted entirely to Beckett, *A Reader's Guide to Samuel Beckett* (1973), is aimed at beginners, but it would be a rare scholar who could not derive pleasure or knowledge from Kenner's lucid and witty chapters on individual works.

Among the more notable volumes that appeared in the next four years were Ruby Cohn's *Samuel Beckett: The Comic Gamut* (1962), Frederick J. Hoffman's *Samuel Beckett: The Language of Self* (1962), Richard Coe's brief *Samuel Beckett* (1964), John Fletcher's *The Novels of Samuel Beckett* (1964), and Raymond Federman's *Journey to Chaos: Samuel Beckett's Early Fiction* (1965). All subsequent studies of Beckett are in some sense indebted to these pioneering works. Cohn is concerned first and foremost with comic elements in Beckett's work—everything from slapstick effects to punning and satire. Along the way, she provides her readers with detailed outlines and analyses of the works through *Happy Days* as well as a separate chapter—one of her best—on Beckett as "self-translator." In contrast to Cohn's close readings we have Hoffman's attempt to place Beckett within the literary and intellectual traditions of the past century, particularly the tradition of alienation and pessimism that runs from Dostoevsky's *Notes from Underground*, through Kafka's stories, and up to the plays of Eugene Ionesco. Some of Hoffman's judgments now seem odd (as when he says that "Proust offered a useful point of departure, though Beckett was not significantly influenced by him"), but in general this study remains an important contribution to Beckett scholarship.

Coe's *Samuel Beckett* is concerned largely with the treatment of rationality and being in the novels, although a concluding chapter demonstrates how these themes are developed in the dramatic works. Despite limitations of space, Coe's brief book (118 pages including bibliography) is an intelligent and useful guide to Beckett's "art of failure"; among its many virtues is its emphasis on Beckett's own statements about artistic expression and awareness, both in his *Proust* and in the "Three Dialogues." John Fletcher's longer and far more detailed *The Novels of Samuel Beckett* examines the fiction (the novels plus *More Pricks Than Kicks*, the *Nouvelles*, and the *Textes pour rien*) from a number of angles. Fletcher also provided Beckett's readers with summaries and analyses of the then-unpublished *Mercier et Camier* and the still-unpublished *Dream of Fair to Middling Women*; the first of these abandoned works had been subjected only to cursory analysis by previous critics while the second was generally unknown prior to Fletcher's book. Federman's *Journey to Chaos* is even more restricted in its range (it deals only with the fiction written before the trilogy: the English works, *Mercier et Camier*, and the *Nouvelles*), but in tracing the elements of alienation and absurdity in Beckett's work—as well as Beckett's rejection of fictional conventions—Federman's study describes a "paradoxical creative system" that remains important in the development of the later works.

Among the other books on Beckett that appeared in the 1960s, three volumes in English deserve special mention: *Samuel Beckett's Art* by John Fletcher (1967), Ihab Hassan's *The Literature of Silence: Henry Miller and Samuel Beckett* (1967), and Michael Robinson's *The Long Sonata of the Dead: A Study of Samuel Beckett* (1969). While Fletcher's earlier book contained extended analyses and explications of individual novels, the later book focuses on aspects of artistic form in the works. The chapter on "The Art of the Dramatist," for example, begins with a discussion of Beckett's relationship to Artaud and the "new theatre" and continues with sections on the elements of the drama: setting, characterization, gesture and movement, language, and the like. The book as a whole is clear and well balanced, suggestive without being dogmatic; among the parts that seem particularly important are the chapter on Beckett's French style and the succinct commentaries on Beckett's use of Dante and his relationship to Descartes and Geulincx. Hassan's study deals separately with Miller and Beckett as apocalyptic writers, simultaneously "intimates of silence" and "obsessive babblers" whose works illustrate "the new hollow speech" of anti-literature. This brilliant and radically original book anticipates the line of argument in Hassan's *The Dismemberment of Orpheus* (1971), which traces a tradition of alienation and fragmentation from the Marquis de Sade to Beckett. Robinson's *Long Sonata*, on the other hand, belongs to the more conservative school of Beckett criticism; it is essentially an extended reader's guide, a lucid and persuasive commentary on the themes of the works.

Throughout the 1960s, French criticism of Beckett lagged far behind criticism written in English: all too often, French critics seemed unable to escape from the straitjackets of the series for which their books were written, and the commentaries are generally rather elementary. Examples include André Marissel's *Samuel Beckett* (1963), Pierre Mélèse's *Beckett* (1966), and Ludovic Janvier's *Beckett par lui-même* (1969). That the trouble is at least partly due to the series formats of these books is suggested by the fact that Janvier's earlier study, *Pour Samuel Beckett* (1966), is an astute assessment of the works from a highly individualistic point of view. The other major French volume of the decade was Olga Bernal's *Langage et fiction dans le roman de Beckett* (1969), a philosophically sophisticated commentary on style in Beckett's fiction, especially in the trilogy. The 1970s saw some improvement in this situation, although the more interesting criticism in French often originated outside of France: the Canadian arts council supported work on Fernande Saint-Martin's *Samuel Beckett et l'univers de la fiction* (1976) and Brian T. Fitch's *Dimensions, structures et textualité dans la trilogie romanesque de Beckett* (1977), while Aldo Tagliaferri's *Beckett et la surdétermination littéraire* (1977) is a translation of an Italian study published a decade earlier.

1970 saw the publication of several new books, three of which deserve special mention: *Samuel Beckett Now*, edited by Melvin J. Friedman—possibly the best of the collections of essays "by divers hands"; *Samuel Beckett: His Works and His Critics* by Raymond Federman and John Fletcher—an indispensable, although immediately outdated, bibliographic study; and *Samuel Beckett: Poet and Critic* by Lawrence E. Harvey. Harvey's book, one of the most substantial yet produced, centers on what to many people seems an insignificant aspect of Beckett's career, his poetry and criticism (although Harvey adopts a broad enough definition of "poet and critic" to be able to include an extended discussion of *Watt*), but it performs the essential service of demonstrating beyond a doubt that the poetry and criticism, although relatively unimportant for their own sakes, provide us with significant insights into the fiction and drama.

Despite the undoubted importance of the Federman-Fletcher bibliography and the seminal volume by Lawrence Harvey, the early 1970s marked a decline in the overall quality of Beckett scholarship; as Melvin Friedman noted in a thoughtful and well-balanced 1973 review of current scholarship, "some of the recent books prove disappointing when measured against those splendid studies by Hugh Kenner, Frederick J. Hoffman, Ruby Cohn, Raymond Federman, and John Fletcher."[8] Friedman cited exceptions, including David H. Hesla's *The Shape of Chaos: An Interpretation of the Art of Samuel Beckett* (1971), Sighle Kennedy's *Murphy's Bed: A Study of Real Sources and Surreal Associations in Samuel Beckett's First Novel* (1971), John Fletcher and John Spurling's *Beckett: A Study of His Plays* (1972), and H. Porter Abbott's *The Fiction of Samuel Beckett: Form and Effect* (1973). While agreeing with Friedman's positive response to these books, I would suggest that the studies by Hesla and Abbott are closer than the others to the standards set by the best scholars of the 1960s. Had Friedman written only a few months later, he would have had another distinguished volume to add to his list: Ruby Cohn's *Back to Beckett* (1973) which, if anything, is superior to her fine pioneering volume in its steady attention to the works and their effect on readers and audiences. Cohn's books—most recently her *Just Play: Beckett's Theater* (1980), a study of theatrical effects in the drama—are among the finest yet written on Samuel Beckett; as in the best of Beckett criticism, they open up possible avenues of response to the works without being overly schematic in their methodology.

Friedman's feeling that the critics of the 1970s were falling short of the standards set in the 1960s was certainly borne out by many of the studies that appeared in the next few years. Despite the appearance of a few very distinguished works focusing on specialized areas of interest—notably Clas Zilliacus's *Beckett and Broadcasting* (1976), S. E. Gontarski's *Beckett's Happy Days: A Manuscript Study* (1977), and James Knowlson and John Pilling's *Frescoes of the Skull: The Later Prose and Drama of Samuel Beckett* (1979)—the period 1974–79 saw the appearance of only one general study of undoubted importance: John Pilling's *Samuel Beckett* (1976). Pilling is at times overly eager to pass judgment on Beckett's critics and works alike: his preface announces that his first reason for writing the book was "that I was dissatisfied with all the other available accounts, which, however helpful they were in one area, seemed misleading, or insensitive, in others," and his assessment of *Film* is that it "is one of [Beckett's] least successful works, marred by technical ineptitude as much as deliberate technical limitation, and needlessly obscure for those spectators who have not had the benefit of consulting the shooting-script beforehand."[9] Yet even when Pilling's judgments seem wrong—as this evaluation of *Film* seems to me—they are at least refreshingly honest, and throughout the book there are numerous original insights into the works.

While Pilling's book combines the critic's personal response with a balanced and disinterested analysis and evaluation of the works, Vivian Mercier's idiosyncratic *Beckett / Beckett* (1977) all too often seems to be about Mercier / Mercier. Actually, though, in one sense the point of the title is well taken; Beckett's art is often contradictory or paradoxical, and the works often seem to operate out of a fundamental dialectic such as those suggested by Mercier's chapter titles: "Thesis / Antithesis," "Ireland / The World," "Gentleman / Tramp," "Classicism / Absurdism," "Painting / Music," "Eye / Ear," "Artist / Philosopher," and "Woman / Man." The briefest of these chapters, "Classicism / Absurdism," seems to me also the best, which is perhaps a key to the book's real weakness: any set of critical categories eventually comes into conflict with Beckett's work itself, and the elaboration of virtually any argument runs the risk of imposing a critical straitjacket on the works.

Even more serious flaws mar two other books of the late 1970s, Deirdre Bair's *Samuel Beckett: A Biography* (1978) and Barbara Reich Gluck's *Beckett and Joyce: Friendship and Fiction* (1979). Major problems with Bair's biography were pointed out in reviews by such eminent scholars as Richard Ellmann (*New York Review of Books*, 15 June 1978), Hugh Kenner (*Saturday Review*, August 1978), Martin Esslin (*Encounter*, March 1979), and John Calder (*Journal of Beckett Studies*, Spring 1979); for the most part, these critics complained about errors and inconsistencies in the book and about what Calder considers "the embarrassingly bad taste in the wealth of intimate private detail revealed" by the biography. A further problem might be suggested by Bair's prefatory remark that she wrote the book because she "was dissatisfied with existing studies of his writings" and believed that a biography would answer "the need for a factual foundation for all subsequent critical exegesis."[10] The implication seems to be that Beckett's works are largely autobiographical and that future studies of the fiction and drama will focus on the way Beckett translates his life into his works; but while it is interesting to know, for example, that a passage in "From an Abandoned Work" refers to a walk that Beckett took with his father in 1933,[11] the information has had little bearing on my own reading of the story.

Gluck's book also deals to some extent with the relationship between Beckett's life and works, but the focus is narrower and the results generally more satisfactory. What is perhaps disappointing about Gluck's book is that it does not really do enough with its subject. In a study of the Joyce-Beckett nexus we might at least have expected a reasonably thorough list of recognizable Joycean echoes or allusions in Beckett's works, but my own spot check reveals five probable references to *A Portrait of the Artist* that are nowhere mentioned in Gluck's book: (1) the quotation from Shelley's "To the Moon," first cited in *Proust* and repeated in *Waiting for Godot*, probably occupies such a prominent place in Beckett's work because the same quotation appears in the *Portrait*;[12] (2) the description of Murphy's first encounter with Celia—"A little short of half way, grateful for the breather, he arrested the movement and gazed at Celia. For perhaps two minutes she suffered this gladly . . ."—parodies Joyce's bird-girl sequence: "when she felt his presence and the worship of his eyes her eyes turned to him in quiet sufferance of his gaze, without shame or wantonness. Long, long she suffered his gaze . . .";[13] (3) for the most part, Moran's method of running "with my head flung back, my teeth clenched, my elbows bent to the full and my knees nearly hitting me in the face" reminds us of Stephen's running "in the style Mike Flynn favoured, his head high lifted, his knees well lifted and his hands held straight down by his sides";[14] (4) in *How It Is*, the narrator's boast, "I'll quicken [Pim] you wait and see how I can efface myself behind my creature when the fit takes now my nails," recalls Stephen's description of the dramatic mode of art in which "The artist, like the God of the creation, remains within or behind or beyond or above his handiwork, invisible, refined out of existence, indifferent, paring his fingernails";[15] and (5) "To relieve oneself in bed is enjoyable at the time, but soon a source of discomfort," an observation on life taken from *First Love*, is transparently based on Stephen's infantile reflection that "When you wet the bed first it is warm then it gets cold."[16] Although omissions such as these indicate that work on the Joyce-Beckett relationship is far from over, it must be added that Gluck has certainly advanced our understanding of that relationship.

Among the books on Beckett published in the early 1980s, three stand out: Ruby Cohn's *Just Play*, to which I have already referred; Eric P. Levy's *Beckett and the Voice of Species* (1980), and J. E. Dearlove's *Accommodating the Chaos: Samuel Beckett's Nonrelational Art* (1982). Cohn's work is, as usual, fresh and stimulating; here she focuses on the performance of Beckett's plays, a subject that is also treated in Sidney Homan's *Beckett's Theaters: Interpretations for Performance* (1984). Levy's book, on the other hand, concerns itself solely with the fiction and focuses on the nature of the Beckettian narrator from *More Pricks Than Kicks* through *Fizzles*. The argument here is cogent and persuasive as Levy demonstrates both the continuity and the evolution of the narrative voice in the fiction. Dearlove, meanwhile, follows in the tradition of Kenner, Coe, Janvier, and Hesla in dealing with the relationship between Beckett's ideas and the artistic development of his work. Her exposition of the "nonrelational" quality of Beckett's art concentrates on the fiction, where the breakup of relationship is most apparent. Although no single vantage point is sufficient for the explication of Beckett's themes, Dearlove's study goes a long way toward showing the inadequacy of "relational" theories of Beckett's art.

Two very recent volumes deserve mention here. Lance St. John Butler's *Samuel Beckett and the Meaning of Being: A Study in Ontological Parable* (1984) is a study of the connection between Beckett's ideas and those of Heidegger, Sartre, and Hegel. Butler occasionally pushes the parallels to the point of critical reductiveness, but he nonetheless provides a solid ontological foundation for future studies. Rubin Rabinovitz's *The Development of Samuel Beckett's Fiction* (1984) is in large part composed of revisions of essays that appeared over the previous decade, and his book demonstrates both the strengths and the weaknesses that one would expect of a book of the sort: the ideas are solid, having been tested over a substantial period of time before being incorporated into the book, but the emphasis on "development" promised by the title is largely lost as Rabinovitz focuses, instead, on loosely related aspects of the fiction through *Watt*. Even so, the book is valuable not only for numerous critical insights but also for two thorough appendices that list repeated elements in *Murphy*.

In compiling this collection of essays on Samuel Beckett, I have of course attempted to choose work of particularly high quality; in addition,

I have tried to include criticism of each major aspect of Beckett's work, while the separate section on the trilogy indicates the regard in which I hold those novels. I have also followed several other guidelines: all of the reprinted selections must be reasonably brief and yet self-contained, whether or not they were originally written as separate articles; the selections should be of interest to Beckett scholars and general readers alike (this eliminates many very specialized articles, no matter how good); and the focus should be on interpretation of the works, not on Beckett's life, the problems in staging his plays, etc. The ready availability of a Critical Heritage volume on Beckett,[17] with numerous reviews of the works, has allowed me to eliminate reviews and concentrate on more substantial critical essays. In general, I have preferred essays that have not appeared in other collections, although in some cases I have made exceptions (most notably for Hugh Kenner's often-reprinted but indispensable "The Cartesian Centaur"). Finally, I have tried to include work by the Beckett scholars whom I most admire, although in some cases, for one reason or another, I have failed in that attempt; I particularly regret my inability to include any examples of the work of H. Porter Abbott, Raymond Federman, or John Fletcher.

The contributions by Susan Brienza, Kay Gilliland Stevenson, and Robert Zaller are published here for the first time. Two other contributions, by Ludovic Janvier and John Pilling, have not previously been available in English. The Janvier essay in particular illustrates the need for English translations of the best French books on Samuel Beckett.

PATRICK A. MCCARTHY

University of Miami

Notes

1. "Dante . . . Bruno . Vico . . Joyce," in Samuel Beckett and others, *Our Exagmination Round His Factification for Incamination of Work in Progress* (1929; New York: New Directions, 1972), p. 5.

2. Hugh Kenner, *Samuel Beckett: A Critical Study*, new ed. (Berkeley: University of California Press, 1968), p. 10.

3. Samuel Beckett, *Molloy*, in *Three Novels* (New York: Grove Press, Evergreen Black Cat Edition, 1965), p. 169.

4. Denis Donoghue, *The Arts Without Mystery* (Boston: Little, Brown, 1983).

5. H. Porter Abbott, "A Poetics of Radical Displacement: Samuel Beckett Coming up to Seventy," *Texas Studies in Literature and Language* 17 (Spring 1975):231.

6. Barbara Reich Gluck, *Beckett and Joyce: Friendship and Fiction* (Lewisburg: Bucknell University Press, 1979), pp. 91–92.

7. Rubin Rabinovitz, *The Development of Samuel Beckett's Fiction* (Urbana: University of Illinois Press, 1984), p. 170 n. 2.

8. Melvin J. Friedman, "Samuel Beckett and His Critics Enter the 1970s," *Studies in the Novel* 5 (Fall 1973):383.

9. John Pilling, *Samuel Beckett* (London: Routledge & Kegan Paul, 1976), pp. ix, 106.

10. Deirdre Bair, *Samuel Beckett: A Biography* (New York: Harcourt Brace Jovanovich, 1978), p. xii.

11. "One day I told [my father] about Milton's cosmology, away up in the mountains we were, resting against a huge rock looking out to sea, that impressed him greatly." *First Love and Other Shorts* (New York: Grove Press, 1974), p. 42; cf. Bair, p. 162.

12. *Proust* (New York: Grove Press, 1970), p. 50; *Waiting for Godot* (New York: Grove Press, 1954), p. 34a; *A Portrait of the Artist as a Young Man*, ed. Chester G. Anderson (New York: Viking Critical Library, 1968), p. 96.

13. *Murphy* (New York: Grove Press, 1957), p. 14; *Portrait*, p. 171.

14. *Three Novels*, p. 144; *Portrait*, p. 61.

15. *How It Is* (New York: Grove Press, 1964), p. 52; *Portrait*, p. 215.

16. *First Love and Other Shorts*, p. 30; *Portrait*, p. 7.

17. *Samuel Beckett: The Critical Heritage*, ed. Lawrence Graver and Raymond Federman (London: Routledge & Kegan Paul, 1979). As a Miamian, I cannot pass up the chance to correct one error in the introduction to this volume: the Coconut Grove Playhouse, where *Godot* had its American premiere, is located in Miami, not (as Graver and Federman say on p. 10) in Miami Beach.

The Early Fiction

The Novels of Samuel Beckett: An Amalgam of Joyce and Proust

Melvin J. Friedman*

Samuel Beckett has said little directly about his own work. He has modestly avoided taking a literary stand or connecting himself with any "school" or movement. But this has not prevented his commentators from associating his plays with those of Adamov and Ionesco, and his novels with those of Kafka, Camus, and Genet. Denied the assent of Beckett, who has so far remained noncommittal concerning his literary forebears, most of these judgments must be relegated to the category of impressionistic criticism.

On two occasions, however, Beckett has made known his opinions of other writers. In 1929 he contributed a twenty-page essay to a volume published in James Joyce's honor, *Our Exagmination round his Factification for Incamination of Work in Progress.* Two years later he published a monograph on Marcel Proust.

The Joyce essay, bearing the tangential yet suggestive title "Dante . . . Bruno . Vico . . Joyce," is clearly the work of a young man. It is original and intuitive but at the same time digressive and facile. Comparison with Joyce's early critical article on Ibsen immediately comes to mind. Beckett shows the same blind dedication to Joyce which Joyce showed to Ibsen twenty-nine years earlier.[1] The youthful pretentiousness of Beckett's title is carried over into the essay: "And now here am I, with my handful of abstractions, among which notably: a mountain, the coincidence of contraries, the inevitability of cyclic evolution, a system of Poetics, and the prospect of self-extension in the world of Mr. Joyce's *'Work in Progress'* " [*Our Exagmination*, Paris, 1929, p. 3]. Indeed the task of reconciling Joyce with the three distinguished Italians with whom Beckett connects him in his title is of herculean proportions. Beckett gets swallowed up in the enthusiasm of his own words and pronouncements. He becomes Joyce's self-appointed champion and cries out against the philistines who have declared the Irish writer too oblique: "On turning to the *'Work in Progress'* we find that the mirror is not so convex. Here is direct expression—pages

*Reprinted from *Comparative Literature* 12 (Winter 1960) by permission of the journal.

and pages of it. And if you don't understand it, Ladies and Gentlemen, it is because you are too decadent to receive it" [p. 13].

Then Beckett breaks into a series of generalizations which set the tone for the remainder of the essay. Such catch phrases as "Here form *is* content, content *is* form" (p. 14), "His writing is not *about* something; *it is that something itself*" (p. 14), "Mr. Joyce has desophisticated language" (p. 15), "a quintessential extraction of language and painting and gesture" (p. 15), set the characteristic pace of the disciple speaking in abstract superlatives about his master.

Most of these comments have a surface brilliance but in the end are probably no more than a clever word game, and cannot really help us find the seeds of Beckett's novels in his early literary criticism. However, he does let slip one crucial observation: "There is one point to make clear: the Beauty of '*Work in Progress*' is not presented in space alone, since its adequate apprehension depends as much on its visibility as on its audibility. There is a temporal as well as a spatial unity to be apprehended" [p. 15]. The space-time, audio-visual connections which are essential to Joyce's work are also present in the novels of his young enthusiast, as will be seen.

Beckett maintained his interest in Joyce's work. He was very helpful with the French translation of the Anna Livia Plurabelle section of *Work in Progress*, published in 1931 in the *Nouvelle Revue Française*. These were the years when Beckett served as "lecteur d'Anglais" at the École Normale Supérieure. He was already seriously considering the step of expatriation which Joyce had taken; he was on the verge of rejecting his native Ireland and seeking permanent refuge in Paris—which he did finally in 1937.

The connection with Joyce takes on a more personal aspect at this time. Peggy Guggenheim, Richard Ellmann, and others report how Beckett served as Joyce's amanuensis. The memoirs of Peggy Guggenheim, *Out of This Century*, are especially revealing. The frequently married heiress had a strong personal attachment for Beckett, which often exceeded the bounds of propriety, and she was naturally anxious to hold his interest. She tells us that in a strange, almost unnatural, way her chief rival for his attentions was James Joyce. (There is certainly no hint of homosexuality, merely a dispossessed son searching for a father, the Stephen Dedalus-Leopold Bloom situation all over again.)[2] It is interesting to have this report, which reaffirms Beckett's early literary gestures in Joyce's behalf. The relationship almost had to be one-sided; the author of a few scattered poems and a volume of short stories[3] was clearly overshadowed by the author of *Ulysses* and of what was to become two years later *Finnegans Wake*.

His hero worship of Joyce the man as well as of Joyce the writer is a very different thing from Beckett's admiration of Proust. There is no puppy-dog servility in the monograph on Proust which appeared in 1931.

Beckett now wrote with genuine detachment, since he had no personal ties with the French writer, who had died nine years earlier.

Still, this step in the Gallicizing of Beckett takes a curious twist—rather like entering through a forbidden back staircase, an approach which has always tempted him. Proust is hardly the writer to turn to if one is looking for a typically French model. His style has been traditionally considered un-French; when *A la recherche du temps perdu* was turned into English by C. K. Scott Moncrieff, the result was so genuine that several critics suggested that Proust had missed his literary vocation by writing in French.

There is certainly more critical maturity in *Proust* than in "Dante . . . Bruno . Vico . . Joyce." Some of the most interesting passages have to do with style. Beckett insists that "for Proust, as for the painter, style is more a question of vision than of technique."[4] One is reminded of the extraordinary powers which Proust attributes to the visual arts—the magical properties which Marcel finds in Elstir's art and the strange fascination which draws Bergotte to his beloved Vermeer painting just before his death. Beckett saw that Proust's style has a more than ordinary concentration of metaphor, a less than ordinary concern with the well-turned phrase or the technically perfect sentence: "The Proustian world is expressed metaphorically by the artisan because it is apprehended metaphorically by the artist: the indirect and comparative expression of indirect and comparative perception. The rhetorical equivalent of the Proustian real is the chain-figure of the metaphor" [*Proust*, pp. 67–68]. He goes on to describe the type of image which predominates in Proust and makes the interesting, if not startling, observation: "It is significant that the majority of his images are botanical. He assimilates the human to the vegetal. He is conscious of humanity as flora, never as fauna. (There are no black cats and faithful hounds in Proust)" [p. 68]. With the long tradition in French literature, especially in poetry, which favors animals—Baudelaire's and Verlaine's cat fixation—this is a departure worth noting.

In one way or another Beckett manages to connect everything in Proust's work with the psycho-literary device of involuntary memory: "Involuntary memory is explosive, 'an immediate, total and delicious deflagration.' It restores, not merely the past object, but the Lazarus that it charmed or tortured . . . But involuntary memory is an unruly magician and will not be importuned. It chooses its own time and place for the performance of its miracle" [pp. 20–21]. "The chain-figure of the metaphor," the "visionary" aspects of the work, both contribute to these special moments when Proust's characters seem to resist successfully the dulling effects of the exterior world. As several critics have suggested, chance encounters with such diverse and unrelated objects as a madeleine, unevenly spaced flagstones, silverware, and a sonata produce this liberating effect—detachment from time.

But Beckett not only approaches Proust's work through the purely literary and psychological dimensions, but also has something to say about the moral. "Here, as always, Proust is completely detached from all moral considerations. There is no right and wrong in Proust nor in his world" (p. 49). This aspect of Beckett's discussion ends with a general statement which might be applied as readily to Greek and existentialist heroes as to Proust's creatures: "The tragic figure represents the expiation of original sin, of the original and eternal sin of him and all his 'soci malorum,' the sin of having been born" (p. 49).

When we reread the 1929 discussion of Joyce and the 1931 monograph of Proust in the light of the novels Beckett wrote later, we make the important discovery that he was perhaps writing as much about what he himself would become as a novelist as about the Irish or the French novelist. It has become almost a commonplace that the creative writer, writing literary criticism, speaks more of his own work than of that of the author he is studying. Gide made new discoveries about himself when he wrote his monograph on Dostoevsky; Mann fashioned a new Olympian man of himself when he wrote on Goethe. Beckett seems to gain both creative vigor and a literary direction from Joyce and Proust. His novels become a kind of meeting ground for the two most original novelists of the twentieth century.

Beckett's first novel, *Murphy* (1938), is curiously unexperimental when one recalls his literary baptism. It is a third-person narrative, written in English, describing the comic antics of an Irishman in London who finally dies in an insane asylum—where he is not an inmate. Murphy is a kind of Leopold Bloom in reverse—he meets disaster by fleeing from women, and is completely free from the long introspective silences of Joyce's hero. But the Irish wit which is so plentiful in Joyce overflows into Beckett's work. Beckett seems unable to resist the temptation of the comic interlude even when it is quite irrelevant to his novel; he has the Irish gift for delineating character in its most amusing dimensions. Witness this description of a quite secondary character in *Murphy*:

> Cooper experienced none of the famous difficulty in serving two employers. He neither clave nor despised. A lesser man would have sided with one or the other, a bigger blackmailed both. But Cooper was the perfect size for the servant so long as he kept off the bottle and he moved incorruptible between his corruptors with the beautiful indifference of a shuttle, without infamy and without praise. To each he made a full and frank report, ignoring the emendations of the other; and made it first to whichever of the two was more convenient to the point at which dusk surprised him. [*Murphy*, pp. 197–198]

The odyssey motif is revived once again in *Murphy*. Murphy is intent on eluding several former mistresses and confidants and gives them a merry chase. His principal pursuers, Miss Counihan and Celia (mistresses) and Wylie and Neary (dubious confidants), follow the almost clueless path to an insane asylum, only to find a dead Murphy. In a characteristically amusing passage, quite irrelevant to the progress of the "action," Beckett describes the bedroom arrangement of the two ladies on the lower floor, the two men above them: "Miss Counihan would not have minded going up to Wylie if Celia had not minded Neary coming down to her. Nor would Wylie have objected in the least to going down to Celia if Miss Counihan had not objected most strongly to going up to Neary. Nor would Neary have been less than delighted to go down to either, or have either come up to him, if both had not been more than averse to his attentions, whether on the first floor or the second" [p. 255].

This mock-logical arrangement, seemingly exhausting all the possibilities of a given situation, is carried over into *Watt.* This novel, also written in English, seems to be an inexhaustible catalogue of possibilities relevant to a sustained period during which Watt was in the employ of a certain Knott. The first floor-second floor interplay in *Murphy* becomes one of the vital issues of this novel. It is a sign of election in the Knott household for a servant to be shifted from the first to the second floor, but it is also, paradoxically enough, a sign that his services will soon be dispensed with. Watt, like all his predecessors, began on the first floor, was transferred to the second after a year, and was dismissed soon afterwards. And this is all the plot that *Watt* sustains. The novel is marred by such unfortunate word plays as "Not that Watt was ever to have any direct dealing with Mr. Knott, for he was not."[5]

The cataloguing device reaches new levels of absurdity in *Watt.* As Joyce describes everything in Bloom's, Molly's, or Stephen's line of vision, often in overelaborate detail, so Beckett supplies us with an exhaustive list of several generations of a family, with a full analysis of the physical peculiarities of each member, and with a detailed catalogue of word inversions executed by Watt, involving the reversal of letters in the words, of words in the sentences, and of sentences in the paragraphs. Even Leopold Bloom's mind is never subjected to the type of scrutiny which we find in a characteristic passage such as the following:

> And to those who objected that neither Ann's charms, nor her powers of persuasion, could be compared with Bridie's, or with a bottle of stout's, it was replied that if Tom had not done this thing in a fit of depression, or in a fit of exaltation, then he had done it in the interval between a fit of depression and a fit of exaltation, or in the interval between a fit of exaltation and a fit of depression, or in the interval between a fit of exaltation and another fit of exaltation, for with Tom depression and exaltation were not of regular alternance, whatever may have been said to the contrary, but often he emerged from one fit of depression only to be seized soon after by another, and frequently he shook off one fit of exaltation only to fall into the next almost at once, and in these brief intervals Tom would sometimes behave most strangely, almost like a man who did not know what he was doing. [*Watt*, pp. 118–119].

Watt carries the plotless novel to new lengths; unfortunately, it seems to be a stopping place; it indicates no "new directions" in the novel form. Beckett finished the novel in 1944, though it was not published until 1953. About this time in his career he made two radical departures from his accustomed manner. One is that all his fiction after the completion of *Watt* is written in French. The other is that he now changes over from the influence of Irish wit, with Joyce as his model, to a more sober, introspective type of novel, closer to Proust.

These classifications, however neat and convincing, are only relative. First of all, another side of Joyce will keep reappearing alongside of Proust in the novels written in French. Second, the new type of hero who appears in these recent Beckett novels is really a carry-over from Watt—the man who suffers from acute physical deficiencies, with "the more intimate senses greatly below par."[6]

But it can still be said that the trilogy in French, *Molloy, Malone Meurt*, and *L'Innommable*,[7] published between 1951 and 1953, reveals a very different Beckett. It is almost as if a change in language effected a change in literary personality. The trilogy proceeds almost as an unbroken monologue—quite in contrast to the objective narrative approach of his first two novels. The omniscient author has fulfilled Joyce's intention, first proposed in *A Portrait of the Artist as a Young Man*, of being refined out of existence. Beckett leaves everything up to a series of monologuists who, with one exception, seem to speak in a single voice.

The exception is Moran, who narrates the second part of *Molloy*. He is far more conscious of what he is saying than the other "centers of consciousness" of Beckett's trilogy.[8] Moran begins his section very concretely: "It is midnight. The rain is beating on the windows. I am calm" (*Molloy*, New York, 1955, p. 125). This desire to identify one's location, the preoccupation with space-time considerations, beg comparison with the first words pronounced by Proust's narrator. Marcel has the same fear of not being able to establish his identity, particularly in a temporal sense. "There is a temporal as well as a spatial unity to be apprehended," as Beckett wrote in the 1929 essay on Joyce.

Despite the failure of the other monologuists of Beckett's trilogy to apprehend reality as concretely as Moran, they are still all of a kind. The soliloquies of the trilogy are the thoughts and words of thoroughly desperate men. All have serious physical defects—they are lame, deaf, dumb, blind, or suffer from a combination of these ailments. Proust's neurasthenic narrator is better off than Beckett's succession of cripples, though he suffers an occasional failure of lucidity, as attested by the opaque, digressive opening pages of *A la recherche du temps perdu*.

This type of "sickness" in Proust gives the narrator a heightened awareness of the things about him. Everything is expressed through complex interrelationships which result in what Beckett labeled "the chain-figure of the metaphor" in his monograph on Proust. Beckett's characters, on the other hand, although they grope in this poetic direction, depend finally on what they can immediately perceive. They often go through elaborate rituals of identification of the various objects in their line of vision or touch. The dying Malone is intent upon identifying things about him, things which to the ordinary person appear inconsequential but to him have a strange kind of importance. The stub of pencil which keeps eluding him exerts this kind of special, almost plastic appeal: "What a misfortune, the pencil must have slipped from my fingers, for I have only just succeeded in recovering it after forty-eight hours (see above) of intermittent efforts" (*Malone Dies,* New York, 1956, p. 48). This is not peculiar to Malone; the narrators of the other parts of the trilogy have fixations with curious objects. Molloy, for example, has a series of "sucking stones" which preoccupy a good many of his waking hours. Perhaps this fascination with "things" is in some way connected with the physical deficiencies of Beckett's characters.[9] For them the act of seeing, feeling, and touching perfectly routine objects is as creative as the more imaginative, intuitive responses of the ordinary person.

The irresistible urge to identify everything as it becomes apparent to the senses is, then, at the heart of Beckett's aesthetic. Malone's search for the pencil stub is the same kind of experience as Swann's interest in Vinteuil's "petite phrase," only Malone's investigation is conducted on a more primitive level. Both experiences are concerned with the dimension of time which Proust has linked with "involuntary memory." Proust's characters, as has often been noted, seem to resist successfully the dulling effects of the outside world through these chance encounters with unrelated "things"—these objects seem to have magical properties and exert special effects on his creatures.

For Beckett, however, involuntary memory is not the traumatic thing that it was for Proust. Beckett's characters never feel that they can systematically rid themselves of the destructive effects of time, though they are staunch supporters of the creative aspect of memory. They attach themselves to objects in much the same way that Stephen Dedalus carries an ashplant and Leopold Bloom holds on to his shriveled potato, because they feel the urge to attach themselves to "things." It is obvious, then, that Beckett's Molloy, Moran, and Malone have reached a level of existence several notches below that of Proust's Marcel, Bergotte, and Elstir. Beckett's characters lack the temperament for imagining that it is possible to escape reality through an artistic experience, through an "involuntary memory"; they are just existentialist enough to believe that there is no way out.

This existentialist type has become increasingly more unfashionable, to the point where Camus recently modified his "l'homme absurde" in favor of "l'homme révolté." Yet Beckett tenaciously holds on to "l'homme absurde" and even exaggerates his disproportion with society; he is guilty of what Beckett refers to in the Proust monograph as "the sin of having been born."

This delight in reviving the outmoded turns up in quite another way in the trilogy. The sustained reproduction of continuous, almost unbroken thoughts through three volumes places *Molloy, Malone Dies,* and *The Unnamable* in the same fictional category as *A la recherche du temps perdu* and *Ulysses*. Only, as Kenneth Allsop was quick to point out, Beckett came rather too late on the introspective scene: "He is not, in France where he has lived and been known about for years, thought of as being a particularly 'daring' experimental writer. His harsh, desolate, denuded style is entirely and unmistakably his own, but his literary 'form,' the stream-of-consciousness device which most young British writers wouldn't dream of using nowadays for fear of being thought quaint, derives from his years as secretary to James Joyce" [*The Angry Decade*, New York, 1958, p. 38]. It took several decades before the stream-of-consciousness form of fiction became an essential part of Beckett's technique, when, if we are to believe Kenneth Allsop and other critics, it was already moribund. Yet the results testify to a convincing "posthumous" application of a technique which was supposed to have been exhausted with the publication of *Finnegans Wake* in 1939.

It is perhaps appropriate in any case for Beckett to use an outmoded technique in his trilogy, since his characters seem to survive through the memory of past achievement; they linger on in a world which ungratefully ignores their existence. Using very recent terminology, we might call these creatures "picaresque saints."[10] Molloy, Malone, and the unnamed narrator of *The Unnamable* are all engaged in some sort of quest. Molloy fruitlessly searches for his mother whom he is destined never to find; Moran has no idea why he must find Molloy, although he continues to search for him;[11] Malone is not sure why he is confined to a bed and knows relatively little about his surroundings; the unnamed narrator is not certain of his name or whether he is alive or dead, but is intent on making some form of self-discovery. They are all constant wanderers—even if the wandering never quite gets beyond the mind with Malone and the unnamable. The "saint" and the "outlaw," as R. W. B. Lewis has written in another connection, seem to combine to form those people who deny themselves worldly goods because they are only on the fringes of society.

A part of the unnamable's soliloquy has the distinctly "d'outre-tombe" quality of vagueness and uncertainty which pervades the entire trilogy: "It's of me now I must speak, even if I have to do it with their language, it will be a start, a step towards silence and the end of madness, the madness of having to speak and not being able to, except of things that don't concern me, that don't count, that I don't believe, that they have crammed me full of to prevent me from saying who I am, where I am, and from doing what I have to do in the only way that can put an end to it, from doing what I have to do" [*The Unnamable*, New York, 1958, p. 51]. Even the existentialist hero seems to have more purpose and design than this person. Yet this groping towards a new way of expressing himself indicates a kind of awareness which we have long associated with the symbolist poets and with Proust and Joyce. In the two "lettres du Voyant" and elsewhere, Rimbaud roundly refuses "to do it with their language." Proust's long novel and *Ulysses* and *Finnegans Wake* are even more convincing protests; *Finnegans Wake* especially, Beckett would agree, is an important "step towards silence."[12]

A passage such as that quoted above from *The Unnamable* seems to carry to fruition many of the remarks Beckett had made earlier in reference to Joyce and Proust. "Dante . . . Bruno . Vico . . Joyce" and *Proust* stand almost in the relationship of program notes to the finished piece, the *Molloy–Malone Dies–Unnamable* trilogy.

Beckett's most recent work, *Nouvelles et Textes pour rien,*[13] has the same ring of despair we have come to expect from his fiction written in French. The title conveys the listless quality of the prose and the sense of aimlessness. At one point (p. 40) the narrator writes: "Je ne sais pas pourquoi j'ai raconté cette histoire. J'aurais pu tout aussi bien en raconter une autre. Peut-être qu'une autre fois je pourrai en raconter une autre. Ames vives, vous verrez que cela se ressemble." The person speaking seems to lack the vigor of Beckett's other narrators. He has less curiosity about himself and his whereabouts. *Nouvelles et Textes pour rien* is somewhat of a disappointment after the trilogy; its fragmentary structure, put together like a series of fugitive pieces, leaves the reader with a sense of incompleteness.

Because Samuel Beckett came to the fictional marketplace relatively late, we can be fairly certain that he has not yet burned himself out,[14] though Kenneth Allsop's claim "that he is in his technique an obsolete writer"[15] probably has to stand for the time being at least. He still seems to be in the uncomfortable position of the imitator looking frantically for a way of escape.

On the one hand, Beckett is indebted to Proust for his narrative point of view. His characters seem to have the sense of time which Proust found in Bergson and transformed into literary terms. The ability to "recapture" certain moments of their past, though in a far less convincing way than Proust's narrator, saves such lost souls as Molloy and Malone from total extinction of consciousness. The ritual of self-identification which each of Beckett's monologuists goes through is all part of a complicated memory pattern which makes the confused reality about them more meaningful. The sickness of Proust's narrator gives him a more artistic way of looking at the world, while illness among Beckett's characters seems to dull their sensibilities. Proust's imagination sustains an unbridled flow of metaphor, while the less conscious narrators in Beckett are barely articulate. But the search for identity through successive flirtations with "pure time" is carried on in the work of both authors. It is perfectly realized in *A la recherche du temps perdu*, bitterly and disappointingly unrealized in the Molloy trilogy.

On the other hand, Beckett seems indebted to Joyce for his concentration on "things."[16] In *Murphy* and *Watt* the concern with the purely physical is handled comically; in the novels written in French the preoccupation becomes a more serious matter. Murphy's rocking-chair exercises, which are so elaborately explained at the beginning of the novel, are not very different from Molloy's bicycle jaunt, except that the latter is treated quite seriously. Joyce had the gift, particularly in *Ulysses*, of making a situation appear both tragic and comic at the same time. Beckett, when he abandoned his native English for his adopted language, seems to have rejected his Irish wit in favor of a more sober, introspective approach. But Dedalus' ashplant and Bloom's potato, both in their comic and tragic dimensions, are echoed in Molloy's "sucking stones" and Malone's pencil stub. This holding on to objects, for Beckett's characters as for Joyce's, is a way of survival.

Joyce's work is filled with a sharp concentration on "things." *Ulysses* is on occasions a catalogue of the physical properties of the city of Dublin. Joyce cleverly places these bits of Dubliniana in the midst of Bloom monologues. This technique, as has been pointed out before, divides the concentration between Bloom's mind and the city surrounding him. Malone's inmost thoughts are interrupted by a haunting awareness of the objects about him; he repeatedly catalogues the objects in his possession. Beckett seems to have learned from Joyce a method for artistically blending the inmost thoughts of his characters with their exterior surroundings. To Proust's gift of temporal awareness has been added Joyce's gift of spatial awareness.

Notes

1. "Ibsen's New Drama," *Fortnightly Review*, LXXIII (1900), 575–590.

2. Peggy Guggenheim describes a year-long love affair with Beckett, whom she fondly calls Oblomov (his indolence seems to have reminded her of Goncharov's hero). "In spite of the fact that I took every consolation which crossed my path, I was entirely obsessed for over a year by the strange creature whom I shall call Oblomov. He came into my life the day after Christmas, 1937. I had known him slightly. He had been to our house in the Avenue Reille. I knew that he was a friend of James Joyce, that he had been engaged to his daughter and had caused her great unhappiness." On the following page she writes that "Oblomov was a sort of slave to Joyce." *Out of This Century* (New York, 1946), pp. 194, 195.

3. The best known of Beckett's works up to this time were the long poem, *Whoroscope* (1930), the collection of short stories, *More Pricks than Kicks* (1934), and the poems contained in *Echo's Bones* (1936).

4. *Proust*, p. 67. Proust makes a similar remark in one of his letters: "Le style n'est nullement un enjolivement, comme croient certaines personnes, ce n'est même pas une question de technique, c'est comme la couleur chez les peintres, une qualité de vision . . ." *Lettres de Marcel Proust à Bibesco* (Lausanne, 1949), p. 177.

5. *Watt* (Paris, 1958), p. 73.

6. *Watt*, p. 223.

7. Beckett himself translated these novels into English as *Molloy, Malone Dies, The Unnamable*—collaborating with Patrick Bowles on *Molloy*. Beckett's developed bilingual tendencies serve him in good stead as a translator of his own work, a somewhat unique literary phenomenon.

8. Molloy narrates the first half of *Molloy*; Malone tells all of *Malone Dies*; the narrator of *The Unnamable*, appropriately enough, goes unnamed.

9. See J. Robert Loy, " 'Things' in Recent French Literature," *PMLA*, LXXI (1956), 27–41.

10. Patrick Bowles uses the expression "psychological picaresque" in reference to *Molloy* (see "How Samuel Beckett Sees the Universe," *The Listener*, June 19, 1958, p. 1011). Yet R. W. B. Lewis' expression, which he does not use in connection with Beckett, strikes me as a more appropriate term.

11. See Warren Lee, "The Bitter Pill of Samuel Beckett," *Chicago Review*, X (1957), 77–87.

12. All of the important commentators on Joyce, Stuart Gilbert and Harry Levin being probably the most penetrating, mention this aspect of his work. Jean-Jacques Mayoux in his "Le Théâtre de Samuel Beckett," *Études Anglaises*, X (1957) 366, makes the important point: "Comme Joyce, Beckett est un chercheur d'absolu; d'être dans un monde contingent, voué au contingent jusque dans la création imaginative, l'exaspère."

13. Paris, 1958. Parts of the work had appeared in various forms earlier.

14. In 1959 his talents took a new turn, when he translated a large number of Mexican poems—beginning with a sixteenth-century sonnet and ending with a 1910 lyric—into English for inclusion in *An Anthology of Mexican Poetry* (with the critical blessing of a preface by C. M. Bowra). We cannot be sure what new literary feat Beckett will perform next.

15. *The Angry Decade*, p. 37.

16. William York Tindall touches on this rapproachement between Beckett and Joyce in his excellent article, "Beckett's Bums," *Critique*, II, 1958. He perceptively remarks "that Beckett's trilogy, in one sense, is a kind of portrait of the artist—as an old man; and that *Molloy* is a parody of *Ulysses*" (p. 10). Kenneth Hamilton also touches on the problem in "Boon or Thorn? Joyce Cary and Samuel Beckett on Human Life," *Dalhousie Review*, XXXVIII (1959), 437–438.

Style and Obscurity in Samuel Beckett's Early Fiction

Rubin Rabinovitz*

Obscurity in the works of Samuel Beckett raises many problems of interpretation. Even in his early fiction, Beckett confronts his readers with passages which after persistent scrutiny seems to yield no meanings. Many of the difficulties in these works arise when Beckett dispenses with the techniques of the traditional novel in a refusal to permit content to dominate form. Early in his career he noted that many readers, condi-

*Reprinted from *Modern Fiction Studies* 20 (Autumn 1974); © by Purdue Research Foundation, West Lafayette, IN 47907. Reprinted with permission.

tioned by traditional fiction, considered the form of a work no more than a peripheral adjunct to its content. In an essay defending *Finnegans Wake*, Beckett set out to re-educate these readers: "You are not satisfied unless form is so strictly divorced from content that you can comprehend the one almost without bothering to read the other. This rapid skimming and absorption of the scant cream of sense is made possible by what I may call a continuous process of copious intellectual salivation. The form that is an arbitrary and independent phenomenon can fulfil no higher function than that of stimulus for a tertiary or quartary conditioned reflex of dribbling comprehension."[1]

A principal reason for public hostility to *Finnegans Wake*, Beckett argued, was that Joyce's audience did not know what to make of a work where form and content were united. "Here form *is* content, content *is* form. You complain that this stuff is not written in English. It is not written at all. It is not to be read—or rather it is not only to be read. It is to be looked at and listened to. His writing is not *about* something; *it is that something itself*."[2] Two years later, in his book on Proust, Beckett made a similar point: "For Proust, as for the painter, style is more a question of vision than of technique. Proust does not share the superstition that form is nothing and content everything, nor that the ideal literary masterpiece could only be communicated in a series of absolute and monosyllabic propositions. For Proust the quality of language is more important than any system of ethics or aesthetics. Indeed he makes no attempt to dissociate form from content. The one is a concretion of the other, the revelation of a world."[3] If Proust's writing is like painting in its marriage of form and content, Beckett's fiction, like abstract painting, permits form to gain the upper hand.[4] The narrator's description of obscure incidents in *Watt*, "of great formal brilliance and indeterminable purport," indicates this dominance of form.[5]

The long, boring passages in *Watt*, listing the arrangements of Mr. Knott's furniture or the glances exchanged by members of a committee, have formal uses, but they impede the progress of the story. They serve the content in showing that the deceptiveness of superficial reality is masked by oceans of tedium, tedium which conventional literature usually bridges with an *et cetera*. A traditional writer would summarize boring details, but Beckett's method is to refrain from descriptions when he can offer demonstrations. This is one of the qualities he admired in Joyce's fiction: "When the sense is sleep, the words go to sleep," Beckett writes. "When the sense is dancing, the words dance."[6]

Beckett's lists reproduce the anxiety Watt feels about the rules at Knott's house when they force the reader to consider skipping to the bottom of a boring passage; they are designed to increase the reader's impatience and confusion, and they do. By using these techniques Beckett indicates his willingness to abandon the seemingly indisputable aesthetic principle that art must always be pleasing.

His refusal to heed the dictum that art must be pleasing and his formalism are only two aspects of Beckett's comprehensive rejection of old literary modes. His fiction can be seen as an attempt, as radical as Joyce's, to revolutionize the novel. Beckett's parodies and reversals of traditional novelistic techniques, like Joyce's, also contribute to the obscurity of his fiction. As his comments about *Finnegans Wake* indicate, Beckett will not simplify his works in order to appease those who read only for "dribbling comprehension."

An announcement of this revolutionary outlook comes in *Murphy*, when Neary says, "Let our conversation now be without precedent in fact or literature, each one speaking to the best of his ability the truth to the best of his knowledge" (p. 214). The comment is made ironically, and the hyperbole contributes to the humor; but Beckett's jest is in earnest. He does feel that literature often misrepresents reality, and he is committed to a scrupulous truthfulness in his own works.

One way that literature misrepresents reality is in its use of verisimilitude to blur the distinction between imaginative and historical events. Verisimilitude forces the novelist to pretend that he is describing action which originates in the world and not in his own imagination; this is justified as a way of increasing the realism of literature. The implication is that the untethered imagination would drift off irretrievably if its earthly connections were severed. Beckett feels that verisimilitude restrains the imagination; his goal is an imaginative literature freed from its obligation to represent mundane reality. He, therefore, frequently uses devices which remind the reader that he has before him not life, but a book by Samuel Beckett. In *More Pricks Than Kicks*, for example, he mentions himself as the author of a well-turned phrase (p. 176).

This sort of technique also gives Beckett's works a quality of honesty which is lost when writers insist that fictional events really occurred. The old Platonic argument that artists are liars is usually considered simplistic, but a connotation of mendacity persists in words like *fiction*, *artful*, *romance*, *acting*, *fable*, or *device*. The opinion that artists are in some sense liars seems pervasive, if only at a popular level.

Beckett, in emphasizing the distinction between historical and imaginative events, meets even this literal criterion of truthfulness. He also takes seriously the argument in the last book of *The Republic* that its mimesis makes art subservient to the material world. The artist who portrays objects in the material world, says Plato, tacitly admits that his works occupy a lower plane of reality than his subject matter. Beckett's art abandons mimesis and proclaims its independence from the material world.

For Beckett, the reality that art presents is one of the few alternatives to the deception and error that are entailed by existence in the material world. Art can indicate the deficiencies of material existence and occasionally may offer an escape from its vicissitudes.

This critical view of the material world is an important theme in Beckett's writing. Lawrence Harvey says that Beckett once remarked that two quotations will help a critic to understand his work: "Ubi nihil vales ibi nihil velis" (Geulincx) and "Nothing is more real than nothing" (Democritus). To these quotations Harvey adds another which is important for Beckett, Berkeley's "essere est percipi."[7] The first comment warns of the futility of volitional activity in the material world; the second indicates that a rational understanding of the material world founders on paradox; and the third is the crux of an argument which denies real existence to the material world. Beckett's rejection of materialism on volitional, rational, and phenomenological grounds is a logical counterpart to his aesthetic critique of materialism. Here Beckett follows Schopenhauer, both in rejecting materialism and in holding that art provides a path to a higher plane of reality.[8]

Beckett argues in his essay on Proust (where he also pays homage to Schopenhauer's aesthetic theories) that the artist creates a world which liberates him from the prison of the material world.[9] The need for the world of art to free itself from the strictures of materialism is often expressed in Beckett's fiction. In *More Pricks Than Kicks* the narrator toys with his obligation to follow space-time rules: "Let us call it Winter," he says, "that dusk may fall now and a moon rise" (p. 20). In *Murphy*, physical laws are violated and the violation is underlined: "Miss Carridge's method of entering a private apartment was to knock timidly on the door on the outside some time after she had closed it behind her on the inside. Not even a nice hot cup of tea in her hand could make her subject to the usual conditions of time and space in this matter" (p. 68).

In *Watt*, Beckett describes fish which "are forced to rise and fall, now to the surface of the waves and now to the ocean bed." He then anticipates the reader who doubts the verisimilitude of the description and asks, "But do such fish exist?" The reply to this is: "Yes, such fish exist, now" (p. 120). Questioning the existence of these creatures in the material world is irrelevant; they do exist in the world of the novel. Again, after a passage in *Watt* which mentions that Kate Lynch is a bleeder, Beckett uses a footnote to proclaim the independence of his art: "Haemophilia is, like enlargement of the prostrate, an exclusively male disorder. But not in this work" (p. 102).

An aesthetic theory which frees art from the obligation to represent events as they occur in the material world has broad implications for literature. When there is no longer a need for verisimilitude, devices like characterization, appropriate dialogue, motivation, chronological sequence, and descriptions of locale may be dispensed with; for these are all controlled by an obligation to make the work conform to outside reality.

In addition, some of these devices, like motivation and characterization, promote the illusion that it is possible for an author to understand the behavior and personality of other human beings. Such insights, Beckett believes, are either misleading or trivial. Only the microcosm of his own mind is accessible to any person.[10] The intrinsic self of another human being is unknowable; we see others as objects in time and space, phenomena in the macrocosm. In *Proust* Beckett agrees with Schopenhauer that the macrocosm a person perceives is in reality no more than a projection of his own will.[11] Hence, even when a realistic writer attempts to portray characters as if they were composites of people from the outside world, he succeeds only in presenting images which ultimately originate in his own mind. The intrinsic self of a person (in Schopenhauer's philosophy, his aspect as a thing-in-itself) always remains hidden from others.

Where his characters began to resemble people from the outside world too much, Beckett, therefore, used techniques to diminish this aspect of verisimilitude. In *Watt*, for example, the characters who become vivid because their thoughts are described—Hackett, Watt, and Sam—are given names that remind the reader of Beckett's. At the same time, the novel's peripheral figures are denied the rounding effect of conventional characterization and become contrived author's dummies.

Dylan Thomas made a similar point about *Murphy:* Neary is a failure as a character, says Thomas, because he is "a slap-stick, a stuffed guy, when he moves; his mind is Mr. Beckett's mind."[12] But this stereotype is the result of Beckett's refusal, and not his inability, to provide conventional characterizations. Beckett was aware of the effect he was producing, as a line of the novel indicates: "All the puppets in this book whinge sooner or later, except Murphy, who is not a puppet."[13]

Beckett's earliest published story, "Assumption," though innovative in other respects, does use traditional methods of character description.[14] In *More Pricks Than Kicks*, which appeared six years later, there are occasional playful refusals to characterize. "There was nothing at all noteworthy about his appearance," the narrator says of one character; and the description of another is interrupted by, "But it would be a waste of time to itemise her" (pp. 27, 105).

In this book Beckett also begins to grow reticent about the motivation of his characters. With an ironic concern about verisimilitude, his narrator speaks of the hero's impending suicide attempt: "we feel confident that even the most captious reader must acknowledge . . . the verisimilitude of what we hope to relate in the not too distant future. For we assume the irresponsibility of Belacqua, his faculty for acting with insufficient motivation, to have been so far evinced in previous misadventures as to be no longer a matter for surprise" (p. 89). A tap of the wand, and the reader is urged to believe that this sleight of hand has transformed a lapse in narration into a shining example of consistent characterization.

For the conventional narrator, a suicide attempt is an occasion for extensive spiritual and psychological probing; but Beckett's narrator only shrugs: "how he had formed this resolution to destroy himself we are quite unable to discover. The simplest course, when the motives of any deed are found subliminal to the point of defying expression, is to call that deed *ex nihilo* and have done. Which we beg leave to follow in the present instance" (p. 89). Behind the ironic tone there is again a hint that the intrinsic self of another person is unknowable.

Similarly, the characters in *Murphy* often seem unknowable. Mr. Endon is inscrutable; Celia's body measurements are listed in lieu of a characterization; Ticklepenny is introduced with a dismissal: "This creature does not merit any particular description" (pp. 84–85). Murphy himself is portrayed in an unusual way. One learns little about his superficial qualities, but his mind is described in a special chapter where the reader with a good knowledge of the works of Bruno, Descartes, Geulincx, Malebranche, Leibniz, Berkeley, and Schopenhauer will have only moderate difficulties.

These characterizations are less whimsical than they first appear. Because the narrator has access to Murphy's mind, he describes it in detail; but since he sees Celia from the outside, he must content himself with an external description. No one can know another's mind with the same immediacy that he perceives his own, but one's idea of his physical self is often distorted (by mirror images, for example). Beckett, therefore, does not claim to have perfect knowledge both of the bodies and minds of his characters; and when he portrays a character's inner life, he does not conceal the connections between his own mind and the one he is describing. This is also true in *Watt*, when Beckett uses names that resemble his own for characters whose minds he describes.

Beckett here is attacking the time-honored convention of the omniscient narrator. This device permits an author to give complete physical and mental description of his characters; but such omniscience has no counterpart in human experience. In keeping with the sort of literary truthfulness he hopes to achieve, Beckett does not pretend that his narrators have access to knowledge which he himself could never acquire. This leads to extensive descriptions of the mental qualities of those characters whose minds are like Beckett's, whereas only cursory portrayals are given for the others. As the narrator of Murphy indicates, the peripheral characters in that book are puppets.

There is an additional parody of conventional techniques in this novel when Mr. Kelly asks Celia to tell him about Murphy; this device for presenting inobtrusive characterizations must have been shopworn when in the *Iliad* Priam questioned Helen about Agamemnon. Like a well-trained student writer, Mr. Kelly asks the proper questions about Celia and Murphy: "the who, what, where, by what means, why, in what way and when" (p. 17). The narrator compares Mr. Kelly to Quintilian, and the allusion indicates Beckett's familiarity with the rhetorical rules he has set out to violate. Though Mr. Kelly is unrelenting in his curiosity, the most important detail Celia can offer him is that Murphy is Murphy. This she repeats. A tautology is safest when the interrogator is persistent and the question unanswerable.

A similar refusal to describe the superficial characteristics of the hero occurs in *Watt*. Here Mr. Hackett hopes to get biographical details about Watt from Mr. Nixon: "Nationality, family, birth-place, confession, occupation, means of existence, distinctive signs," says Hackett, "you cannot be in ignorance of all this" (p. 21). But Nixon can be. He says he knows nothing about Watt, that nothing is known. Hackett's quest for Watt's haecceity is frustrated by Nixon's *nichts*; Kelly will search in vain for the *quel* of amorphous Murphy.[15]

Just after the Nixon-Hackett conversation there is another incident in *Watt* involving characterization. During a scuffle Watt loses his hat; a news agent called Evans returns it to him. Unlike Watt, Evans' appearance is described in detail: "He seemed a man of more than usual acerbity, and to suffer from unremitting mental, moral, and perhaps even physical pain. One noticed his cap, perhaps because of the snow-white forehead and damp black curly hair on which it sat. The eye came always in the end to the scowling mouth and from there on up to the rest. His moustache, handsome in itself, was for obscure reasons unimportant" (pp. 25–26). In addition, we learn that Evans always keeps his cap on; that he is a cyclist and chess-player. Hats, caps, bicycles, chess—readers familiar with the symbolism of Beckett's earlier works will expect this character to play an important role in the forthcoming action. Evans never appears again.

Beckett repeats this joke with a character who appears later in the same novel: "The postman, a charming man, called Severn, a great dancer and lover of greyhounds, seldom called. But he did sometimes, always in the evening, with his light eager step and his dog by his side, to deliver a bill, or a begging letter" (p. 69). This passage constitutes the entirety of Mr. Severn's sole appearance in the novel.

Beckett's technique of undermining characterization leads to another innovation: when the characters' vividness is diminished the reader becomes more involved in the work. At first glance, the opposite would seem to be true. One of the justifications of conventional characterization is that it increases the emotional intensity of a work: by making a character life-like, the author hopes to persuade the reader to identify with him and thus be drawn into the work emotionally. But when conventional characterization is used, the reader is induced to believe in a figure who is actually an intermediary between the reader and the action in the work; moreover, the quality of his emotional response is limited by the reader's ability to identify with a particular character.

In Beckett's works the characterization is weakened so that the reader may directly experience events which are described. Though he may identify to some extent with Beckett's characters, the reader is himself forced to struggle with the work in a manner which subtly duplicates the ordeal of the characters. In this fashion, Beckett can transmit the emotional quality of fictional events without relying on intermediary figures alone. Form and content have been united; the pretense that fictional characters have material existence has been abandoned; and as the reader experiences events in the book with this immediacy, he himself takes on the role of a character in the work.[16]

When he begins to participate in the action, the reader often finds that Beckett's characters are expressing emotions similar to those evoked in him by the work. Hackett and Kelly, when they demand characterizations, give voice to a desire the reader accustomed to traditional novelistic devices would feel. In Beckett's drama, when characters like Vladimir and Estragon speak of their boredom while waiting for Godot, they anticipate the audience's reaction to the lack of action in the play. In *Watt*, the hero's need to learn about Knott and the anguish he feels when he is frustrated are duplicated when the reader's intense curiosity about Knott is never satisfied.

This is a reason why Beckett cannot tell his audience who Godot is or what Knott represents. If the reader takes it upon himself to assign an arbitrary meaning to these characters, an important dimension of Beckett's art is lost when the frustration involved in waiting for Godot, or in attempting to define the ineffable Knott, is diminished. In this fashion, Beckett uses obscurity to confront his readers with emotions like those his characters feel when they encounter obscurity in their search for ultimate reality.

In some modern works, the obscurity creates a barrier between audience and author; only a reader with the patience and sophistication necessary to interpret such works can succeed in understanding them. Such works become vulnerable to the charge that they use obscurity for its own sake; they capitalize on an aura of exclusiveness which flatters the successful reader.

Beckett, especially in his later fiction, attempted to avoid this sort of obscurity. In *Watt* and the works that came after it, he began to use a simpler vocabulary and a less allusive style. In the later works, when the reader is forced to struggle with obscure passages, it is usually because of innovative techniques or the difficulty of representing ineffable reality. Beckett similarly struggles with subjects that are no less difficult to describe than they are to read about. Ultimately, reader, author, and characters all confront the same obscurity, the obscurity of reality; and all eventually feel the same despair when they are unable to penetrate it.[17]

Notes

1. Samuel Beckett, "Dante . . . Bruno. Vico . . Joyce." *Our Exagmination Round His Factification for Incamination of Work in Progress* (London: Faber and Faber, 1961), p. 13. This essay appeared in *transition* 16–17 (June 1929), 242–253.

2. Beckett, p. 14. The italics are Beckett's.

3. Samuel Beckett, *Proust* (New York: Grove Press, 1957), p. 67. *Proust* was originally published in London by Chatto and Windus in 1929.

4. Useful discussions of the form-content question may be found in Lawrence Harvey, *Samuel Beckett, Poet and Critic* (Princeton University Press, 1970), p. 435; John Fletcher, *Samuel Beckett's Art* (London: Chatto and Windus, 1967), p. 12; and Tom Driver, "Beckett by the Madelaine," *Columbia University Forum*, 4 (Summer 1961), 23.

5. Samuel Beckett, *Watt* (New York: Grove Press, 1959), p. 74. Future references to Beckett's works which appear in the text are to the Grove Press editions. *Watt* was completed about 1944; it was first published in Paris by the Olympia Press in 1953. *More Pricks Than Kicks* (1970) was first published in 1934 by Chatto and Windus in London; *Murphy* (1957) in 1938 by Routledge in London.

6. *Our Exagmination*, p. 14. The deceptive quality of the lists has been demonstrated by John Mood in " 'The Personal System'—Samuel Beckett's *Watt*" *PMLA*, 86 (March 1971), 255–265.

7. Harvey, pp. 267–268. The Geulincx quotation appears in *Murphy* (p. 178); "esse est percipi" appears in the notes for *Film*.

8. For material dealing with the influence of Schopenhauer on Beckett's poetry, see Harvey, pp. 73–78; on *Murphy*, David Hesla, *The Shape of Chaos* (Minneapolis: University of Minnesota Press, 1971), Ch. 11; on *Watt*, my article, "*Watt* from Descartes to Schopenhauer," in *Modern Irish Literature, Essays in Honor of William York Tindall*, edited by James Brophy and Raymond Porter (New York: Twayne Publishers, 1972); on *Waiting for Godot*, F. N. Lees, *Memoirs and Proceedings of the Manchester Literary and Historical Society*, 1961–1962, p. 39.

9. *Proust*, pp. 8, 66–69.

10. In *Proust* (pp. 6–7) Beckett writes, "Moreover when it is a case of human intercourse, we are faced by the problem of an object whose mobility is not merely a function of the subject's, but independent and personal: two separate and immanent dynamisms related by no system of synchronisation."

11. *Proust*, p. 8.

12. Dylan Thomas, "Documents: Recent Novels," *James Joyce Quarterly*, 8 (Summer 1971), 291 (reprinted from the *New English Weekly*, March 17, 1938).

13. *Murphy*, p. 122. Murphy, however, did whinge on page 37; the "except" may exclude Murphy from being a puppet, but not from whingeing.

14. "Assumption," *translation*, 16–17 (June 1929), 268–271.

15. Sidney Warhaft, in "Threne and Theme in *Watt*," *Wisconsin Studies in Contemporary Literature*, 4 (Autumn 1963), 267, connects Hackett with *haecceitas*, Watt with *quidditas*. Beckett uses the word haecceity in *More Pricks Than Kicks*, p. 147.

16. H. Porter Abbott makes a similar point in the third chapter of his study, *The Fiction of Samuel Beckett* (Berkeley: University of California Press, 1973).

17. This essay was completed with the assistance of grants from the Columbia University Council on Research in the Humanities and the National Endowment for the Humanities.

Belacqua

Michael Robinson*

> "Brother," said he, "what use to go up yet?"
> Dante

In 1934 Beckett published a group of ten short stories under the general (and suggestive) title, *More Pricks Than Kicks*. The stories originally formed part of an unfinished and unpublished first novel, *Dream of Fair to Middling Women*, an apprentice work which was begun and abandoned during his post-Dublin *wanderjahre*. The *Dream* furnished Beckett with the hero and several episodes in the stories, and a passage from it was also published in *Transition* under the title *Sedendo et Quiescendo*.[1] In their present form the stories are uneven in quality and evidently the work of a young man intent on exploring the possibilities of his learning and early impressions. Nevertheless *More Pricks Than Kicks* is remarkable for the way in which it already suggests the majority of Beckett's later preoccupations, and at least two of the stories reveal the presence of an individual and disturbing sensibility. They trace the career of Belacqua Shuah—student, philanderer, failure and anti-hero—through a series of grotesque situations that end with his accidental and needless death upon an operating table. The various stories unite to create the total personality of Belacqua, the initial guise of the Beckett hero, whose origins and nature are important to one's understanding of his later evolution. Indeed, much that seems obscure in Beckett's mature writing is illuminated by the name which his first hero inherits.

The opening lines of the first story, *Dante and the Lobster*, read: "It was morning and Belacqua was stuck in the first of the canti of the moon. He was so bogged that he could neither move backward or forward." Here, on his first appearance, the Beckett hero is discovered in his now familiar condition of stasis. He is, moreover, reading Dante, and his own Christian name has been taken from the fourth canto of the *Purgatorio*. The original Belacqua was in real life a lute maker of Florence whom Dante had known as notorious for his indolence and apathy. In the poem he has been placed on the second terrace of Ante-Purgatory, the dwelling of the late-repentant who have postponed their reconciliation with God until the last moment—*in articulo mortis*. As a punishment they are obliged to wait at the foot of the mountain through a time as long as their lives on earth, enduring the indolence in which they used to indulge, before making the ascent that will prepare them for Paradise. In the relevant lines Virgil has just warned Dante not to rest before his journey's end when the poets are arrested by a voice:

*Reprinted from *The Long Sonata of the Dead: A Study of Samuel Beckett* (New York: Grove Press, 1969) by permission of the publisher.

He'd hardly spoken when, from somewhere fast
  Beside us, came a voice which said: "Maybe
  Thou'lt need to sit ere all that road is passed."

At this we both glanced round inquiringly,
  And on our left observed a massive boulder,
  Which up till then we had not chanced to see.

This, when explored, revealed to the beholder
  A group of persons lounging in the shade,
  As lazy people lounge, behind its shoulder.

And one of them, whose attitude displayed
  Extreme fatigue, sat there and clasped his knees,
  Drooping between them his exhausted head.

"Oh good my lord," said I, "pray look at this
  Bone-lazy lad, content to sit and settle
  Like sloth's own brother taking of his ease!"

Then he gave heed, and turning just a little
  Only his face upon his thigh, he grunted:
  "Go up then, thou, thou mighty man of mettle."

I knew him then; and proved that, though I panted
  Still from the climb, I was not so bereft
  Of breath, I could not reach him if I wanted.

When I drew near him he would scarcely shift
  His head to say: "Nay, hast thou, really though,
  Grasped why the sun's car drives upon thy left?"

My lips twitched at the grudging speech, and slow
  Gestures. "Belacqua," I began, "I see
  I need not grieve for thee henceforward; no

But tell me: why dost thou resignedly
  Sit here? Is it for escort thou must wait?
  Or have old habits overtaken thee?"

"Brother," said he, "what use to go up yet?
  He'd not admit me to the cleansing pain,
  That bird of God who perches at the gate.

My lifetime long the heavens must wheel again
  Round me, that to my parting hour put off
  My healing sighs; and I meanwhile remain

Outside, unless prayer hasten my remove—
  Prayer from a heart in grace; for who sets store
  By other kinds, which are not heard above?"[2]

This passage evidently made a deep impression on Beckett during his own reading of Dante for its influence is discernible throughout his works. Dante's Belacqua, who does not appear unduly distressed by his penance, becomes the prototype for all Beckett's heroes and the persistence of his image, from the first stories to the plays some twenty years later, suggests that his significance exceeds the youthful plagiarism of his name. In fact the true importance of Belacqua in Beckett's work is not yet apparent in *More Pricks Than Kicks* where he appears as a character: only in the trilogy does Beckett begin to explore the real implications of his waiting and remembering at the foot of Mt. Purgatory.

Belacqua's favoured position, described in the fourth verse above, is adopted by his namesake in the story *A Wet Night*. Returning home after a miserable and intemperate evening he is afflicted with severe stomach pains and "disposed himself in the knee-and-elbow position on the pavement." Beckett's Belacqua is by nature "sinfully ignorant, bogged in indolence, asking nothing better than to stay put," and if he does not lie under the shadow of a rock he finds an agreeable substitute in a low public house where he is not known. It is in such a place that he makes his apathetic and reluctant attempt at salvation with its overtones of the theology on which Dante based his fourth canto. In the story *Ding-Dong* he is approached by a hatless woman who offers him two seats in heaven: " 'Seats in heaven,' she said in a white voice, 'tuppence a piece, four for a tanner.' " Belacqua is struck by her face, "it was so full of light . . . it bore no trace of suffering and in this alone it might be said to be a notable face." The woman persists and, mortified by the stares of the other drinkers, Belacqua overcomes his indolence. He buys four, a needless extravagance, and asks: "have you got them on you?" In reply the woman tells him that heaven goes round and round: " 'Rowan,' she said, dropping the d's and getting more of a swing into the slogan, 'rowan an' rowan an' rowan.' " Her words recall Belacqua's explanation to Dante: that the heavens must revolve about him his lifetime long before St. Peter will admit him to "the cleansing pain."

Although Belacqua, as a character, disappears with the stories, his name is evoked as that of a respected antecedent in several of the later novels. *Molloy* opens with the hero in the shadow of a rock under which "I crouched like Belacqua, or Sordello, I forget,"[3] and Murphy has what he terms his "Belacqua fantasy" in which he dreams of being released by death into the inaction of Ante-Purgatory. There he will sit in "embryanal repose, looking down at dawn across the reeds to the trembling of the austral sea."[4] The "knee-and-elbow position," or state of "embryanal repose," approximates to the foetal image of the unborn. (Peggy Guggenheim records that Beckett himself "retained a terrible memory of life in his mother's womb.")[5] The security and apparent peace of this position attract almost all the heroes in moments of especial suffering or at the height of their longing for nothingness. To be in the womb is, of all the attitudes they have experienced, the nearest terrestrial analogy to the timeless and spaceless ideal of being a speck in the Void. Belacqua declares, "I want very much to be back in the caul, on my back in the dark forever"; Watt is so overcome by weariness that he "settled himself at the edge of the path, with his hat pushed back and his bags beside him, and his knees drawn up, and his arms on his knees, and his head on his arms";[6] and in *The Unnamable* the most extreme incarnation of the hero, Worm, is literally in embryo, enclosed in the womb. He is motionless and perhaps timeless but not ideally so: as Beckett ironically observes, "it would be to sign his life-warrant to stir from where he is."[7] Once again the Dante prototype is recalled—"Brother," said he, "what use to go up yet?"

The significance of Beckett's debt to Dante, however, transcends the particulars of Belacqua's position in the shadow of the rock. His heroes are suspended between time and timelessness, fragment and whole, actual and ideal. They have an impression of that final, glorious release towards which they struggle, but are halted at an impasse which forever denies them entrance. They have been expelled into life and so committed "the original and eternal sin . . . the sin of having been born."[8] At first their condition appears reminiscent of Milton's fallen angels, scouring hell in search of relief only to discover everything inhospitable, monstrous and perverse. The angels find their progress barred in every direction and the Miltonic "mournful gloom" seems to foreshadow the perpetual greyness of the Beckett landscape. Satan's followers, like Beckett's hero, search for a dimension of life (or death) that will give purpose and meaning to their exile from Paradise. Some entertain themselves with feats of arms, some by celebrating their heroic deeds in song, while:

> Others apart sat on a hill retir'd,
> In thoughts more elevate, and reason'd high
> Of Providence, Foreknowledge, Will and Fate,
> Fixt Fate, Free Will, Foreknowledge absolute,
> And found no end, in wan'dring mazes lost.[9]

They turn in despair to the succour of reason and find that without the grace of God reason not only does not remove their problems but complicates them still further. All Hells have one quality in common. Whether the punishment is in the mind or the body nature is irrevocably a meaningless round, and endless marking-time. In hell the sinners symbolize their sin throughout eternity, perpetually relive the past or else stay fixed—grotesquely mounted specimens—in horrible parody of their guilt, tormented by a memory of "the only Paradise that is not the dream of a madman, the Paradise that has been lost."[10]

Such a place seems at first to compare with the futile, distorted activity or sterile inactivity of Beckett's world. In Dante, the grovelling of the Gluttonous and the aimless fisticuffs of the Wrathful in the Marsh of the Styx, the ceaseless change and interchange of forms among the

Thieves, and the Violent against God, Nature and Art stretched on a desert of burning sand, appear to stand behind the geography of *How it is*, the flux in identity of the hero of *The Unnamable*, and the plight of Winnie in *Happy Days* respectively. But the transference of the Belacqua episode into Beckett's thought belies this apparently feasible and frequently made identification as to the location of his world. Beckett's heroes are not in Hell but Purgatory: a Purgatory of waiting on the verge of timelessness. It is a grimmer place than that imagined by Dante and at times—in *Endgame* or *How it is*—almost indistinguishable from Hell. In Dante's *Purgatorio* eventual ascent, the toil uphill, was certain for even the most indolent of its inhabitants, but in Beckett there is no certitude; only the confusion and doubt of a limbo with no known end and no discernible path. What perhaps misleads is the appearance of Belacqua, a character from the *Purgatorio*, as one of Beckett's central images, against a landscape which often relies heavily upon the imagery of the *Inferno*. Yet in Hell one pursues one's monotonous activities without reason through all eternity, while in Beckett's cosmology a shred of hope remains. Paolo and Francesca, tossed and flailed upon a howling wind, are for ever hopeless; the hero of the trilogy, aware that one of the thieves was saved even upon the cross, and prompted by the mysterious intervention of the Hypothetical Imperative, still anticipates an ultimate relief.

The Beckett hero progresses to the edge of timelessness where he is compelled to wait, like Hamm, for "the moments to mount up to a life."[11] Again Dante's Belacqua provides the image, Belacqua who is also trapped at an impasse by his late repentance and unable to ascend. Belacqua's dilemma, that of a man whose life is over but not yet ended, reliving his existence on his foothold at the base of Mt. Purgatory, becomes the dilemma of the hero in the trilogy. For example Molloy who puzzles over the contradiction of his life as something over and yet continuing—"My life, now I speak of it as something over, now as a joke which still goes on, and it is neither, for at the same time it is over and it goes on, and is there any tense for that?"[12] and Malone who, on the brink of departure, goes over his life yet again.

In the end Beckett's heroes are left waiting, like the figures in Dante's Ante-Purgatory, for the gate to be unlocked and the angel to guide them on their way to Paradise, but with the important difference that waiting remains the limit of their progress. The stasis is unrevoked; the angel, like Godot, does not come.

> VLAD: Well? Shall we go?
> EST: Yes, let's go.
>
> *They do not move*
>
> CURTAIN[13]

Yet neither does their life in time regress; earth is the purgatorial now between before and after, the contingent present encircled by the void.

Out of Belacqua's inactive position overlooking what Beckett calls "the austral sea," emerges the tremor of an archetypal association which extends this image of Purgatory. For the sea, which stretches away from the earth into the unknown and against which man is as nothing, has repeatedly aroused overtones of the eternal. On earth man is finite—three score years and ten—but in the sea he finds an image for the eternity from which he has come and to which he will soon return. From the Epic of Gilgamesh to Baudelaire's *Le Voyage* the earth-confining sea has been viewed with awe, and poetry has often given to it a significance that outweighs even its natural, implacable force. The hero of the Gilgamesh epic crosses the ocean to find Utnapishtim the Faraway who alone knows the secret of everlasting life, and Baudelaire enlists the aid of Death himself to weigh anchor and captain the ship that will take him "Into the unknown in search of the new!" The rock where Belacqua and Beckett's heroes shelter also appears to be on the verge of this eternal ocean of release. Several of the heroes make their way to the sea-shore where they experience moments of unusual peace. Beckett himself stands there in the four, short Dieppe poems;[14] Henry in *Embers*, attempts to contact the dead from his past while the waves claw at the shingle on which he sits; and Malone ends the story of Macmann with the boatful of lunatics drifting out into the immensity of the ocean, significantly at the moment when he himself crosses over from life into death.[15]

But the most trenchant of these examples is Molloy's journey to the seaside in search of sucking stones. He recalls that "Much of my life has ebbed away before this shivering expanse,"[16] and describes some of the advantages of life on the sea-shore: the excitement of digging holes in the sand, how one's sight improves with the uninterrupted view, and the pleasure of living in caves. Then briefly he remembers an instance when he journeyed on the sea itself: "And I too once went forth on it, in a sort of oarless skiff, but I paddled with an old bit of driftwood. And I sometimes wonder if I ever came back, from the voyage. For if I see myself putting to sea, and the long hours without landfall, I do not see the return, the tossing on the breakers, and I do not hear the frail keel grating on the shore."[17] This disappearance into the unseen distance of the ocean is as close as Molloy comes to being a speck in the void, at one with nothingness. It raises one of the frequent imponderables in Beckett's work, and creates the poetry of uncertainty which gives to his writing those moments of intimation with their suggestion of a half-forgotten, preconceptual and non-rational truth.

Thus Dante, in the person of Belacqua, gave Beckett an image for the condition which he has explored with obsessive honesty throughout his work. Belacqua with his certainty of eternity and Beckett's hero with his dubious hope, both cling tenaciously to the rock overlooking the infinite sea where they dream again the events of their past and suffer the Purgatory of waiting for the final voyage into bliss. In Beckett's beginning is his end for, true to the dictum he applauded in *Proust*, his later writing is a descent into the area originally suggested by the character and fate of a one-time lute maker of thirteenth-century Florence.

Notes

1. *Transition*, The Hague, no. 21, pp. 13–20.
2. *Purgatorio*, Canto 4, 1.97–139, trans. Dorothy Sayers, Penguin Classics, 1955.
3. *Molloy*, p. 11.
4. *Murphy*, p. 56.
5. *Out of this Century*, Dial Press (New York), 1946, p. 205.
6. *Watt*, p. 31.
7. *The Unnamable*, p. 361.
8. *Proust*, p. 67.
9. *Paradise Lost*, II, 557–61.
10. *Proust*, p. 74.
11. *Endgame*, p. 45.
12. *Molloy*, p. 36.
13. *Waiting for Godot*, p. 94.
14. *Poems in English*, p. 47.
15. Note also this fragment from the addenda to *Watt*: "dead calm, then a murmur, a name, a murmured name, in doubt, in fear, in love, in fear, in doubt, wind of winter in the black boughs, cold calm sea whitening, whispering to the shore, stealing, hastening, swelling, passing, dying, from naught come, to naught gone" (*Watt*, p. 247).
16. *Molloy*, p. 68.
17. *Ibid.*, p. 69.
18. *The Novels of Samuel Beckett* (Chatto and Windus), 1964, p. 15.

Belacqua in the Moon: Beckett's Revisions of "Dante and the Lobster"

Kay Gilliland Stevenson*

The first sentence of Samuel Beckett's "Dante and the Lobster"—"It was morning and Belacqua was stuck in the first of the canti in the moon"[1]—gives the reader pause. Or it should. Some ideal combination of information and ignorance is demanded by the story. Those experienced in Beckett's fiction may know too much, or assume they do, about his early collection of stories and therefore find it difficult to feel again the edge of wrongness in that opening sentence. Belacqua "stuck in the first of the canti in the moon"? How the hell did he get there? And in the morning, as well. In the context of Dante's *Commedia* the time is wrong, the place is

*This essay was prepared for this volume and is published here for the first time.

wrong, and the action—or kind of inaction "stuck" establishes—is, if not quite wrong, certainly not quite right. It is precisely noon (*Paradiso* I. 43–45) when Dante enters the sphere of the moon, where those inconstant in their vows glow and rejoice now in the grace which saved them. Belacqua does not belong in the canti of the moon, *Paradiso* II–V, at all; Dante met him far away, back in the fourth canto of *Purgatorio*, waiting with others late in repentence for a span of time equal to his earthly life before he can enter purgatory proper. He is waiting with striking stillness and lassitude—"more indolent than if sloth were his sister"[2]—but this immobility has a completely different quality from that of "stuck." That would be an odd verb even in relation to *Purgatorio* and it is absurd for *Paradiso*, explicitly absurd given that in the second of the canti in the moon Piccarda and other blessed shades smile at Dante's ignorance when he asks whether they don't desire a higher place; she corrects his assumption that they might feel stuck in this lowest sphere of paradise: "In His will is our peace. It is that sea to which all things move" (*Paradiso* III.85–86).

Though "impatient to get on to Piccarda," Belacqua slams shut his book when he hears midday strike. Here Belacqua of Dublin is distinguished from Belacqua of Florence, but with a minimum of circumstantial evidence. In later stories of *More Pricks Than Kicks* he acquires a surname, a "strong weakness for oxymoron" (p. 41), and various girlfriends. Knowing such details is far from necessary; indeed they can obscure the achievements of "Dante and the Lobster," the first story in the collection and one of the few which Beckett was willing to see reprinted for more than three decades.[3] Students of Beckett too familiar with Belacqua Shuah may treat him with contempt. Raymond Federman, who considers all the stories of *More Pricks Than Kicks* together, describes Belacqua as if he were a consistent character and asserts that his "pedantry, arrogance, egocentricism, and morbidity reject the compassion aroused by Beckett's later heroes."[4] He is, in "Dante and the Lobster," less easily summed up. Furthermore, a number of the changes Beckett made in revising the story between its first appearance in *This Quarter* (Winter 1932) and *More Pricks Than Kicks* (1934) work to increase the balance, or ambiguity, of Belacqua's presentation, and thus increase the tension between judgment and charity which is a major theme. Any single pronouncement about Belacqua would be as inappropriate as a single view of the moon, which presides over all three clearly marked sections of the story.

When Ruby Cohn briefly surveys the revisions made between the 1932 and 1934 printings, she concludes that "the main purpose of revision was to sharpen the comic."[5] Despite admiration for Beckett's "early elegance," she finds the three incidents of the story inadequately unified and focused: "Each . . . is described in such meticulous and sardonic detail that the underlying theme, the difficulty of reconciling divine mercy with divine justice, frequently fades away."[6] Concerned with comic techniques, she underestimates the seriousness of the story.[7] I think that more needs to be said about the revisions, in relation to Belacqua, to the question of unity, and to the stylistic elegance which is a source of the comic and troubling effects. Both the instances she cites of comic incongruity arising from "an image that is ludicrously out of key with what it describes" will repay further exploration: "In 'Dante and the Lobster,' there are several examples of incongruity which are sharpened in the revised version: 'to feel his fangs break through the splendid hard crust of toast into a yielding zone' becomes 'to feel his teeth meet in a bathos of pith and dough.' Similarly 'so that the whole presented an appearance of a diamond and square with common centre' is changed to 'so that the whole resembled the Japanese flag.' "[8]

In the first of Cohn's examples, Beckett is naming explicitly a central rhetorical device for "Dante and the Lobster." From the title onward, equilibrium in the reader is troubled by juxtaposition of the grand and the commonplace. What have Dante and a lobster to do with each other, coupled in a coordinate phrase? Bathos is, again, wittily dominant in Beckett's play on the significance of the moon, as Belacqua moves from the blessed souls of *Paradiso* to a sandwich of green cheese. The bathetic and profound jostle in Belacqua's day: as his "three large obligations" of lunch, lobster, and Italian lesson parody Dante's trinitarian structures, as the story links the deaths of McCabe, Christ, and a lobster, and as his thoughts swing from banality ("We live and learn, that was a true saying") to theological questions ("Why not piety and pity, even down below? Why not mercy and Godliness together?").

The pattern of a Japanese flag, in Cohn's second example, contributes not simply to incongruity in general, but to the single most important image unifying Belacqua's progression through lunch, lesson, and lobster. After Beckett has changed the shape of Belacqua's loaf of bread from square to round, thus providing a new pattern on his toaster, Japan's rising sun is mirrored by the charred, seared moon on whose spots Beckett continues to muse. Beginning in the moon of *Paradiso*, "Dante and the Lobster" is as moonstruck as *A Midsummer Night's Dream*, and it triumphantly combines materials as diverse. Dante's moon underlies the high seriousness of the story, for in *Paradiso* the moon figures both the salvation of Piccarda and the wanderings of Cain (since Dante includes this folklore identification of the man in the moon by having Beatrice refute it). Lower comedy, and a different folklore about the moon, appear in Belacqua's exuberant, obsessive examination of the central ingredient in his lunch. It lacks any odor of sanctity: "He rubbed it. It was sweating. That was something. He stooped and smelt it. A faint fragrance of corruption. What good was that? He didn't want fragrance, he wasn't a bloody gourmet, he wanted a good stench. What he wanted was a good green stenching rotten lump of Gorgonzola cheese, alive, and by God he would have it" (pp. 13–14). For the third section of the story, the moon makes a final, more puzzling appearance. "Let us call it Winter," says Beckett, "that dusk may fall now and a moon rise" (p. 20). Now this is a bit like the scarves in *Murphy*; it simply doesn't work out. Twice a year in the Northern Temperate Zone, thus in Dublin, sunset and moonrise coincide—for a few days around full moon at the autumnal equinox ("harvest moon") and again at the next full moon ("hunter's moon"). Neither could be called "Winter," and if there is definitely no autumnal fruition in the story, at least it is not the moon of Cain, tiller of the field. What Beckett provides here is typically Beckettian, in its wintry but not entirely dark setting, and in its fictive impossibility. It is also highly Dantean. At first I was inclined to think that Beckett was deliberately creating something entirely new. Reflection, however, produced—reflection. This winter moonrise is equal and opposite to the Dante's first sunrise. In the *Commedia*, the moon sets as the sun rises on Good Friday 1300. But scholars searching for a cluster of astronomical facts which will fit the descriptions find that "there is no day in the year 1300 which meets all these conditions"[9] established by Dante for the sun and moon. Like Dante, Beckett creates an ideal rather than a naturalistic pattern.

In so moonstruck a story, it is natural that Belacqua should have some tinges of lunatic, lover, and poet. The virtuosity with which Beckett plays with his identity is not confined to the initial double-take, Belacqua of Florence and Belacqua of Dublin. In curious ways, at various points, he is associated with Dante and with the lobster, with Christ and with Cain.

Studying Beatrice's different explanation of spots on the moon, Belacqua is something of a model for the literary critic: "Still he pored over the enigma, he would not concede himself conquered, he would understand at least the meanings of the words, the order in which they were spoken and the nature of the satisfaction that they conferred on the misinformed poet, so that when they were ended he was refreshed and could raise his heavy head, intending to return thanks and make formal retraction of his old opinion" (p. 9). In that sentence, "he" is at first firmly linked with Belacqua but becomes Dante by the end. The grammatical slippage does not occur in the *This Quarter* version; one of Beckett's revisions supplies the parallel series of verbs: "he would not concede . . . he would understand" to "could raise his heavy head." Moreover, in 1932 the next sentence, opening paragraph two, begins unequivocally "Belacqua" but in 1934 "He."

Dante's *Convivio*, from which Beckett had quoted shortly before, in his contribution to *Our Exagmination* . . . (1929), provides a link between verbal structures and the recurrent, changing moon. Dante associates the planetary spheres with the seven liberal arts, and the moon is the sphere of grammar. The kind of literary criticism with which Belacqua starts is that of the grammarian—the meanings of the words, the order in which they were spoken. What satisfactions follow? If one picks up a copy of *Paradiso* to check on the passage over which Belacqua is poring, finding there Dante raising his heavy head after Beatrice's explanation, and reads on to the appearance of Piccarda, one finds a gently ridiculous picture of Dante adjusting his view. When Piccarda appears, Dante takes her for a reflection, a mirror image, and he turns around, looking behind him. Reading "Dante and the Lobster" demands similar readjustments, recognition of mirroring relationships, the discovery of congruity in incongruous materials. Here is wit in Locke's sense, perception of likeness in unlike objects. Moreover, Beckett induces in the reader something like the habitual self-corrections, the scrupulous rejections of easy formulations, which he gives his most moving major characters.

A paragraph on moonspots (identical in the 1932 and 1934 versions) is sandwiched without transition between paragraphs describing Belacqua madly, methodically charring bread for his sandwich: "For the tiller of the field the thing was simple, he had it from his mother. The spots were Cain with his truss of thorns, dispossessed, cursed from the earth, fugitive and vagabond. The moon was that countenance fallen and branded, seared with the first stigma of God's pity, that an outcast might not die quickly. It was a mix-up in the mind of the tiller, but that did not matter. It had been good enough for his mother, it was good enough for him" (pp. 11–12). Something odd is going on with the pronouns again. In "he had it from his mother," who is "he" and what is "it"? Is it the explanation of moonspots Belacqua had from his mother (the explanation which Beatrice rejects in the first of the canti in the moon), or is the mother not Belacqua's but Eve, and "it" the original sin Cain inherits from her? As the first of Beckett's footsore protagonists ("his feet were in ruins, he suffered with them almost continuously"), Belacqua has other links with wandering Cain. The description of his charred toast as "burnt . . . offering" (p. 12) could make him equally close to Cain or to Abel – as the name of condemned criminal McCabe makes him son of Abel or son of Cain.

He is curiously close to the lobster as well, partly because of marine metaphors. He "suddenly dived into a little family grocery" (p. 13) and goes "diving into the public, as usual" (p. 16); he reflects that "all had gone swimmingly" (pp. 16–17) with lunch and the collection of the lobster. In revising the first paragraph between 1932 and 1934, Beckett expands watery images. The phrase "complicated and up in the air" is abandoned; "straightforward" is replaced by "plain sailing." In 1932 Belacqua "was bogged, and could not get on." In 1934, "He was so bogged that he could move neither backward nor forward." A reader may recollect that one of the striking characteristics of lobsters is their swimming backward, and further reflect that Belacqua's movement in the story is in some sense a backwards version of Dante's pilgrimage, regressing from Paradise in the early paragraphs "down into the bowels of the earth, into the kitchen in the basement" for the final pages. There, in his shock at finding that lobsters are boiled alive, Belacqua mirrors "Dante's rare moments of compassion in Hell" with distant punning on the phrase he had quoted in his Italian lesson: "qui vive la pietà quando è ben morta," that is, "here pity lives when by rights it is dead."

The lobster is twice compared with Christ. Belacqua and his aunt contemplate it "cruciform on the oilcloth" (p. 21). Earlier, he identifies it for the French teacher as a fish, with a play on the Greek anagram ΙΧΘΥΕ: "He did not know the French for lobster. Fish would do very well. Fish had been good enough for Jesus Christ, Son of God, Saviour. It was good enough for Mlle. Glain" (p. 19).

Belacqua's name, according to Hugh Kenner, is "compounded from Dante and gutter-Irish (Bollocky)."[10] Amorous activity, prominent in other stories of *More Pricks Than Kicks*, plays little part in "Dante and the Lobster," except insofar as Belacqua's sentimental and flirtatious relationship to his Italian teacher, a middle-aged woman "who had found being young and beautiful and pure more of a bore than anything else" (p. 18), remotely parodies Dante's relationship to Beatrice. The qualities, and the quality, of "Dante and the Lobster" are apt to be obscured when *More Pricks Than Kicks* is discussed as a collection in which "In the main, Belacqua is involved in adventures with various ladies."[11] While "Bollocky" possibilities are not developed, literal translations of the name into English and Irish underline the unity and the contradictions of the story. The epithet "Blissful Beatrice" in the opening paragraph encourages a reader to translate names directly. In English, Belacqua as "beautiful water" is ironically appropriate for the lobster's violent end. In Irish, the name changes to *fionn uisce* or Phoenix (the transformation by which Phoenix Park got its name), evoking one of the traditional symbols of Christ, as the phoenix which once in a thousand years bursts into flame and arises again from the ashes.

In both versions of the story, Belacqua's identity is fluid, as befits his name. In the second version, however, there occurs what might be called an improvement in his character. Some phrases are toned down: "a vicious piece of hooliganism" (1932, p. 225) becomes "hooliganism pure and simple" (1934, p. 12). Given the etymological precision with which other words are employed, the disappearance of "vicious" is particularly significant. When Belacqua "deployed an old Herald," the verb has the full sense of *dis-plicare*, unfold, and a white slice of bread is literally a "candidate." Belacqua does not, of course, become fully virtuous by such a revision, but he becomes more ambiguous. A few sentences of no great importance, but generally unsympathetic, disappear completely: "His mind was tired, it could not be bothered carrying him beyond the lesson. . . . He did not feel like fake enthusiasm at the moment" (*This Quarter*, pp. 223, 230). In both versions, his lunch is "spiced" by the news that McCabe will hang at dawn. But in 1932, "If anything was wanted to crown that exquisite gastronomical experience, it was just such a piece of news" (p. 231), while in 1934 zest gives way to unspecified pungency: "Belacqua, tearing at the sandwich and swilling the precious stout, pondered on McCabe in his cell" (p. 17).

When Belacqua calculates his timetable for picking up the lobster, "Assuming that his aunt had given her order in good time . . . so that her nephew should on no count be delayed" becomes more roughly phrased: "aunt" becomes "lousy old bitch of an aunt," and "nephew" becomes "blackguard boy." Curiously, however, the two derogatory phrases almost cancel each other; if Belacqua (or the narrator) is casually abusive about the aunt, he is also jocularly dismissive about the nephew. Furthermore, "blackguard" may be a small etymological joke: the equal and opposite of "candidate"; the first definition for "blackguard" in the *OED* reads: "The lowest menials of a royal or noble household, who had charge of pots and pans and other kitchen utensils, and rode in the wagons conveying these during journeys from one residence to another; the scullians and kitchen-slaves." One sentence added in 1934 is more ambiguous. After "He had burnt his offering, he had not fully dressed it," Beckett inserts, "Yes, he had put the horse behind the tumbrel" (p. 12). First, by turning a proverbial phrase around so that the cart is not (verbally) ahead of the horse, Beckett is neatly repeating and exemplifying the idea of lobster-like progress backwards. Secondly, however, the substitution of "tumbrel" for "cart" links Belacqua not with the lobster, innocent as Abel, but with executioners. There are many of these in the story: Cain, God as punisher of Cain, Ellis the hangman crossing from England to dispatch McCabe, and Belacqua's aunt matter-of-factly lifting the lobster into the pot.

Perhaps influenced by Joyce, Beckett radically simplified punctuation in the 1934 edition. One result is to make the distinction between Belacqua and the narrator, which is fine in both versions, even harder to draw. Beckett leaves such tags as "He thought," but removes the quotation marks which in 1932 mark the ends of internal direct discourse: "At the corner of the street a horse was down and a man sat on its head. I know, thought Belacqua, that that is considered the right thing to do. But why? A lamplighter flew by on his bike, tilting with his pole at the standards, jousting a little yellow light into the evening" (p. 20). The inquiring spirit of Belacqua, one of his attractive qualities, is clear. It is not, however, clear whether the metaphoric perception of the lamplighter as a knight belongs to him or to the narrator. In 1932 quotation marks signpost "But why?" as the end of Belacqua's conscious thought, but here as in other paragraphs the modulation between Belacqua's consciousness and the narrator's is subtle or disconcerting. Except for the third-person pronoun, a description of Belacqua's eagerness to "avoid being accosted" seems to be his own view of the situation, idiosyncratic but engagingly vigorous: "To be stopped at this stage and have conversational nuisance committed all over him would be a disaster" (p. 13). Two sentences later, Beckett changes the 1932 phrasing "hunger—obviously more of mind than of body" to "hunger, more of mind, I need scarcely say, than of body," and thus jostles a reader not only by the shift from vivid hyperbole to cliché but also by the insistent, intrusive *I*.

In 1934, the triangle of asterisks which set off the three sections of the story disappear, although a few centimeters of white space are left. Any reasonably alert reader can see without the help of the asterisks that, like the *Commedia*, the story is tripartite. Belacqua lists the major units—lunch, lesson, and lobster—and the second and third sections begin with the same phrase: "Belacqua drew near to the school . . . Belacqua drew near to the house of his aunt." Given a reference to McCabe's last supper (p. 20), the phrase thus emphasized by position and repetition suggests the liturgical "Draw near with faith." For a reader steeped in Scripture, and alerted to echoes of the Bible by references to burnt offerings, Cain, Pilate, and Jonah, the phrase may recall Abraham's protesting at the destruction of Sodom: "And Abraham drew near and said, Wilt thou also destroy the righteous with the wicked?" (Genesis 18:23). It could also evoke Luke 15, a chapter in which Jesus tells three parables about God's mercy or his rejoicing over the saved, the parables of the lost sheep, the lost coin, and the prodigal son: "Then drew near unto him all the publicans and sinners to hear him" (Luke 15:1). God's awareness of even the fall of a sparrow (though Belacqua sweeps away crumbs "as though there were no such thing as a sparrow in the wide world," p. 11) and the story of "Jonah and the gourd and the pity of a jealous God on Nineveh" (p. 20) on which Belacqua ponders are among the clear Biblical allusions. Belacqua refrains from mentioning one obvious Biblical story, even more watery than Jonah's: by omitting the Flood he keeps the balance of justice and mercy tilted, precariously, toward mercy.

Simplified punctuation in 1934 shows Beckett trusting a reader to catch the allusion to Keats near the end of the story. In 1932, a snatch of the "Ode to a Nightingale," l. 54, is set off with quotation marks and followed by ellipsis marks: "Take into the air my quiet breath . . . ," thus sending one off to look at its richly ironic context. Within the stanza, "easeful Death" (l. 52) and "To cease upon the midnight with no pain" (l. 56) contrast with the lobster's boiling; in the larger pattern, wishful imagination is defeated by experience. The quotation appears in 1934 without any signal, except the shift from "it" to "my," that Belacqua's train of thought about the lobster has been complicated: "In the depths of the sea it had crept into the cruel pot. For hours in the midst of its enemies, it had breathed secretly. It had survived the Frenchwoman's cat and his witless clutch. Now it was going alive into the scalding water. It had to. Take into the air my quiet breath" (p. 21). I vaguely wondered whether the line was the refrain of a sentimental Irish tenor's song, and felt shocked and chastened when I finally placed it.[12]

The longest addition to the story consists of two sentences inserted into the paragraph about Gorgonzola cheese: "He knew a man who came from Gorgonzola. He had been born in Nice but all his youth had been spent in Gorgonzola" (p. 13). These apparently random recollections reinforce Beckett's equally casual introduction of the *Herald*, the newspaper on which Belacqua slices his loaf. Dublin's *Evening Herald* is a major newspaper but hardly the only one he could have had at hand; it's the *Telegraph* that is mentioned in "Fingal." No messenger is to appear in this story with tidings of joy or a ram caught in a thicket, but the *Herald* and Angelo together join other oblique references to Dante and the moon. Angels proper, as distinct from the more elevated seraphim, cherubim, thrones, dominions, virtues, powers, principalities, and archangels, are the order presiding over the sphere of the moon. Dante catalogues the nine orders in *Paradiso* XXVIII.

Not quite the first published narrative by Beckett, "Dante and the Lobster" would be almost too neat a beginning for his career: dark but not completely dark, elegant and deliberately banal, comic and troubling, carefully crafted and calling attention to its artifice. In the penultimate sentence, Belacqua hopefully ameliorates the lobster's fate: "Well, thought Belacqua, it's a quick death, God help us all." Beckett's justly famous last sentence reproves easy resolutions.

Notes

1. Samuel Beckett, *More Pricks Than Kicks* (London: Calder, 1970). This is substantially a reprint of the 1934 text. Subsequent references are given in parentheses after quotations.

2. *The Divine Comedy of Dante Alighieri*, Italian text with English translation and commentary by John D. Sinclair (New York and Oxford, 1961), 3 vol. *Purgatorio* IV.110–11. From this canto of *Purgatorio* Belacqua brings a general aura of amusement, mockery, and affection; he brings very little hard information about his identity, since little except his indolence and some friendship with Dante is provided in the poem, and editors' notes are cautiously laconic ("Said to have been a musical instrument maker of Florence with whom Dante was familiar," says Sinclair, in full). The figure of Belacqua recurs in Beckett's later fiction, most recently in *Company* (London: Calder, 1980): "So sat waiting to be purged the old lutist cause of Dante's first quarter-smile and now perhaps singing praises with some section of the blest at last" (p. 85). His huddled position is familiar to Beckett's readers, who might not be surprised to find him anywhere. For a perceptive survey of Beckett's use of Dante, see Michael Robinson, "From Purgatory to Inferno: Beckett and Dante Revisited," *Journal of Beckett Studies*, no. 5 (Autumn 1979):69–82.

3. Raymond Federman and John Fletcher, *Samuel Beckett: His Works and His Critics, An Essay in Bibliography* (Berkeley, Los Angeles, and London: University of California Press, 1970), pp. 13–14 list one reprint for "The Smeraldina's Billet Doux" and "Yellow," and four for "Dante and the Lobster." They note that the 1934 edition of *More Pricks Than Kicks* "is now rare," but that "Mr. Beckett has so far not been willing to authorize its republication." The mimeographed typescript editions issued by Calder and Boyars in 1966 and 1967 were labelled "Special edition Hors Commerce for Scholars." A commercial reprint did not appear until 1970.

4. Raymond Federman, *Journey to Chaos: Samuel Beckett's Early Fiction* (Berkeley and Los Angeles: University of California Press, 1965), p. 53.

5. Ruby Cohn, *Samuel Beckett: The Comic Gamut* (New Brunswick: Rutgers University Press, 1962), pp. 18–19.

6. Ibid., pp. 18–19.

7. Ibid,, pp. 30–31.

8. Ibid., p. 31. Her page references to the 1934 edition have been omitted.

9. Philip H. Wicksteed, notes to the Temple edition of *The Inferno* (London, 1900), p. 396. Cf. the ideally symmetrical cosmos in some of Beckett's later prose pieces (e.g. *Imagination Dead Imagine*, 1965).

10. Hugh Kenner, *Samuel Beckett: A Critical Study* (London: Calder, 1962), p. 39.

11. Cohn, p. 18. Cf. Brian Finney, "What is distinctive about this first book of short stories is its concentration on Belacqua's sexual misadventures," "Beckett's Shorter Fiction," in *Beckett the Shape Changer*, ed. Katherine Worth (London: Routledge and Kegan Paul, 1975), p. 66.

12. For emphasis on the significance of "Ode to a Nightingale" for Beckett's work in general, see Barbara Hardy, "The Dubious Consolations in Beckett's Fiction: Art, Love and Nature," in *Beckett the Shape Changer*, p. 117.

Appendix: The opening paragraphs of "Dante and the Lobster" in 1932 and 1934.

This Quarter (Winter 1932)

Belacqua was stuck half-way through the first of the great Moon Canti. He was bogged, and could not get on. Blissful Beatrice was there, and Dante, and she explained the spots on the moon to him. First she showed him where he was at fault, then she put up her own explanation. She had it from God, so he could rely on its being accurate in every particular. It was only a question of following the argument, step by step. The first part, the refutation, was straightforward. She made her point clearly, she said what she had to say without fuss and without loss of time. But the second part, the demonstration, was so complicated and up in the air that Belacqua could not make head or tail of it. The disproof, the reproof—that was neat, fleet and lucid. But then came the proof—a dense, involved showing forth of the real facts of the case; and Belacqua was bogged. Also, he was bored. He was in a great hurry to get on to Piccarda. Still, he pored over the enigma, resolved not to give in just yet, stiffy resolved to understand at least the meaning of the words, and the order in which they were spoken, and the nature of the satisfaction that they conferred on the misinformed poet, so that when they were ended he was refreshed and raised his heavy head, intending to return thanks and make formal retraction of his old opinion.

More Pricks than Kicks (1934, reprint 1970)

It was morning and Belacqua was stuck in the first of the canti in the moon. He was so bogged that he could move neither backward nor forward. Blissful Beatrice was there, Dante also, and she explained the spots on the moon to him. She showed him in the first place where he was at fault, then she put up her own explanation. She had it from God, therefore he could rely on its being accurate in every particular. All he had to do was to follow her step by step. Part one, the refutation, was plain sailing. She made her point clearly, she said what she had to say without fuss or loss of time. But part two, the demonstration, was so dense that Belacqua could not make head or tail of it. The disproof, the reproof, that was patent. But then came the proof, a rapid shorthand of the real facts, and Belacqua was bogged indeed. Bored also, impatient to get on to Piccarda. Still he pored over the enigma, he would not concede himself conquered, he would understand at least the meanings of the words, the order in which they were spoken and the nature of the satisfaction that they conferred on the misinformed poet, so that when they were ended he was refreshed and could raise his heavy head, intending to return thanks and make formal retraction of his old opinion.

The Utopia of Mr. Knott's House

Lawrence E. Harvey*

Arsene's parting words tell us a good deal about the situation in which, a man like Watt, at a certain age, may find himself. . . . It is a situation defined in essentially negative terms. Watt's arrival means first of all an end to blind wandering: "The dark ways all behind. . . ." Movement does not cease altogether, but it is no longer a flight or a search or a social commitment. Instead it has become "a stirring beyond coming and going." Activity does not come to a halt, but there are no more questions, orders, explanations, for the sounds that come "demand nothing, ordain nothing, explain nothing" (p. 39).[1] Even though the new arrival in Knott's house does not find, as he hoped he would, "a situation where to do nothing exclusively would be an act of the highest value, and significance," quite different from the "superficial loitering" and "disinterested endeavour" that tormented and horrified him, respectively, in the past, he is soon reconciled to a service of "unquestionable utility . . . [and] exceptional fruitfulness" (p. 41) that benefits him even more than his master. It is significant that the work done for Mr. Knott ("he peels the potato and empties the nightstool") is of a routine, manual nature, requiring no decisions and exempt from anxiety. Knott's servant goes about his tasks "calm and glad" (p. 42). Knott's home is a "refuge" (p. 39) and, as the etymology of the term implies, a retreat or flight back to the source. We are therefore hardly surprised to find figures of a return to the womb along with related images incorporating softness, warmth, darkness, or enclo-

*Reprinted from *Samuel Beckett: Poet and Critic, 1929–1949* (Princeton: Princeton University Press, 1970).

sure. Approaching Knott's house, Watt feels weak and rests by the side of the road, assuming the foetal position (p. 33). Earlier, a clearly positive value is attached to the "warm nest of books and periodicals" (p. 25) of the news agent who witnesses Watt's run-in with the porter in the railway station. At the end, in the insane asylum, Watt enjoys the "separate soundless unlit warmth" of his padded cell. On the level of irony, the conditions obtaining in the mind of Mr. Thomas Nackybal, the Visicelt brought back by Mr. Ernest Louit from western Ireland in support of his dissertation, "The Mathematical Intuitions of the Visicelts," compose a metaphorical correlative of the ideal state to be found in the womb. Apart from an almost instinctive "knowledge of how to extract, from the ancestral half-acre of moraine, the maximum of nourishment, for himself and his pig, with the minimum of labour," his mind is "an ecstasy of darkness, and of silence" (p. 175).

In the amusing hoax perpetrated by Mr. Louit, Beckett takes advantage of a variant form of the myth of the good savage to satirize academia and, indirectly, man's obsessive need to know. At the same time he suggests a link between what Murphy called the microcosm of the mind and the prenatal state. Under the proper conditions perhaps the former can approximate the latter, can become, that is, a place in which one can live. The utopia of Mr. Knott's house has much in common with the "little world" of Murphy's mind. Indeed, the author employs the identical term to describe it when he writes of "the little world of Mr. Knott's establishment" (p. 85). Often enough, however, the focus narrows still further to the microcosm inside Watt's skull. There, when thought stops and the body is placated and quiet, Watt experiences, in auditory terms, something closely akin to Murphy's "pure forms of commotion" (*Murphy*, p. 112): "He lay on the seat, without thought or sensation, except for a slight feeling of chill in one foot. In his skull the voices whispering their canon were like a patter of mice, a flurry of little grey paws in the dust" (p. 232). Such an experience, the enjoyment of pure form, is conditional upon an absence of thought or meaning. It can arise spontaneously in the mind if circumstances are favorable, or it can come from the song or speech of Mr. Knott: "The words of [Mr. Knott's] songs were either without meaning or derived from an idiom with which Watt, a very fair linguist, had no acquaintance. . . . Mr. Knott talked often to himself too, with great variety and vehemence of intonation and gesticulation, but this so softly that it came, a wild dim chatter, meaningless to Watt's ailing ears. This was a noise of which Watt grew exceedingly fond. . . . while it sounded he was gladdened, as by the rain on the bamboos . . ." (p. 209). The phrase "rain on the bamboos" recalls the poem "Alba" and by thematic association "Dortmunder" as well, and the state of contemplative ataraxy produced in both poems through the influence of music, i.e., nonreferential sound, pure form. As we shall shortly see, the ghost of Schopenhauer, invoked in "Dortmunder," is with us still in *Watt*.

A number of other images are used to describe the utopia of *Watt*, all of them in one way or another suggesting a negation. On several occasions life is rendered inanimate or scaled down from the human or animal to the vegetable level. Arsene imagines himself "longing to be turned into a stone pillar or a cromlech" (p. 49) and the fate of Daphne, metamorphosed into a laurel tree, is envisioned not with sadness but rather as an altogether happy way out of a disagreeable situation (p. 44). Images of freedom *from* and separation *from* are further indications of a continuing process of stripping away, not unrelated to Arsene's description of the three kinds of laughter as "successive excoriations of the understanding" (p. 48). Existence in the macrocosm is like existence on a ladder, a constant mounting and descending, an organized relation between one thing and another, between one step and another, a logical, practical, tiring business. Life in Knott's house, at least at times, is equivalent to "existence off the ladder" (p. 44). In this context the joke "Do not come down the ladder, Ifor, I haf taken it away" (p. 44) suggests a utopian situation. Treadmill existence has been replaced by isolation, nonrelation, reduced mobility, and possibly a greater sense of enclosure—recalling the womb, Knott's house, and life in the mental microcosm. Much later in the novel we find a related passage with images that suggest Belacqua's cup or funnel: "one is in the pit, in the hollow . . . at the foot of all the hills at last, the ways down, the ways up, and free, free at last . . ." (p. 202). Arsene's sentiments were identical when he spoke of the "sites of a stirring beyond coming and going," of a being "light and free," of "the secret places where nobody ever comes" (p. 39).

The logical culmination of the tendency to reduce, negate, eliminate is *le néant*, and we do indeed find that images of nothingness, beginning with the house of Mr. Knott, are very frequent. When Beckett finishes describing Watt's aversions, little is left: "For if there were two things that Watt disliked, one was the moon, and the other was the sun" (p. 33). And very shortly thereafter, "And if there were two things that Watt loathed, one was the earth, and the other was the sky" (p. 36). Arsene speaks of a being that is "as the being of nothing" (p. 39). Much later we learn that "In empty hush, in airless gloom, Mr Knott abode. . . . And from it this ambience followed him forth, and when he moved, in the house, in the garden, with him moved, dimming all, dulling all, stilling all, numbing all, where he passed" (p. 200). The middle years, between the contrary yearnings of youth and the decay of old age, are like Mr. Knott's house, a kind of respite between torments where "the gnashing ends" and "one is . . . nothing at last" (p. 202). Belacqua had his "womb-tomb," his "limbo," as Murphy had his "little world," but they were occasional escapes; Mr. Knott's house, for a time at least, is Watt's world, and everything else is peripheral. When Arsene speaks of the transition from the outside world of youth to the inner world of middle age, his words describe a Belacqua, the "border man," becoming a Watt: "he will be in his midst at last, after so many tedious years spent clinging to the perimeter" (p. 41). A similar figure involving the circle occurs later on in the same context of alienation from the integration into one's proper context. The painting in Erskine's room, of a circle and a point, causes Watt to wonder "how long it would be before the point and circle entered together upon the same plane. . . . if they had sighted each other . . . [whether] the artist had intended to represent . . . a circle and its centre in search of each other, or . . . a circle and a centre not its centre in search of a centre and its circle respectively, in boundless space, in endless time . . . and at the thought that it was perhaps this . . . Watt's eyes filled with tears that he could not stem . . ." (p. 129).

All the externals that are stripped away are "other." Together they make up the illusory, insubstantial outside world. They distract. They clutter the context called Nothing, in which a man can be at home, perhaps discover the true nature of his own being. As Arsene explains, in Knott's abode the wanderer reaches his destination. Finally, for the first time, the alien, the misfit, is "the right man, at last" and "in the right place, at last" (p. 40). The theme of untimeliness . . . in the poetry recurs in *Watt*. It is a temporal form of the spatial out-of-placeness that Lucky evokes in *Godot* when he refers to "l'air la terre, faits pour les pierres" (and not, he implies, for man). Outside are "the languor and the fever of the going of the coming too late, the languor and the fever of the coming of the going too soon. But to Mr Knott, and with Mr Knott, and from Mr Knott, were a coming and a being and a going exempt from languor, exempt from fever, for Mr Knott was harbour . . ." (p. 135). Beckett's dualistic vision, in which the two halves exist in uneasy, inappropriate alliance, for once, even if briefly, gives way to a kind of mystical harmony between man and nature. Arsene describes the moment when one arrives at Mr. Knott's house and feels the "premonitions of harmony . . . , of imminent harmony, when all outside him will be he, the flowers . . . the sky . . . the earth . . . , and all sound his echo . . ." (pp. 40–41). Arsene would seem to accent his creator's adaptation of the insight of Democritus that nothing is more real than nothing (*Murphy*, p. 246), for in his opinion "it was not an illusion, as long as it lasted, that presence of what did not exist, that presence without, that presence within, that presence between . . ." (p. 45).

If Nothing is a state more real than the one in which man finds himself in the world beyond Mr. Knott's house and garden, it is nevertheless defined primarily in negative terms. And the principal precondition for the "presence of what did not exist," to which we now come, is the absence of desire, need, will. Once Arsene "was in the sun, and . . . was the sun . . . and the wall and the step, and the yard, and the time of year, and the time of day." His "personal system was so distended . . . that the distinction between what was inside it and what was outside it was not at all easy to draw." Then "something slipped," and he finds himself back in the old dualistic fix, in an alien land as before, with the old needs, the old yearnings. The metamorphosis has been reversed: "The Laurel into Daphne" (pp. 42–44). Especially as it relates *Watt* to the central predicament of Belacqua, the invocation of the myth is of the utmost importance. Belacqua was torn between two desires, figured by Apollo and Narcissus or the need to go out to the other and the need to retreat into the self, pursuit of the girl (for youth, the emblem par excellence of desire) and flight from her. Limbo was the abolition of both needs. The laurel occupies the same place in *Watt*. Devoid of need, conscious need in any case, the tree is a part of nature and in harmony with it. There is no longer any distinction between subject and object. Turned back into Daphne, this being reenters a world of attractions and repulsions, loves and hates, comings and goings determined by needs positive and needs negative, desires for association and yearnings for solitude.

How much better would life be without *atra cura*, the "black want" of the poems. "And yet it is useless not to seek, not to want, for when you cease to seek you start to find. . . ." Satisfaction of needs merely gives rise to other needs. And fulfillment itself is considerably less desirable than the state of wanting: "when you cease to want, then life begins to ram her fish and chips down your gullet until you puke, and then the puke down your gullet until you puke the puke, and then the puked puke until you begin to like it." For Arsene, at least, the depressing fact is that the closest one can get to happiness is the state of unfulfilled desire, "to hunger, thirst, lust, every day afresh and every day in vain, after the old prog, the old booze, the old whores . . ." (p. 44). And yet Beckett, with Schopenhauer, makes it clear enough that the root of our misery is desire, that its ablation would be felicity. Influenced no doubt by the torments of Swann needing Odette, of the narrator wanting Gilberte, Beckett ends his introduction to *Proust* with a quote from Leopardi that gives away his own view of the dilemma: "non che la speme, il desiderio è spento."

Although Arsene rejects fulfillment as a way out, it seems to play some part in the ideal hypothetical solution that the author sets up. For Mr. Knott is perhaps above all the one who does *not* need. He provides the standard against which all other attempts to establish a utopian mode of existence must be measured. "For except, one, not to need, and, two, a witness to his not needing, Knott needed nothing, as far as Watt could see." Mr. Knott seems to maintain his happy state of indifference by doing things—even though he has no need to do them—that, were they left undone, might have the power to create needs in him. He wears many varieties of clothes, for example, clothes for all seasons and occasions, but indiscriminately, without regard to the season or occasion. So it is with his other activities. They are invariably explainable by his nature: that of a non-needing being. "If he ate and he ate well; if he drank, and he drank heartily; if he slept, and he slept sound; if he did other things, and he did other things regularly, it was not from need of food, or drink, or sleep, or other things, no, but from the need never to need, never never to need, food, and drink, and sleep, and other things" (p. 202).

Knott's mode of being has an effect on the surroundings. "This ataraxy covered the entire house-room, the pleasure-garden, the vegetable-garden and of course Arthur [Watt's successor on the ground floor]" (p. 208). In referring to the root condition of the utopia he calls "Nothing" Watt speaks of "the longing for longing gone, the horror of horror" (p. 202). Not only have attraction and repulsion, or positive and negative desire, vanished. The need for desire has also been abolished, and that is the crux of the matter. Man not only desires, he desires to desire—which is disastrous. He seems incapable under ordinary conditions of living in limbo. He seeks to want. His comings and goings are purposeful, and he is forever coming and going. Only Knott "seems to abide" (p. 58). And yet human progress is no progress at all, as Watt's vision after leaving Knott's house indicates. Since the flame of desire is eternally rekindled from its own ashes, all our comings and goings, which in *Watt* are figures of the needs that propel us, are futile. All motion is equivalent to stasis, since it brings us right back to the starting point: need. With Estragon and Vladimir, we move in place.

In the metaphoric structure of the novel, the sojourn in Knott's house is a time of staying and a time of nonwilling. It represents in general an end to the comings and goings that are outward manifestations of desire. The comings and goings in Knott's house are of a different nature. They are not determined by Watt. He is a servant who follows the rules of the establishment. He is not expected to make decisions.[2] His status as an obedient servant is a principal prerequisite to the tranquility of indifference (p. 39), to the "willlessness" that is the *summum bonum*. Watt enjoys Knott's "wild, dim chatter," but he is not sorry when it ceases nor glad when it begins again (p. 209). When he leaves Knott's house, he does so "with the utmost serenity." Only after he has left the premises does "he burst into tears" (p. 208). While in Mr. Knott's house he suffers "neither from the presence . . . nor from [the] absence" of his master (p. 207). And yet Watt is by no means always exempt from the common condition of need, even in Knott's house. The novel, then, appears to pose the following question: "Is there a place, like the house of Mr. Knott, in which the normal condition of need can be transcended?"

Notes

1. Page numbers of *Watt* (New York: Grove Press, 1959) will be cited parenthetically.

2. Cf. Belacqua in "Ding-Dong." Incapable of deciding which direction to take, he must wait for a sign.

Mercier and Camier

Ludovic Janvier*

Mercier and Camier make a couple. "Pseudo-couple" a subsequent character will later call them, condemning the work as a pseudo-work rather than condemning their association. Despite certain schematic inperfections, an association does indeed exist between this pair. They decide *together* to leave the town because it flaunts and bullies them both, they travel together by train or on foot, either toward or in the Irish countryside, they make acquaintances together in an inn, they come back to the town together because apparently they cannot really leave it . . . and, together, they try to leave again, do leave, then come back finally to separate there in the rain that softly falls just as it did during the first departure.

This coupling of two wanderering paths is also, we suspect, the coupling of two solitudes, though in a slightly different way than in Beckett's preceding work. Mercier and Camier are associated like Watt and Sam, of course, and sustain and complete each other. (A character named Watt makes an ambiguous appearance at the end of *Mercier and Camier*, implicitly drawing attention to the already palpable link between different motifs: physical discomfort, lack of meaning, the desperateness of solitude.) But also, and here is the decisive change, this couple rends itself. Ultimately, they will break up. They love each other but make each other suffer. They need one another, fall to tears and to prostration though separated by only a few feet, if it looks like their community might end; but, back together, they can exchange insults, fight, and mutually reproach the condition that the weighty presence of the other imposes. A trial at fraternity, their naive association is the first sketch of a friendship that will fail—perhaps because Beckett has not yet found the savage mold that will save Vladimir and Estragon, but also because at this point separation and failure constitute the only possible outcome for an adventure with a twosome. In the earlier novel, Watt merely stopped along his way at Sam's. His own adventure, in *Watt*, required the stop, just as the adventure of *Mercier and Camier*, set in motion by the narrator named Beckett, requires that the individual be by himself. Mercier and Camier make a pseudo-couple because they come too soon. Their solution is too easy—hence null and void—because it dodges around the central problem: the confrontation of the individual, *alone*, with the world, and the elocution of the main issue of this drama.

Mercier and Camier abounds nonetheless in important landmarks. The first of these is the appearance of the Irish countryside. Henceforth, each work will recall more or less the soil, the grass, the sky, the rain

*Translated, by permission of the publisher, from *Pour Samuel Beckett* (Paris: Editions de Minuit, 1966). Translated for this volume by Gordon Browning, University of Miami.

(already so present in *Watt*): that is, on the one hand, a dire earthbound necessity that will take as its ultimate and monstrous forms the mud of *How It Is* and the mound where Winnie lives half buried in *Happy Days*, and, on the other hand, the movement that goes from the mud to the blue sky: "With what relief the eyes from this clutter [move] to the empty sky" (40).[1]

Next is the opening out of this space onto the incommensurateness of time. A new curse, foreseeable already in *Watt* but now completely acknowledged, strikes the individual: that is, the feeling of never being able to get out of an enormous time where the present is drowned; as one of the characters says, "past and future merged in a single flood and closed, over a present for ever absent" (32). Other images can be grouped here that denounce this emptiness which is also a prison, from time as "Balue in his cage," meaning by that a time "so short it is not worth their while beginning, too long for them not to begin" (76), up to the realization that the vastness of each instant is such, and the distance needed to catch up with time, to catch up with one's self in time, is so long (cf. Belacqua) that one can only resign oneself, out of despair and calmly, "once and for all to thirsting in the darkness" (87). The sound of this voice will reoccur.

In addition we have now the definitive making of the bum. Mercier and Camier are Watt, twicefold and down to the details. They make three of a kind, enough to form the line-up of these run-down characters which henceforth we will never get away from. Decked out as hobos, dirty, stinky, ridiculous silhouettes outlined against a background of the countryside or standing out among the city dwellers for whom their very presence is an insult, they live in front of us, proposing as the only answer to their derisory destiny a parody of their own behavior. The word destiny is no exaggeration, since, as we have noted, it is *Mercier and Camier* which first uncovered so forcefully the enormous stretch of time that human existence is called to fill. Just as Watt, frightened by the emptiness of reality, fills the space of possibilities with his reasoning, here the enormous stretch of time is furrowed, slowly, consciously, but uselessly, by the double paths of the couple. Consciously—for they take their time, even measure out the space-time which is alotted to them. But uselessly also because there is no progress in the gigantic circular time into which we are plunged. Hence the trip's immobility. Hence also the usefulness of conversation. The high degree of humor in their exchanges is not enough to define the use they make of words. We must add this as a justification for the platitudes and quaint expressions they shamelessly string along: "Gab was my salvation, every day a little more, a little better" (38).

Here then is their final contribution, stressing the "acted" character—inherited from Watt—of their double existence. They go, but never arrive. They leave, only to come back. They speak, but to no purpose.

In summary, the Beckettien type has been born, for we may say that it comes to life, even in this couple that fails, as the cruel and radical experience of the Monad.

Note

1. Quotes from Samuel Beckett, *Mercier and Camier* (New York: Grove Press, 1974).

The Trilogy

The Cartesian Centaur

Hugh Kenner*

. . . whilst this machine is to him. . .
—*Hamlet*

Il n'y a plus de roues de bicyclette.
—*Fin de Partie*

Molloy had a bicycle, Moran was carried on the luggage rack of a bicycle, Malone recalls the cap of the bell of a bicycle, bicycles pass before Watt's eyes at the beginning and at the end of his transit through the house of Knott; Clov begged for a bicycle while bicycles still existed, and while there were still bicycles it was the wreck of a tandem that deprived Nagg and Nell of their legs. Like the bowler hat and letter M, the bicycle makes at irregular intervals a silent transit across the Beckett *paysage intérieur*, whether to convince us that this place has after all an identity of sorts, or else like the poet's jar in Tennessee to supply for a while some point about which impressions may group themselves. If it is never a shiny new substantial bicycle, always a bicycle lost, a bicycle remembered, like Nagg's legs or Molloy's health, that is a circumstance essential to its role; like the body it disintegrates, like the body's vigor it retires into the past: *Hoc est enim corpus suum*, an ambulant frame, in Newtonian equilibrium.

Molloy is separated from his bicycle as the first stage in a disintegration which entails the stiffening of one leg, the shortening of the other leg which had previously been stiff, the loss of the toes from one foot (he forgets which), a staggering in circles, a crawling, a dragging of himself flat on his belly using his crutches like grapnels, brief thoughts of rolling, and final immobility, in a ditch. "Molloy could stay, where he happened to be." Formerly, while he possessed the bicycle, he had a less derelict posture in which to stay where he happened to be: "Every hundred yards or so I stopped to rest my legs, the good one as well as the bad, and not only my legs, not only my legs. I didn't properly speaking get down off the machine, I remained astride it, my feet on the ground, my arms on the

*Reprinted from *Samuel Beckett: A Critical Study* (New York: Grove Press, 1961) by permission of the Sterling Lord Agency, Inc.

handle-bars, and I waited until I felt better." In this tableau man and machine mingle in conjoint stasis, each indispensable to the other's support. At rest, the bicycle extends and stabilizes Molloy's endoskeleton. In motion, too, it complements and amends his structural deficiencies: "I was no mean cyclist, at that period. This is how I went about it. I fastened my crutches to the cross-bar, one on either side, I propped the foot of my stiff leg (I forget which, now they're both stiff) on the projecting front axle, and I pedalled with the other. It was a chainless bicycle, with a free-wheel, if such a bicycle exists. Dear bicycle, I shall not call you bike, you were green, like so many of your generation, I don't know why. . . ." This odd machine exactly complements Molloy. It even compensates for his inability to sit down ("the sitting posture was not for me any more, because of my short stiff leg"); and it transfers to an ideal, Newtonian plane of rotary progression and gyroscopic stability those locomotive expedients improbably complex for the intact human being, and for the crippled Molloy impossible.

In various passages of the canon, Beckett has gone into these expedients in some detail. For more than half a page he enumerates the several classes of local movement entailed by "Watt's way of advancing due east, for example"; the protagonist of "L' Expulsé" devotes some 500 words to a similar topic, noting that every attempt to modify his somewhat awkward methods "always ended in the same way, I mean by a loss of equilibrium, followed by a fall," while the characteristic progression of the protagonist of "Le Calmant" "seemed at every step to solve a statodynamic problem without precedent." "The hands and knees, love, try the hands and knees," cries Winnie in *Happy Days*. "The knees! The knees! (*Pause.*) What a curse, mobility." For the human body is to the Newtonian understanding an intolerably defective machine. It possesses, in the upright position, no equilibrium whatever; only by innumerable little compensatory shiftings does it sustain the illusion that it is standing motionless, and when it moves forward on its legs it does so by periodic surrender and recovery of balance, in a manner too hopelessly immersed in the *ad hoc* for analytic reconstruction. Every step is improvised, except by such dogged systematizers as Watt. And this was the kind of machine whose union with the pure intelligence puzzled Descartes, who invented the mode of speculation in which all Beckett's personages specialize. "But there is nothing which that nature teaches me more expressly than that I have a body which is ill affected when I feel pain, and stands in need of food and drink when I experience the sensations of hunger and thirst, etc. And therefore I ought not to doubt but that there is some truth in these informations."

That last sentence, despite Descartes' proclaimed certainty, has Molloy's tone, and the whole passage—it is from the Sixth Meditation (1641)—prompts comparison with certain speculations of The Unnamable: ". . . Equate me, without pity or scruple, with him who exists, somehow, no matter how, no finicking, with him whose story this story had the brief ambition to be. Better, ascribe to me a body. Better still, arrogate to me a mind. Speak of a world of my own, sometimes referred to as the inner, without choking. Doubt no more. Seek no more. Take advantage of the brand-new substantiality to abandon, with the only possible abandon, deep down within. And finally, these and other decisions having been taken, carry on cheerfully as before. Something has changed nevertheless." These fiats and revulsions come closer to the Cartesian spirit than Descartes himself; for Descartes, when he took his attention away from the immutable truths of mathematics, could resolve manifold confusions about the human estate "on the ground alone that God is no deceiver, and that consequently he has permitted no falsity in my opinions which he has not likewise given me a faculty of correcting." But this premise comes from outside the System, and a Molloy or a Malone have little confidence in it; to say nothing of The Unnamable, who assumes that the superior powers deceive continually. The Beckett protagonists would accord the classic resolutions of the Cartesian doubt a less apodictic weight than Descartes does; and notably his conclusion that the body, "a machine made by the hands of God," is "incomparably better arranged, and adequate to movements more admirable than is any machine of human invention." For unlike that of Molloy, the Cartesian body seems not subject to loss of toes or arthritis of the wrists.

So committed is Descartes to this perfect corporeal mechanism, that the question how a fine machine might be told from a man requires his most careful attention, especially in view of the circumstance that a machine can do almost anything better: "A clock composed only of wheels and weights can number the hours and measure time more exactly than we with all our skill." His answer is far from rigorous, based as it is on just that interpenetration of body and reason which he is elsewhere so hard put to explain. Molloy or Malone would have less difficulty with this question. The body, if we consider it without prejudice in the light of the seventeenth-century connoisseurship of the simple machines, is distinguished from any machine, however complex, by being clumsy, sloppy, and unintelligible; the extreme of analytic ingenuity will resolve no one of its functions, except inexactly, into lever, wedge, wheel, pulley, screw, inclined plane, or some combination of these. If we would admire a body worthy of the human reason, we shall have to create it, as the Greeks did when they united the noblest functions of rational and animal being, man with horse, and created the breed to which they assigned Chiron, tutor of Asclepius, Jason, and Achilles. For many years, however, we have had accessible to us a nobler image of bodily perfection than the horse. The Cartesian Centaur is a man riding a bicycle, *mens sana in corpore disposito*.

This being rises clear of the muddle in which Descartes leaves the mind-body relationship. The intelligence guides, the mobile wonder obeys, and there is no mysterious interpenetration of function. (The bicycle, to be sure, imposes conditions; there is no use in the intelligence attempting to guide it up a tree. God in the same way cannot contradict His own nature.) Down a dead street, in "Le Calmant," passes at an unassignable time a phantom cyclist, all the while reading a paper which with two hands he holds unfolded before his eyes. So body and mind go each one nobly about its business, without interference or interaction. From time to time he rings his bell, without ceasing to read, until optical laws of unswerving precision have reduced him to a point on the horizon. Across the entire Beckett landscape there passes no more self-sufficient image of felicity.

It grows clear why for Molloy to describe his bicycle at length would be a pleasure, and why Moran "would gladly write four thousand words" on the bicycle his son buys, which must once have been quite a good one. Though neither of these descriptions is ever written, we do receive a sufficiently technical account of the mode of union—not to say symbiosis—between each of these bicycles and its rider. ("Here then in a few words is the solution I arrived at. First the bags, then my son's raincoat folded in four, all lashed to the carrier and the saddle with my son's bits of string. As for the umbrella, I hooked it round my neck, so as to have both hands free to hold on to my son by the waist, under the armpits rather, for by this time my seat was higher than his. Pedal, I said. He made a despairing effort. I can well believe it. We fell. I felt a sharp pain in my shin. It was all tangled up in the back wheel. Help! I cried. . . .") The world is an imperfect place; this theme deserves to be explicated on a more ideal plane. Let us try.

Consider the cyclist as he passes, the supreme specialist, transfiguring the act of moving from place to place which is itself the sentient body's supreme specialty. He is the term of locomotive evolution from slugs and creeping things. Could Gulliver have seen this phenomenon he would have turned aside from the Houyhnhnms, and Plato have reconsidered the possibility of incarnating an idea. Here all rationalist metaphysics terminates (as he pedals by, reciprocating motion steadily converted into rotary). The combination is impervious to Freud, and would have been of no evident use to Shakespeare. This glorified body is the supreme Cartesian achievement, a product of the pure intelligence, which has preceded it in time and now dominates it in function. It is neither generated nor (with reasonable care) corrupted. Here Euclid achieves mobility: circle, triangle, rhombus, the clear and distinct patterns of Cartesian knowledge. Here gyroscopic stability vies for attention with the ancient paradox of the still point and the rim. (He pedals with impenetrable dignity, the sitting posture combined with the walking, *sedendo et ambulando*, philosopher-king.) To consider the endless perfection of the chain, the links forever settling about the cogs, is a perpetual pleasure; to reflect that a specified link is alternately stationary with respect to the sprocket, then in motion with respect to the same sprocket, without hiatus between these conditions, is to entertain the sort of soothing mystery which, as Moran remarked "with rapture" in another connection, you can study all your life and never understand. The wheels are a miracle; the contraption moves on air, sustained by a network of wires in tension not against gravity but against one another. The Litany of the Simple Machines attends his progress. *Lever, Pulley, Wheel and Axle*: the cranks, the chain, the wheels. *Screw*, the coaster brake. *Wedge*, the collar that attends to the security of the handlebars. And the climax is of transparent subtlety, for owing to the inclination of the front fork, the bicycle, if its front wheel veers left or right, is returned to a straight course by the action of an invisible sixth simple machine, the *Inclined Plane*; since so long as it is not holding a true course it is troubled by the conviction that it is trying to run up hill, and this it prefers not to do. Here is the fixation of childhood dream, here is the fulfillment of young manhood. All human faculties are called into play, and all human muscles except perhaps the auricular. Thus is fulfilled the serpent's promise to Eve, *et eritis sicut dii*; and it is right that there should ride about France as these words are written, subject to Mr. Beckett's intermittent attention, a veteran racing cyclist, bald, a "stayer," recurrent placeman in town-to-town and national championships, Christian name elusive, surname Godeau, pronounced, of course, no differently from Godot.[1]

Monsieur Godeau, it is clear from our speculations, typifies Cartesian Man in excelsis, the Cartesian Centaur, body and mind in close harmony: the mind set on survival, mastery, and the contemplation of immutable relativities (*tout passe, et tout dure*), the body a reduction to uncluttered terms of the quintessential machine. From the Beckett canon it is equally clear that M. Godot, this solving and transforming paragon, does not come today, but perhaps tomorrow, and that meanwhile the Molloys, Morans, and Malones of this world must shift as they can, which is to say, badly. Cartesian man deprived of his bicycle is a mere intelligence fastened to a dying animal.

The dying animal preserves, however, stigmata of its higher estate. Molloy, after his bicycle has been abandoned, does not then resign himself to the human shuffle and forego that realm where arc, tangent, and trajectory describe the locus of ideal motion. No, even in his uncycled state he is half mechanized; he can lever himself forward, "swinging slowly through the sullen air." "There is rapture, or there should be, in the motion crutches give. It is a series of little flights, skimming the ground. You take off, you land, through the thronging sound in wind and limb, who have to fasten one foot on the ground before they dare lift up the other. And even their most joyous hastening is less aerial than my hobble." ("But these are reasonings, based on analysis," he is careful to add, locating but not submitting to the tragic flaw in the Cartesian paradise.) After his legs give out he is able to adapt the principle of the rack and pawl: "Flat on my belly, using my crutches like grapnels, I plunged them ahead of me into the undergrowth, and when I felt they had a hold, I pulled myself forward, with an effort of the wrists." Periodically, as he crashes forward in this way, like the prototype of a moon-camion, he improves on the analogy with a bicycle of some inefficent pattern by blowing his horn ("I had taken it off my bicycle") through the cloth of his pocket. "Its hoot was fainter every time."

Reciprocating motion, it seems, is a characteristic of Molloy's, whether mounted on his bicycle or not. The unusual chainless bicycle, transmitting power apparently locomotive-fashion by the reciprocating rod,[2] accents this motif. Nor is he the only person in these books whose mode of progression is a studied and analyzed thing, distinct from human inconsequence. It is oddly relevant to say of Beckett characters, as of Newtonian bodies, that they are either at rest or in motion; and in the Beckett universe, motion, for those who are capable of setting themselves in motion, is an enterprise meriting at least a detailed description, and more likely prolonged deliberation. Malone's creature Macmann, for example, commences to roll on the ground, and finds himself "advancing with regularity, and even a certain rapidity, along the arc of a gigantic circle probably," one of his extremities being heavier than the other "but not by much." "And without reducing his speed he began to dream of a flat land where he would never have to rise again and hold himself erect in equilibrium, first on the right foot for example, then on the left, and where he might come and go and so survive after the fashion of a great cylinder endowed with the faculties of cognition and volition."

Malone himself, on the other hand, is at rest; and so far is the Cartesian mechanism dismantled, that it would take, he estimates, several weeks to re-establish connection between his brain and his feet, should there be any need for that. He has, needless to say, no bicycle, and nowhere speaks of a bicycle; but he includes among his possessions not only half a crutch but the cap of his bicycle bell: the least rudiment, like the knucklebone of a dinosaur. Yet to him too occurs the idea of playing at Prime Mover: "I wonder if I could not contrive, wielding my stick like a punt-pole, to move my bed. It may well be on castors, many beds are. Incredible I should never have thought of this, all the time I have been here. I might even succeed in steering it, it is so narrow, through the door, and even down the stairs, if there is a stairs that goes down." Unhappily at the first trial he loses hold of the stick instead, and meditating on this disaster claims intellectual kinship with another speculative Mover: "I must have missed my point of purchase in the dark. Sine qua non. Archimedes was right."

Let Archimedes' presence disconcert no one: the Beckett bicycle can orchestrate all the great themes of human speculation. Since the Beckett people transact their most palpable business in some universe of absence, however, it is without surprise that we discover the bicycle to have put in its most extended and paradigmatic appearance in a novel which has not been published. This is the composition of *c.* 1945 which details certain adventures of what The Unnamable is later to call "the pseudocouple Mercier-Camier." I translate from a French typescript:

> You remember our bicycle? said Mercier.
> Yes, said Camier.
> Speak up, said Mercier. I hear nothing.
> I remember our bicycle, said Camier.
> There remains of it, solidly chained to a railing, said Mercier, that which can reasonably be said to remain, after more than eight days' incessant rain, of a bicycle from which have been subtracted the two wheels, the saddle, the bell, and the carrier. And the reflector, he added. I nearly forgot that. What a head I have.
> And the pump, naturally, said Camier.
> You may believe me or you may not, said Mercier, it is all the same to me, but they have left us our pump.
> Yet it was a good one, said Camier. Where is it?
> I suppose it was simply overlooked in error, said Mercier. So I left it there. It seemed the most reasonable course. What have we to pump up, at present? In fact I inverted it. I don't know why. Something compelled me.
> It stays just as well inverted? said Camier.
> Oh, quite as well, said Mercier.

This exchange bristles with problems. Having undergone a Molloy's dismemberment, has the bicycle at some stage rendered up its identity? Or is it identifiable only as one identifies a corpse? And in no other way? In some other way? Again, assuming that a bisected rhomboid frame of steel tubing equipped with handlebars and a sprocket is recognizably a bicycle, has this congeries of sensible appearances relinquished its essence with the removal of the wheels? From its two wheels it is named, on its two wheels it performs its essential function. To what extent ought a decisiveness of nomenclature persuade us to equate function, essence, and identity? These are matters to agitate a schoolman; they would certainly have engaged the careful attention of Watt. Mercier, *homme moyen sensuel*, is sufficiently schooled in precision to acknowledge in passing the problem, what can reasonably be said to remain of a bicycle thus reduced, but insufficiently curious to pursue this investigation. His attention lingers instead, a bit antiseptically, on two human problems, the first perhaps ethical (whether, since the anonymous autopsist has presumably only forgotten the pump, it ought not to be left for him) and the second hermeneutic (why, having chosen to leave it, he himself did not forbear to turn it upside down).

These several classes of questions, as it turns out, are of greater formal brilliance than practical import. The Mercier-Camier universe is soured by unassignable final causes, as in their astringent laconism the two of them seem half to acknowledge. They are in the presence, actually, of an archetypal event, or perhaps a portent, or perhaps a cause: there is no telling. In retrospect, anyhow, one thing is clear: from the dismemberment of their bicycle we may date the disintegration of Mercier and Camier's original lock-step unity. In the final third of this novel they gradually become nodding acquaintances, like the two wheels which were once sustained by a single frame but are now free to pursue independent careers. This separation is not willed, it simply occurs, like the dissolution of some random conjunction of planets: "pseudo-couple," indeed.

For The Unnamable there is no stick, no Archimedes, no problem whatever of the Malone order, or of the Mercier-Camier order, chiefly because there is no verifiable body; and there is no mention of a bicycle nor reflection of a bicycle nor allusion to a bicycle from beginning to end of a novel, in this respect as in others, unprecedented in the Beckett canon. Nor is this unexpected; for *The Unnamable* is the final phase of a trilogy which carries the Cartesian process backwards, beginning with a bodily *je suis* and ending with a bare *cogito*. This reduction begins with a journey (Molloy's) and a dismembering of the Cartesian Centaur; its middle term (*Malone Dies*) is a stasis, dominated by the unallayable brain; and the third phase has neither the identity of rest nor that of motion, functions under the sign neither of matter nor of mind because it evades both, and concerns itself endlessly to no end with a baffling intimacy between discourse and non-existence.

This is not to say, however, that the fundamental problems of a seventeenth-century philosopher, and notably the problems of bodies in motion, do not confront The Unnamable in their baldest form. The first body in motion is, unexpectedly, Malone, appearing and disappearing "with the punctuality of clockwork, always at the same remove, the same velocity, in the same direction, the same attitude." He may be seated, he "wheels" without a sound; the evidence in fact points to his being borne through this ideal space on some quintessential bicycle. So much for cosmology. We next confront a certain Mahood, under two aspects: Mahood in motion, Mahood at rest. In motion, on crutches but minus a leg, he executes a converging spiral; at rest, he inhabits a jar. In either aspect, he is a Descartes cursed by the dark of the moon. At rest in the jar, he pursues the *cogito* sufficiently to think of demanding proof that he exists ("How all becomes clear and simple when one opens an eye on the within, having of course previously exposed it to the without, in order to benefit by the contrast."). So pursuing "the bliss of what is clear and simple," he pauses "to make a distinction (I must be still thinking)": "That the jar is really standing where they say, all right, I wouldn't dream of denying it, after all it's none of my business, though its presence at such a place, about the reality of which I do not propose to quibble either, does not strike me as very credible. No, I merely doubt that I am in it. It is easier to raise the shrine than bring the deity down to haunt it. . . . That's what comes of distinctions."

The jar, clearly, is what the body, geometrically conceived, is reducible to by the systematizing intelligence. As for the one-legged man with the crutch, he pursues his converging spiral (the first curve to have been rectified by Descartes), complementing with his ideally incommoded motion the other's ideally perplexed cogitation, and so completing a little cosmos pervaded by the two Cartesian functions, movement and thought. He jerks, hops, swings and falls, so remote from the ancient symbiosis with a bicycle as not even to be visited by such a possibility, yet enacting as best the deficiencies of the flesh will allow his intent parody of some obsessed machine. Molloy too progressed in spirals, "through imperfect navigation," and when he was in the woods slyly resolved to outwit the deception which is reputed to draw benighted travelers into involuntary circles: "Every three or four jerks I altered course, which permitted me to describe, if not a circle, at least a great polygon, perfection is not of this world, and to hope that I was going forward in a straight line." Molloy's is plane geometry; the spiral described by the surrogate of The Unnamable is located on the surface of a sphere, and hence, if it originates from a point, can enlarge itself only until it has executed a swing equal to the globe's greatest circumference, and after that must necessarily commence to close in again. When we take up his tale, his global sweep is converging into a very small space indeed, preliminary to the moment when it will have nothing to do but reverse itself for lack of room. At the pole of convergence we are surprised to discover his family, keeping watch, cheering him on ("Stick it, lad, it's your last winter."), singing hymns, recalling that he was a fine baby.

Yet none of the enmired but recognizably human will to prevail that once animated Molloy's progress toward his mother impresses the reader of these later pages. The narrative, for one thing, is no longer impregnated by indefatigable first person energy. Mahood's progress, half something experienced by The Unnamable but half something unreliably told him, is unhitched from his empathic passions, and endeavoring to recall his (or Mahood's) thoughts and feelings he can only report absorption in the technicalities of spiral progression. "The only problem for me was how to continue, since I could not do otherwise, to the best of my declining powers, in the motion which had been imparted to me." The annihilation of his family by poison does not arrest him as he completes his rounds, "stamping under foot the unrecognizable remains of my family, here a face, there a stomach, as the case might be, and sinking into them with the ends of my crutches both coming and going."

The bicycle is long gone, the Centaur dismembered; of the exhilaration of the cyclist's progress in the days when he was lord of the things that move, nothing remains but the ineradicable habit of persisting like a machine. The serene confidence of the lordly *Cogito* . . . is similarly dissociated, in this last phase of the dream of Cartesian man, into a garrulity, vestigially logical, which is perhaps piped into him by other beings: a condition oddly prefigured by the parrot which a friend of Malone's had tried to teach to enunciate the *Nihil in intellectu quod non prius in sensu*, a doctrine it would have travestied whenever it opened its beak. It got no further than *Nihil in intellectu*, followed by a series of squawks. More profoundly than its great forerunner, *Bouvard et Pécuchet*, the Beckett trilogy takes stock of the Enlightenment, and reduces to essential terms the three centuries during which those ambitious processes of which Descartes is the symbol and progenitor (or was he too, like The Unnamable, spoken through by a Committee of the *Zeitgeist*?) accomplished the dehumanization of man. It is plain why Godot does not come. The Cartesian Centaur was a seventeenth-century dream, the fatal dream of being, knowing, and moving like a god. In the twentieth century he and his machine are gone, and only a desperate élan remains: "I don't know, I'll never know, in the silence you don't know, you must go on, I can't go on, I'll go on."

Notes

1. It may calm the skeptical reader to know that my knowledge of this man comes from Mr. Beckett.
2. Mr. Beckett recalls seeing such a bicycle when he was a boy in Dublin.

The Solipsist Voice in Beckett's Trilogy

Ihab Hassan*

The trilogy that includes *Molloy, Malone Dies*, and *The Unnamable* marks the highest achievement of Beckett in fiction. The heroes are no longer simply recumbent like Dante's Belacqua—the prototype of Watt and Murphy—who spends eternity holding his head between his knees; nor are they gradually alienated from the world of men and clouds and trees. The possibilities of motion for them are severely restricted, and their exile from reality is from the start complete. Sealed up in their mental space, they move about, fading, changing voices in the dark; constrained in all else, they lack the constraints of a particular identity. The fundamental categories of time, extension, and being are called into doubt as the fluid ego of one speaker flows into another, threatening the dissolution of all selves. "I could suppose that I had no body, and that there was no world nor any place in which I might be," Descartes states in his *Discourse on Method*, and Beckett reduces the mentalism of his master to absurdity, giving us the Unnamable.[1] The heroes of the three novels are virtually the

*Reprinted from *The Literature of Silence: Henry Miller and Samuel Beckett* (New York: Alfred A. Knopf, 1967) by permission of the author.

same hero; he is—there where the literal and the symbolic meet—ourselves. His immobility is a tension between hope and despair, desire and the void; his career is as much a quest as an escape; against death he can only pit a "hypothetical imperative." We know an aspect of his character as Kafka's K. We see him as a metaphysical seeker, say Q., and realize, Jacobsen and Mueller have noted, that the immutable laws of his quest require that nothing should be significantly altered or fully comprehended.[2] For Q. is the hero of all closed systems, subject to imperceptible decay.

Molloy was rejected many times before it was finally published in France by the Editions de Minuit (1951) and became a fine *succès d'estime*. The English translation (1955) by Patrick Bowles in collaboration with Beckett himself tends to be more faithful to the original than the translations made by Beckett alone. This novel, both stylistically and thematically, constitutes the broad foundation on which the trilogy rests. There are two sections in *Molloy*; each, narrated in the first person, depicts an absurd journey, the first by Molloy and the second by Moran. The stories, vaguely parallel, may be construed as anti-epics related to each other as Homer's epic, *The Odyssey*, is related to Virgil's, *The Aeneid*. Taken together, the two stories form a complex statement on human impotence, on the questing consciousness and the creative imagination reduced to an obscene noise.

The first section begins with a series of ambiguities suggesting that one-eyed, toothless Molloy lies crippled in a room that once belonged to his mother; presumably, a man attends to him once a week. Molloy is a stranger to everyone, a stranger even to the hand affixed to his own body. His avowed purpose is "to speak of the things that are left, say my goodbyes, finish dying." "They don't want that," he adds.[3] The simplest facts elude the narrator's certainty; question follows question; nothing is recalled clearly. The narrative moves neither by logic nor by free association but by a process of absurd precision. This is his sole activity: "What I need now is stories, it took me a long time to know that, and I'm not sure of it" [p. 15]. Molloy begins his tale by recalling that he once crouched on a hilltop, "like Belacqua, or Sordello," watching two men, A and C, approach one another on a country road. The two men are perhaps unimportant, like the two thieves on each side of the Cross, but one of them, with a cocked hat, is observed later in the novel by Moran. Molloy himself does not tell us much about these symmetrical creatures; he is more interested in finding his mother "who brought me into the world, through the hole in her arse if my memory is correct. First taste of the shit" [p. 20]. (Both Molloy and his mother are ageless, sexless, sharing the same faulty memories and rancors; she calls him Dan and he calls her Mag; and they communicate by knocking on each other's skull.) Molloy's quest involves riding with crutches on a chainless bicycle, wandering through town and country, confronting the police who force him to recall his name. These trivial events seem eternal to Molloy who suddenly turns on the reader and says: "I speak in the present tense, it is so easy to speak in the present tense, when speaking of the past. It is the mythological present, don't mind it" [p. 34]. The doctrine of eternal recurrence in myth, we see, is parodied by Molloy's doctrine of eternal non-occurrence in Beckettian story; for all such stories are really versions of the same solipsistic dream. As he lies in the real ditch in which he has really fallen, Molloy begins to think that all the world has died but for himself.

The antithesis of solipsism is love; love for Molloy, however, is an absence. On his quest for his mother, Molloy runs over the dog of a woman named Lousse, and he ends as her captive. His testicles droop, he is crippled, sterile, and impotent, yet Lousse "makes propositions" to him in the manner of Circe or Calypso, offering him love potions. (The only sexual experience Molloy recalls is with a woman, or perhaps a man, called Edith or Ruth, whom he meets in a garbage dump. "Perhaps after all she put me in her rectum," Molloy wonders. "A matter of complete indifference to me. . . . But is it true love, in the rectum?" [p. 76].) If love is not repugnant, it must be passive. Molloy does not even know why he stays with Lousse. Is it because he wants to free himself internally by accepting external bondage, as a man may feel free by walking eastward on the deck of a ship moving west? "I who had loved the image of old Geulincx, dead young, who left me free on the black boat of Ulysses, to crawl towards the East, along the deck" [p. 68]. When Molloy finally leaves Lousse, he discovers similar freedom at the beach where he collects pebbles and sucks them in every possible order to stay his hunger. "I always had a mania for symmetry," he admits [p. 114]. The deadpan repetition of meaningless rituals, with hat or crutch or stone, is of course a parody of all rhythm and order; the conception of the body as a machine is a denial of organic life; and the confusion of erotic and excremental functions is a repudiation of the vital, binding instinct. Toward the end, Molloy meets a charcoal burner who offers him undesired attentions. Molloy kicks and clobbers him almost to death, and then crawls back, via a ditch whence he is rescued, to his mother's room. Cruelty in word or deed is a Beckettian correlative of impotence.

The second part of the novel focuses on Moran, a cold, precise, punitive man, who masturbates in front of a cheval-glass, carries a bunch of keys weighing over a pound, and likes to bully his thirteen-year-old son, called, like his father, Jacques. Moran confesses: "I was not made for the great light that devours, a dim lamp was all I had been given, and patience without end, to shine it on the empty shadows" [p. 147]. On a Sunday morning in the town of Turdy, a certain Gaber, sent by the mysterious Youdi, comes to Moran with orders to find Molloy. The fastidious life of Moran is gradually disrupted; he begins the day by missing Mass and ends it by experiencing a sharp pain in the knee, while giving his son an enema. He nevertheless makes elaborate preparations for his journey, delivering himself constantly of somber reflections on human destiny. It becomes obvious that he knows something of Molloy and that his relation to him is as obscure as the relation of Youdi is to everyone else. This is what Moran says:

> I knew then about Molloy, without however knowing much about him. . . .
>
> He had very little room. His time too was limited. He hastened incessantly on, as if in despair, towards extremely close objectives. Now, a prisoner, he hurled himself at I know not what narrow confines, and now, hunted, he sought refuge near the center.
>
> He panted. He had only to rise up within me for me to be filled with panting.
>
> Even in open country he seemed to be crashing through jungle. He did not so much walk as charge. In spite of this he advanced but slowly. He swayed, to and fro, like a bear. [pp. 154f.]

As Moran goes on, it becomes apparent that he is not describing Molloy, nor even Moran, but a mythical creature that encloses both of them. In his utter self-ignorance—he thinks of himself as gentle and generous—Moran gives the lie to what he says; Molloy, on the other hand, in his utter uncertainty, gave the lie to the very possibility of knowledge. Obviously, Moran is far behind his quarry, Molloy, in grasping the wizened kernel of truth. When he comments on the excesses of verbal discourse, he intends nothing metaphysical; he is simply boasting of his laconic nature.

With his son, however, Moran takes the northern road toward the "Molloy country," traversing a market town called Bally or Ballyba, after warning his readers: "And it would not surprise me if I deviated, in the pages to follow, from the true and exact succession of events. But I do not think even Sisyphus is required to scratch himself, or to groan, or to rejoice . . . at the same appointed places" [p. 182]. One of his digressions refers to the "rabble in his head," a "gallery of moribunds": Murphy, Watt, Yerk, Mercier and all the others, avatars of the Beckettian hero, who also assayed the same futile quest. As might be expected, the adventures of Moran are arbitrary: his knee is stricken by anchylosis; he dispatches his son to procure a bicycle; he meets C, or someone like him, carrying a club; he meets a short man, who vaguely resembles Moran himself, and beats him to a pulp with a heavy stick like C's; his son returns three days later with a bicycle. After a violent quarrel with Moran, the son vanishes, and Gaber suddenly appears with orders for Moran—who is now wasting away—to return home. The journey home is as painful as Molloy's. The whole realm of matter conspires to balk and resist him. When Moran, now utterly decrepit, reaches his house in the spring, he finds everything empty, locked. He lives on, hobbling about on crutches, renouncing all things of this world. "I have been a man long enough, I shall not put up with it any more, I shall not try any more. I shall never light this lamp again," he states [p. 240]. Outside, it is midnight and raining; or is it neither raining nor midnight? A voice persuades him to write a report.

In *Molloy*, Beckett is obviously employing two closed, interlocking structures that reflect one another. Molloy begins his story in his mother's room and ends it there with some ironic pastoral meditations. Moran records his search for Molloy, beginning his report in his room at midnight while it is raining and ending it there. Molloy does not change much; he is what Moran will become. Moran loses his health, possessions, confidence, and knowledge, and comes to realize, like Molloy, that language subsumes the futility of human existence. Moran, therefore, follows Molloy and turns into an absurd creator in his report. In this, Moran follows Beckett himself who wrote the story of both Molloy and Moran, putting the reader in the same overseeing relation to Moran that Moran is placed to Molloy. Thus the futility of endless reflection may be recognized as infinite.

Molloy is a serious and original work. In it, Beckett introduces us for the first time to the hero as absurd narrator, a voice droning in the wilderness of its solipsism. In doing so, Beckett casts doubt not only on the evidence of the senses or the value of logical analysis; he further subverts the powers of the imagination. For Beckett's creatures are as suspicious of their creator as they are themselves contemptuous of whatever they can create; their creative acts are debased games that merely mirror another game, ad infinitum. The originality of the work also derives from its vision of shifting, merging beings, called by various proper names, who strain toward one another, seeking desperately a whole "I." This is apparent in the correspondences between the careers of Molloy and Moran, in their dim yet persistent awareness of each other, and in their occasional self-forgetfulness, as if their identities would suddenly dissolve into that of a mysterious self, like Youdi's. Finally, *Molloy* presents us not only with a reflexive image of itself but also with an inverted image of the world. Its cosmology is "inside out," its rituals are, like those of the Black Mass, parodies of church rituals. The excremental takes the place of the sacramental as Molloy speculates about his anal birth and constantly evokes the fecal associations of love. We move in a cone-like *Inferno*, the inverse below of what lies in the heavens above, which comes to a point in Satan's crotch. In keeping with this black cosmology, Beckett suggests Youdi as a parody of God and permits Moran to parody the Lord's Prayer: "Our Father who art no more in heaven than on earth or in hell, I neither want nor desire that thy name be hallowed, thou knowest best what suits thee" [p. 229]. In short, *Molloy* embodies all the parodic impulses of Beckett in a form more complete than any he has hitherto devised. The form, nevertheless, deeply unsettles our views of language and structure, self and society, mind and nature; for it scoffs at all possibilities of human order.

Malone Dies (1956) follows easily from *Molloy*; both novels actually came out the same year (1951) in France. The English version, however, tends to be harsher than the French; as self-translator, Beckett took liberties with his text that betray the austerity he felt with the years. Malone is still a more "advanced" case than Molloy or Moran. Thus he begins: "I SHALL SOON BE QUITE DEAD AT LAST IN SPITE OF ALL. . . . Yes, I shall be natural at last. I shall suffer more, then less, without drawing any conclusions, I shall pay less heed to myself, I shall be neither hot nor cold anymore, I shall be tepid, I shall die tepid, without enthusiasm. I shall not watch myself die. . . ."[4]

It soon becomes apparent that Beckett is presenting us with a portrait of the artist as malicious player. For Malone forgives no one: "I wish them all an atrocious life and then the fires and ice of hell and in the execrable generations to come an honoured name" [p. 2]. And Malone decides to do nothing but play to death: "Now it is a game, I am going to play. I never knew how to play, till now. . . . Perhaps as hitherto I shall find myself, abandoned in the dark, without anything to play with. Then I shall play with myself" [pp. 2f.]. Toothless, nearing a century of decay, Malone is fed soup by an old woman in his room—"Dish and pot, dish and pot, these are the poles"—unbeknown to his "stupid flesh" [pp. 7, 9]. With the help of a long stick, hooked at the end, he controls the world of matter in the skull-like space around him. His finicky mind takes endless inventories of his goods and reels out stories; what he writes is what we read.

The stories concern a number of fictional characters who become fused and confused with their creator who hopes to gain reality through them. First, there is an earnest school boy, called Sapo or Saposcat. "Nothing is less like me than this patient, reasonable child, struggling all alone for years to shed a little light upon himself, avid of the least gleam, a stranger to the joys of darkness," Malone solemnly states [p. 17]. Sapo the child, however, is father to Malone the man; "try and live, cause to live, be another, in myself, in another," the dying Malone says [p. 19]. Sapo is then transmogrified into the aged and reptilian Macmann, found first sitting on a bench in the heart of town and later prostrate on the ground under heavy rain. Macmann ends in an asylum where he peeps on a copulating couple across the way and carries on an "affair" with his haggish nurse, Moll. The affair, of course, is a hideous parody of love. Moll dies of an excess of "dry and feeble clips" with the impotent Macmann, and Lemuel, the male nurse, replaces her. Lemuel is a sadistic figure of power; he beats Macmann and butchers two sailors on an island excursion organized by a Lady Pedal. As the sun sets, Lemuel pushes off in the boat, which contains Macmann, among others. The night is strewn with absurd lights. Lemuel raises his bloody hatchet; but his hand can never come down precisely because Malone's pencil has stopped moving. The story has ended, and with it the man who can live only so long as he can tell it: "never anything . . . there . . . anymore" [p. 120].

Malone's stories, however, are interspersed by dark mutterings and reflections. Statements like "Nothing is more real than nothing" rise up from the pit of his consciousness and threaten to drag him down. Echoes of childhood songs call forth ironic thoughts of Easter and the Resurrection of Christ who saved him "twenty centuries in advance." The idea that he may be already dead returns to haunt Malone, as do memories of the time he changed into a thick mud-like liquid. Exactly at the mid-point of the novel, Malone halts his narrative to declare dramatically: "I feel it's [death?] coming. . . . I wanted to be quite sure before I noted it," and a little later he adds: "Then it will be all over with the Murphys, Merciers, Molloys, Morans and Malones, unless it goes on beyond the grave" [pp. 60, 63]. But again and again he pauses to cry: Quick, quick, my possessions! Malone ends by admitting to the reader: "All is pretext, Sapo . . . Moll, the peasant . . . my doubts which do not interest me, my situation, my possessions . . ." [p. 107].

In *Malone Dies*, then, Beckett is not using two narratives, each reflecting the other; he is forcing the same narrative to reflect itself in the course of its own progress. (This reflexive quality is sometimes demonstrated in the same sentence, wherein the second part may comment on the writing of the first part.) Moreover, Malone, more than Molloy or Moran, depends for his existence on the act of narration; the absurd creator has no reality whatsoever outside the act that he condemns as absurd. When Malone ceases to scrawl, Lemuel is petrified; when Lemuel ceases to move, hatchet raised in the hand, Malone dies. And Beckett, who is behind Malone as Malone is behind Lemuel, by implication cancels himself out. Such are the prestidigitations of anti-form.

If the second novel of Beckett's trilogy pushes the idea of anti-form further toward its consummation in silence, its particular motifs and devices revert to his earlier works. The insane asylum of *Malone Dies* is still the complex symbol of inverted consciousness it was in *Murphy*. Reductive parody spares no sacred theme; Moll's earrings represent the two thieves, and Christ is the lone sculptured tooth in her mouth. Objects acquire inordinate importance in the life of people—the stick of Malone and the hat of Macmann are examples. Arbitrary cruelty informs the actions of Lemuel, and sadistic fantasies cheer Malone toward his death. At the same time, the feeling of oppressive guilt, some "immemorial expiation," haunts Macmann as it haunted Molloy. The sense of "unending weariness," of putrescence and decay, or of radical indifference emanates from the limpid sentences of Beckett. "But what matter whether I was born or not, have lived or not, am dead or merely dying, I shall go on doing as I have always done, not knowing what it is I do, nor who I am, nor where I am, nor if I am," Malone states [p. 52].

The stylistic devices of the novel also recall those of *Molloy* and refine them. In the earlier book, Beckett employed verbal repetitions and clichés, circular sentence structures, logical quibbles, paradox, irrelevance, and misplaced concreteness all with subtlety. He could use the obvious, even trivial, detail with a profoundly puzzling effect and spring on the reader, in the most prosaic context, a metaphor of shocking intensity. Above all, Beckett perfected the type of sentence that so hedged or denied its statement that it barely ended with an assertion: "And then doing fills me with such a, I don't know, impossible to express, for me, now, after so long, yes, that I don't stop to enquire in virtue of what principle."[5] *Malone Dies* brings a kind of poetic clarity to these verbal contrivances; at the same time, it shows a new purity of literal statement. Its inventories are but an example of the way reason fondles a phenomenological world, which it is impotent to order. The result of such fondling is to transform objects into numbers in an infinite series and thus abolish the material world.

The contractive art of Beckett contracts closer to naught in *The Unnamable* (1958). In *Malone Dies*, the interludes of self-examination became gradually indistinguishable from the episodes of narrative invention; reality and illusion were blurred in a state of consciousness that also subsumed death and life. Malone's cosmic indifference was really the obverse of cosmic acceptance. In *The Unnamable*, we are closer to the point where all these qualities fuse. Translated brilliantly from the French by Beckett, *The Unnamable* possesses a kind of babbling inevitability that makes paraphrase difficult and criticism superfluous.

The book thus begins: "Where now? Who now? When now? Unquestioning. I, say I. Unbelieving. Questions, hypotheses, call them that. Keep going, going on, call that going, call that on."[6] Space, being, and time are from the start put to question; and so is the process of questioning itself. The narrator proceeds by statements, like the trilogy itself, that spiral toward zero and erase themselves semantically: "The fact would seem to be, if in my situation one may speak of facts, not only that I shall have to speak of things of which I cannot speak, but also, which is even more interesting, but also that I, which is if possible even more interesting, that I shall have to, I forget, no matter" [p. 4]. Yet we do manage to learn a few things about the speaker. He is alone. He is obstinate, determined to "go on," determined at all costs never to cease talking. Never! He is familiar with the other characters of Beckett, whom he calls puppets, surrogates, and "vice-existers": Malone with a brimless hat, passing without casting a shadow, Molloy wearing Malone's hat perhaps, Murphy and all the others. As for his physical situation, we are told that he has always been sitting in the self-same spot, hands on knees, gazing before him, his unblinking eyes streaming with tears.

The sole task of this "big talking ball," who has no sex, no possessions, and no biography, is to keep talking. Trapped in time as he is trapped in space, his only obligation is to "discharge a pensum" before he can be freed; as for his origin, he claims that it coincides with the Beginning. "I am Matthew and I am the angel, I who came before the cross, before the sinning, came into the world, came here," he testifies [p. 18]. Like the hero of an anti-creation myth, the Unnamable becomes the world he creates, becomes the creatures he invents, and takes life from the words they utter. His fictive delegates tell him about the world of men that he has forsaken. Endowed with the perfection of all things fictive, these creatures become, paradoxically, more divine than their creator. "I alone am man and all the rest divine," he says, voicing the feeling that every man must feel in a hermetic universe [p. 16]. The Unnamable ends his preamble with the Berkeleyan resolution to speak of nothing but himself, about whom he knows nothing. What he says from this point on refuses paragraphing.

The ensuing soliloquy invokes the surrogates of the Unnamable. Naturally, these evolve downward, from detested Basil, who somehow becomes Mahood, to Mahood, who becomes irreducible Worm. There is also a good deal of mystifying talk about a "master" who, in the solipsist structure of this novel, could be Beckett himself as well as the ubiquitously absent Godot. The master, the narrator says, "assuming he is solitary, in my image, wishes me well. . . . I want all to be well with you, do you hear me, that's what he keeps on dinning at me. To which I reply, in a respectful attitude, I too, your Lordship. I say that to cheer him up, he sounds so unhappy" [pp. 33f.]. Sometimes the master is conceived as an associate of other masters, equally mysterious, who all wish the Unnamable well. The latter, however, cannot refrain from asking: "Why don't they wash their hands of me and set me free? That might do me good. . . . Perhaps then I could go silent, for good and all" [p. 35]. Here, again, Beckett's ironic play seems a game of mirrors. The Unnamable, understood as the subject of the novel, wants his independence from the "master," the author, in order to cease existing; and the Unnamable, conceived as a creator of such fictions as Mahood and Worm, therefore an author himself, depends on them for his own existence. It is as if Beckett were saying that art and artist long to be free of one another; yet it is only in their mutual bondage that both exist to will their reciprocal destruction.

Pain and laughter freely commingle in this arbitrary narrative, which moves, nonetheless, toward the vanishing point, moves inexorably. The narrator sees himself as an old turkey-hen dying on her feet, her back covered with chickens, and rats spying on her. Next he sees himself as Mahood on crutches, circling ever so slowly the rotunda where his family lives; when he finally arrives there, he finds that his family, dead of sausage poisoning, has decomposed. So much for family life. But the narrator himself fares no better. We see him next as a limbless lump or trunk dumped in a jar that serves as emblem for a chop-house near the Vaugirard shambles.[7] Once a week he is taken out by the proprietress, and as he shrinks and sinks lower into the jar, she fills the bottom with sawdust. Around his neck is a cement ring. As he puts it: "To have forever before my eyes, when I open them, approximately the same set of hallucinations exactly, is a joy I might never have known, but for my cang" [p. 62]. Failing to become one identity, he invents and becomes another and refers to himself alternately in the first and third person. As he says: "no sense in bickering about pronouns and other parts of blather. The subject doesn't matter, there is none" [p. 102]. Quite appropriately, he becomes Worm, the last stage of life that still retains consciousness. Suddenly, a messenger as mysterious as the "master" comes in with an imperious order: Continue. Born obscenely "of a wet dream and dead before morning," the injunction imposes life on a "hero" who brags, "the testis has yet to descend that would want any truck with me, it's mutual, another gleam down the drain" [p. 129]. But the Unnamable does continue even if his words run obscenely in waste and excrement. Beckett, once again, cannot resist the most revolting transportations of birth and death in the "creations" of his storyteller who lets down his trousers to "shit stories" on the whole world.

The Unnamable may be a novel of anal babble. Its hero may continue to summon surrogates even more lowly than Worm—at one point, Worm is almost displaced by a being with doll's eyes and a head splitting with "vile certainties." In the end, however, the book is a metaphysical leg-pull intended, like some Zen *koans*, to cripple the mind. Everything in this anti-novel seems to contradict itself as well as everything else. The narrator neither knows who he is nor what he is doing: "I, who cannot be I, of whom I can't speak, of whom I must speak . . ." [p. 165]. In the same breath he appears a solipsist—"there is no one"—and a nihilist—"no, not me either . . ." [p. 171]. His destiny is to speak always the unspeakable, name the unnamable, averring nothing. His mind casts on the simplest event the shadow of logical impossibility: "This woman," he says, "has never spoken to me, to the best of my knowledge. If I have said anything to the contrary I was mistaken. If I say anything to the contrary again I shall be mistaken again. Unless I am mistaken now" [p. 79]. Though he pretends to be condemned to speech by the masters who control his existence as well as the creatures whose existence he controls, he ends by yearning for his inexistence in "their language." We should not be surprised that the last words of the Unnamable concern the voice of silence:

> you must go on, I can't go on, you must go on, I'll go on, you must say words, as long as there are any, until they find me, until they say me, strange pain, strange sin, you must go on, perhaps it's done already, perhaps they have said me already, perhaps they have carried me to the threshold of my story, before the door that opens on my story, that would surprise me, if it opens, it will be I, it will be the silence, where I am, I don't know, I'll never know, in the silence you don't know, you must go on, I can't go on, I'll go on. [p. 179]

The Unnamable, even more than its predecessors in the trilogy, is a dramatic experience of the mind's search for itself. The search assumes its antithesis in repose, just as words assume their opposite in silence. Thesis and antithesis are perpetuated under the maximum conditions of tension. When the tension breaks, and the Unnamable ceases to speak, Beckett will cease to write.

Viewing the trilogy as a whole, we can discern something more than a pattern of contradictions. The speakers, speaking always in the first person, are all exiled beings, shadows representing the universal drama of the Self. They enact, in the spirit of consummate parody, the ancient struggles between Mind and Matter, Fiction and Fact, Self and Other, Eternity and Time, Light and Dark, Word and Silence. Their struggle turns upon itself like a vortex and threatens to vanish through a central point, leaving us with an absolute blank. Like Cartesian clowns, they play out the farce of human identity in a cosmos turned inside out. They also serve as total satirists of our condition, leaving nothing holy or intact: religion, love, friendship, knowledge, health, society, God. But above all, they are the heroes of a new kind of consciousness, pure voices of subjectivity, recalling those "transcendental reductions" of Husserl that escape all phenomenological definitions. As Husserl put it: ". . . the experiencing ego is nothing that might be taken *for itself* and made into an object of inquiry on its *own* account. . . . it has no content that can be unravelled, it is in and for itself indescribable: pure ego and nothing further."[8] To reflect this new kind of heroic consciousness, Beckett is forced to abandon all the assumptions of the bourgeois novel and to create a fiction as reductive and as transcendental as its hero. Finally, he is forced to reject the possibility that art may ever realize this goal. If, as Ruby Cohn has suggested, *Molloy* reveals the making of the artist, *Malone* the artist making, and *The Unnamable* the artist making comments on art while making it, all three share unequivocally a common destiny: heroic absurdity.[9]

Notes

1. Quoted by Ruby Cohn, *Samuel Beckett: The Comic Gamut* (New Brunswick, N.J.: Rutgers University Press, 1962), p. 117.

2. Josephine Jacobsen and William R. Mueller, *The Testament of Samuel Beckett* (New York: Hill and Wang, 1964), p. 13 ff.

3. *Molloy* (New York: Grove Press, 1955), p. 7. Bracketed page references refer to this edition.

4. *Malone Dies* (New York: Grove Press, 1956), p. 1. Bracketed page references refer to this edition.

5. *Molloy*, p. 61.

6. *The Unnamable* (New York: Grove Presss, 1958), p. 3. Bracketed page references refer to this edition.

7. The restaurant, identified as the Ali Baba, and the squalid real-life setting of this grim fantasy, are noted by John Fletcher, *The Novels of Samuel Beckett* (New York: Barnes and Noble, 1964), p. 184.

8. Edmund Husserl, *Ideas I*, trans. W. R. Boyce Gibson (London: George Allen and Unwin, 1931), p. 233.

9. Cohn, p. 118.

Naming the M/inotaur: Beckett's Trilogy and the Failure of Narrative

Roch C. Smith*

Speaking of the labyrinth in *La Terre et les rêveries du repos*, Gaston Bachelard reiterates his fundamental view that, in a dream, the roles of subject and object are inverted. For the dreamer, what appears to be objective reality never precedes the subjective state but is, instead, shaped by that state. According to Bachelard, ". . . it is not because *the passage is narrow* that the dreamer is *compressed*—it is because the dreamer is *anguished* that he sees the road *get narrower*. . . . Thus, in a dream, the labyrinth is neither seen nor foreseen, it is not presented as a perspective of roads. It must be lived to be seen. The contortions of the dreamer, his contorted movements within the material of the dream leave *a labyrinth in their wake*. . . . Ariadne's thread is a thread of discourse. It belongs to the narrated dream. It is a thread of return."[1] More recently, J. Hillis Miller has offered a similar comparison of Ariadne's thread to what he calls "repetition" of the narrative line—that is, "anything which happens to the line to trouble or even to confound its straightforward linearity: returnings, knottings, recrossings, crinklings to and fro, suspensions, interruptions, fictionalizings."[2] Also like Bachelard, Miller considers that the objective correlative to the subject's vision emerges only after the narrative thread of return has been completely woven. The beast (Bachelard's "object") is not the cause of the chase; rather, the chase (Bachelard's "subject") brings about the beast. "The chase has a beast in view. The end of the story is the retrospective revelation of the law of the whole. That law is an underlying 'truth' which ties all together in an inevitable sequence revealing a hitherto hidden figure in the carpet."[3]

Richard Macksey has seen the dissolution of character in Beckett's trilogy as an imprisonment of the self within a labyrinth.[4] And certainly Miller's definition of narrative repetition seems made to order as a description of the trilogy with its labyrinthine twists, turns, and interruptions. Moreover, in accord with both Bachelard's and Miller's views, Beckett's novelistic labyrinth does not preexist the narration itself. It is not mimetic; rather, it appears as the result of the narrative process. It is the wake left by Molloy turning out his pages, Moran writing his report,

*Reprinted from *Modern Fiction Studies* 29 (Spring 1983). © by Purdue Research Foundation, West Lafayette, IN 47907. Reprinted with permission.

Malone weaving his tales and taking inventory, and the unnamable narrator, whether "I," "he," or Worm, leaving a silky trail, a spider's web of narrative confusion.

Initially, of course, there are stories of physical wandering, particularly with Molloy, whom Ruby Cohn has called the "archetype of the fabulous voyager."[5] And, as the trilogy's narrative is played out, motion that was thought to be linear turns out to be circular. Molloy is forced "to go in a circle, hoping in this way to go in a straight line"[6]; Moran carefully paces in a circle as he waits for his son to return from Hole with a bicycle; and Macmann, rolling upon the ground, discovers that he was advancing "along the arc of a gigantic circle."[7] In *The Unnamable* the narrator's physical wandering has ceased, but we find the narration itself emanating from a sphere—variously described as "an egg" and "a big talking ball"[8]—whose goal, as expressed through the narrator's surrogate, Mahood, is to go on "not always in a straight line" (*U*, p. 320), first a prisoner in a "circular" (*U*, p. 323) building, then on the island he says he never left and where, he tells us, "I wind my endless ways" (*U*, p. 327).

Yet the perambulation is not only circular; it is increasingly cloistered as the rambler finds himself inside dark enclosed places as small as a "head" (*MD*, p. 221) or "my distant skull where once I wandered" (*U*, p. 303), till he can wander no more. He is caught in an inescapable web of words where "to go on means going from here, means finding me, losing me, vanishing and beginning again, a stranger first, then little by little the same as always, in another place, where I shall say I have always been, of which I shall know nothing, being incapable of seeing, moving, thinking, speaking, but of which little by little, in spite of these handicaps, I shall begin to know something, just enough for it to turn out to be the same place as always" (*U*, p. 302).

For the entire trilogy moves toward a gradual replacement of physical wandering, first with the narrator's fictional accounts of the wandering of others and finally with the purely verbal narrative wandering we find in *The Unnamable*, where to "go on" is to write, to produce more words. The narrator's increasingly frequent reminders that he is, and was, telling stories culminate, in *The Unnamable*, in a reduction of all fiction, including earlier tales of wandering, to the words that make it up. Bicycles, crutches, chamberpots, sticks, hats, and jars, even the characters themselves are, after all, but words: "I'm in words, made of words, others' words, what others, the place too, the air, the walls, the floor, the ceiling, all words" (*U*, p. 386). Words overcome the object they were seemingly meant to represent as the stories get tangled in their own verbal web.

Molloy's description of a small silver object made of two crosses joined by a bar serves as a particularly graphic example of this process. The description seems much more detailed than such an innocuous object deserves, especially because, despite all this attention, the object is never identified. Molloy indicates that "the crosses [X's in the original French] of the little object I am referring to were perfect, that is to say composed each of two identical V's, one upper with its opening above, like all V's for that matter, and the other lower with its opening below, or more precisely of four rigorously identical V's, the two I have just named and then two more, one on the right hand, the other on the left, having their openings on the right and left respectively. But perhaps it is out of place to speak here of right and left, or upper and lower" (*M*, p. 63). Molloy further describes this unnamed object as a "strange instrument" (*M*, p. 63) for which he says he felt "affection" and even "veneration" (*M*, p. 64). Moreover, he explains that he "could never understand what possible purpose it could serve" (*M*, p. 63), although he did not doubt "that it had a most specific function always to be hidden from me" (*M*, p. 64).

Because we know that Molloy took the object from Lousse's house along with coffee spoons and other silverware, we may well assume that it is nothing more than a kniferest. Such a conjecture is reinforced by the fact that the narrator in *Malone Dies* makes a specific reference to "a little silver kniferest" (*MD*, p. 258) as the only object of value found in Macmann's pockets. And we know how things have a tendency to reappear from story to story throughout the trilogy. But if we return to Molloy's description, we note that, although it may leave us unsatisfied about the physical identity of the object, it leaves absolutely no doubt about its verbal properties. The object is made of connected letters—X's and V's—and is therefore a *word* at least as much as it is a kniferest. That explains why Molloy, as would any writer, feels affection and veneration for this precious object whose function is both precise and obscure.

The silver kniferest, then, is what Jean Ricardou has called a "structural metaphor"[9] in that it is both an object within the story and an image of the writer's own text. In *Malone Dies* the words themselves, like Macmann's kniferest, are all the narrator has of value. In *Molloy* the symmetrical object-word parallels the rough symmetry of the novel.[10] Its X's and V's like crossroads in the labyrinth offer no guidance as to the correct direction one should take. For in a narrative, Miller reminds us, "any single thread leads everywhere, like a labyrinth made of a single line or corridor crinkled to and fro."[11] Significantly, Miller gives as an example of this phenomenon "the letter X. . . . a letter, a sign, but a sign for signs generally. . . ."[12] Thus the silver kniferest metaphorically summarizes the view implicit in the trilogy that language no longer is an instrument of representation but, as Olga Bernal has expressed it, "the very matter with which literature is at grips. . . ."[13] Beckett's maze is a textual one beyond which there is literally "nothing," not even suffering, as the disembodied narrator of *The Unnamable* reminds us when he refers to this "Labyrinthine torment that can't be grasped, or limited, or felt, or suffered, no not even suffered" (*U*, p. 314). In attempting to "unravel his tangle" (*U*, p. 315), the narrator must follow the maze of words he himself has woven.

Like Theseus, he seeks out the beast hidden somewhere in the loops and twists of this labyrinth. Yet, because the maze is verbal, the monster must be slayed with words; it must be *named* if it is to stop exacting its tribute of words from the hapless narrator. The names multiply to the point that there seem to be many such monsters, yet "there's no getting rid of them without naming them" (*U*, p. 326). This is the fundamental dilemma facing the narrator lost in an increasingly complicated labyrinth of unstoppable words. He can't go on adding more words and increasing the complexity of his narrative labyrinth, yet he must go on because the only way out is through words, or so it seems. So he follows his own exhortation to "weave, weave" (*U*, p. 339). Like a spider in the middle of his web he continues spinning in order to find the word that would end the succession of puppets—the Molloys, Molloses, Morans, Marthas, Macmanns, Molls, Mahoods, Matthews, Marguerites, Madeleines, their predecessors and variants, the Murphys, Watts, Merciers, Worms, and Lemuels, not to mention the mothers and Mags—who people the spirals of his prose with its most striking repetition, the letter M, the M/inotaur of his verbal labyrinth.

For it is part of the narrator's dilemma throughout the trilogy that he is at once the hunter and the hunted, the weaver of the labyrinth and the beast it encloses, Ariadne and Theseus, as well as the unnamable M/inotaur. Like Daedalus, he is caught in the coils of his own creation, a fate shared with many modern artists, as Richard Macksey points out.[14] But it is much worse for Beckett's narrator because, unlike his Athenean forebear, he cannot find a means of escape, and all attempts to do so entangle him further in his verbal prison. The enemy is within, so the narrator must be both executioner and victim. Thus Molloy searches for his mother and finds *himself*; Moran searches for Molloy and ends by uncannily resembling the object of his search to the point that Moran is "devoured" by Molloy, as Ruby Cohn so aptly observed.[15] Later Macmann slowly takes on the characteristics of Malone, including his paralysis and even his hat, whereas Malone, passing silently before the narrator of *The Unnamable*, might be taken for "Molloy wearing Malone's hat" (*U*, p. 293).

None of the trilogy's narrators is able to find an escape from this web of words. Theirs is a narrative doomed to failure. The M/inotaur, even when stripped of his fictional disguises, is forever out of reach, and silence, the only true escape from a labyrinth of words, is therefore impossible, as we see in the following passage from *The Unnamable*: "But now, is it now, I on me? Sometimes I think it is. And then I realize it is not. I am doing my best, and failing again, yet again. I don't mind failing, it's a pleasure, but I want to go silent" (*U*, p. 310).

How widespread is this pleasurable failure? And what is its role in Beckett's trilogy? The narrator fails, of course, to create a fiction that will reveal the truth about his elusive beast and allow him to go silent. But already Moran, whose wanderings mirror the labyrinthine thread of narration, wonders, when his leg begins to slow him down, if he is not "secretly glad that this had happened to me, perhaps even to the point of not wanting to get well?" (*M*, p. 145). And Malone, painfully aware of the failure of his fiction to invent, to name the M/inotaur, rails at "How false all this is. No time now to explain. I began again, no longer in order to succeed, but in order to fail" (*MD*, p. 195). Finally, in *The Unnamable*, the narrator expresses his frustration at the paradox of writing: "What can it matter to me that I succeed or fail? The undertaking is none of mine, if they want me to succeed I'll fail, and vice versa, so as not to be rid of my tormentors" (*U*, p. 347). The point, one that is not fully realized until *The Unnamable*, is that fiction must fail as "storytelling" if it is to have any hope of succeeding as "naming." The narration of fiction, the weaving of a verbal tapestry, multiplies words and carries the narrator further away from the exit of his verbal labyrinth and from the silence he seeks. It is this realization that is behind the gradual disappearance of storytelling as one moves from *Molloy* to *The Unnamable*.

But what replaces the narration of fiction? Here we do well to return to Jean Ricardou, whose theoretical reversal of these two terms—narration and fiction—matches Beckett's practice in the trilogy and provides a means of articulating our experience as readers of these works.[16] For Ricardou, a "new novel" such as Robbe-Grillet's *Project for a Revolution in New York* is marked by a fiction that "emanates from the narrative process and contributes in some way to describing it. Fiction is, most often, a fiction of narration."[17] In such works it is not a question of telling a story about the activities of revolutionaries in New York, for instance, but of telling the story of telling such a story, thereby revealing more about the narrative process than about the story itself. As Ricardou explains, "the novel ceases to be the writing of a story in order to become the story of a writing."[18] Such a novel is deliberately aware of its own workings; it is quite literally "self-conscious." This is particularly true of Beckett's novels where, as Dieter Wellershoff put it, "literature has reached a point at which it is looking over its own shoulders."[19]

The Unnamable is, of course, replete with the stops, twists, and convolutions of the self-conscious novel as the narrator hesitates between the stories of Mahood, Worm, "I," and "he." But pervasive as it is in the last novel of the trilogy, such expressed awareness of the conventions of writing fiction is already a part of earlier works, as Molloy makes clear: "And every time I say, I said this, or I said that, or speak of a voice saying, far away inside me, Molloy, and then a fine phrase more or less clear and simple, or find myself compelled to attribute to others intelligible words, or hear my own voice uttering to others more or less articulate sounds, I am merely complying with the convention that demands you either lie or hold your peace" (*M*, p. 88). The ubiquitous voice, which in *Molloy* and *Malone Dies* begins as an inner murmur or buzzing before turning out intelligible words and whose compulsive power energizes *The Unnamable*, is the voice of narration stripped of its usual fictional baffles by the fiction of narration.

Yet even thus exposed, the fiction of narration does not succeed. Beckett's narrator does not seek merely to bare the word; he seeks to stop it. His goal is not to create novel fictional forms but to still the voice of fiction in order to say "nothing." But, as the narrator of *The Unnamable* ruefully points out, "it seems impossible to speak and yet say nothing, you think you have succeeded, but you always overlook something, a little yes, a little no, enough to exterminate a regiment of dragoons" (*U*, p. 303). It is a task at which he must inevitably fail because it is literally not possible to "say nothing," to express what the narrator of *The Unnamable* calls "the unthinkable unspeakable" (*U*, p. 335). As the narrator resignedly asks near the end of that novel, "how can I say it, that's all words, they're all I have and not many of them, the words fail, the voice fails, so be it" (*U*, p. 413). For, unlike the work of a new novelist like Robbe-Grillet, Beckett's is not merely a fiction of narration but a *fiction of failed narrative*. The trilogy reflects Beckett's view, expressed to Georges Duthuit, "that to be an artist is to fail, as no other dare fail, that failure is his world and the shrink from it desertion. . . ."[20]

Yet, if the trilogy is the story of the narrator's growing awareness of the narrative dilemma, it is also the expression of a fundamental paradox because it is failure itself that makes possible the continuation of narrative, tenuous as that continuation may be. The narrative circularity of *Molloy* is only apparently closed; Malone's pencil lead grows perilously short, but it never runs out; and the "unthinkable unspeakable" may be unnamable, but the narrative thread goes on. The narrator of *The Unnamable* summarizes this paradox when he insists that "the search for a means to put an end to things, an end to speech, is what enables discourse to continue" (*U*, p. 299). Increasingly, the narrator weaves the story of the impossibility of expression, but he does not stop weaving. Whatever hope Beckett's trilogy offers would seem to be found in this unbroken narrative line whose tensile strength barely resists, yet does not break, despite the tugs and pulls of despair. A modern-day Scheherazade, Beckett keeps hope alive solely by telling stories of failed narrative whose nights in "Ballybaba" and the "fresh air of Turdybaba" (*M*, p. 134) ironically echo the traditional storytelling of the *Arabian Nights* and serve as reminders of the transformation of fiction into a labyrinthine quest for silence.

Beckett's narrator lives in what Bachelard, in another context, called a "logosphere" or "universe of the word,"[21] yet, like Derrida, the narrator is wary of a "logocentrism which is also a phonocentrism: an absolute proximity of voice and being. . . ."[22] For Moran it seems that "all language was an excess of language" (*M*, p. 116), and Malone reluctantly resigns himself to the notion that his life is reduced to a "child's exercise book" (*MD*, p. 274), whereas the narrator of *The Unnamable* remarks that "it has not yet been our good fortune to establish with any degree of accuracy what I am, where I am, whether I am words among words, or silence in the midst of silence, to recall only two of the hypotheses launched in this connexion, though silence to tell the truth does not appear to have been very conspicuous up to now, but appearances may sometimes be deceptive" (*U*, p. 389). Thus compelled to utter words, for that is all he has, but uncertain about whether such words have an ontological significance, the narrator will go on. Yet because the ontological question remains unresolved, no fixed figure ever appears in the carpet. Despite it all, or, rather, because of it all, the difficult weaving continues in this fiction of failed narrative that can only exist in the tortuous and tenuous space between logos and silence.

Notes

1. Gaston Bachelard, *La Terre et les rêveries du repos* (Paris: Corti, 1948), p. 215. Unless otherwise noted, translations are mine.

2. J. Hillis Miller, "Ariadne's Thread: Repetition and Narrative Line," *Critical Inquiry*, 3 (Autumn 1976), 68.

3. Miller, p. 69.

4. Richard Macksey, "The Artist in the Labyrinth: Design or *Dasein*," *Modern Language Notes*, 77 (May 1962), 248.

5. Ruby Cohn, *Back to Beckett* (Princeton, NJ: Princeton University Press, 1973), p. 83.

6. Samuel Beckett, *Molloy*, trans. Patrick Bowles, in *Three Novels by Samuel Beckett*, Evergreen Black Cat Edition (New York: Grove Press, 1965), p. 85. Hereafter cited as *M*.

7. *Malone Dies*, trans. by the author, in *Three Novels by Samuel Beckett*, p. 246. Hereafter cited as *MD*.

8. *The Unnamable*, trans. by the author, in *Three Novels by Samuel Beckett*, p. 305. Hereafter cited as *U*.

9. Jean Ricardou, *Problèmes du nouveau roman* (Paris: Seuil, 1967), p. 136.

10. Angela B. Moorjani, in "A Mythic Reading of *Molloy*," in *Samuel Beckett; the Art of Rhetoric*, ed. Edouard Morot-Sir, *et al.* (Chapel Hill: North Carolina Studies in the Romance Languages and Literatures, 1976), sees the kniferest as "a model of the complex ternary and dual configurations of the text" (p. 277).

11. Miller, p. 74.

12. Miller, p. 75.

13. Olga Bernal, *Language et fiction dans le roman de Beckett* (Paris: Gallimard, 1969), p. 177.

14. Macksey, p. 241.

15. Cohn, p. 88.

16. Brian T. Fitch, in the second part of his *Dimensions, structures et textualité dans la trilogie romanesque de Beckett* (Paris: Minard, 1977), makes a very effective use of Ricardou's concepts of narrative in approaching Beckett's trilogy. But, unlike the present analysis, Fitch undertakes a detailed examination of textuality that is deliberately limited to the French text and serves as a contrasting complement to the thematic and structural exploration developed in the first half of his monograph.

17. Jean Ricardou, *Pour une théorie du nouveau roman* (Paris: Seuil, 1971), p. 219.

18. Ricardou, *Problèmes*, p. 166.

19. Dieter Wellershoff, "Failure of an Attempt at De-Mythologization: Samuel Beckett's Novels," in *Samuel Beckett. A Collection of Critical Essays*, ed. Martin Esslin (Englewood Cliffs, NJ: Prentice-Hall, 1965), p. 92.

20. Samuel Beckett and George Duthuit, "Three Dialogues," in *Samuel Beckett. A Collection of Critical Essays*, p. 21.

21. Gaston Bachelard, *Le Droit de rêver* (Paris: Presses Universitaires de France, 1970), p. 216.

22. Jacques Derrida, *De la grammatologie* (Paris: Minuit, 1967), p. 23.

Molloy

Richard Coe*

Molloy (written *c.* 1947) falls into two sections, the second being a form of commentary on the first, the rational attempting—and failing—to explain and as it were catch up with the irrational, the infinite. The first part tells of the journey of Molloy in search of his mother. Concerning his departure, we know all the details:

> I resolved to go and see my mother. I needed, before I could resolve to go and see that woman, reasons of an urgent nature, and with such reasons, since I did not know what to do, or where to go, it was child's play for me, the play of an only child, to fill my mind until it was rid of all other preoccupation and I seized with a trembling at the mere idea of being hindered from going there, I mean to my mother, there and then . . .[1]

but by what means he eventually reaches her, we never discover, although he is in her room already when the story opens. For his journey, which begins on the inevitable bicycle, is interrupted when he runs over a small dog, is arrested, is rescued by the owner of the late animal, "a Mrs Loy, or Lousse"; and the narrative in the end just peters out, leaving Molloy alone in the forest, his bicycle lost and his own body having decayed to the point where he can scarcely crawl, all hope and all desire abandoned: "Molloy could stay, where he happened to be."

If Molloy is the "irrational number," Moran is the integer. To Moran, Molloy's very existence is problematic. "Perhaps I had invented him," he muses, "I mean found him ready-made in my head."[2] Even of the name, "Molloy or Mollose," he is decidedly uncertain—or rather, he is quite certain of the beginning (one *can* be quite certain of the beginning of π), but the end seems strangely difficult to grasp. None the less, Moran—obscurely a cross between a secret agent and a private detective—is ordered by his "Chief," Youdi, to go out in search of Molloy. In spruce and

*Reprinted from *Samuel Beckett* (New York: Grove Press, 1964) by permission of the publisher.

orderly fashion, and accompanied by his son, he sets out; but as soon as he reaches "the Molloy country," his body also begins to decay. He sends his son to buy a bicycle, which in its turn disintegrates, eventually disappears; and so Moran, half staggering, half crawling like Molloy himself, at last reaches home again, his mission unaccomplished.

Between these two parts there is no comparison. Moran remains a contrived and allegorical figure; Molloy from the first transcends his arid intellectual origins and achieves a rich and unforgettable humanity. His "I" seems to embrace the whole of human experience and intellect, the whole of good and evil, poetry and cruelty, which has been assimilated, discarded, ground into the dust of a supreme, contemptuous indifference: "It's a change of muck. And if all muck is the same muck that doesn't matter, it's good to have a change of muck."[3] Yet "indifference" is perhaps inaccurate. "All roads were right for me," he comments, "a wrong road was an event for me"; yet at the same time, all roads lead to suffering, life is an intolerable burden to be borne, birth a worse injustice than death. Suffering is the one incontrovertible fact of life. It *is* existence, it is the proof that "something is taking its course," it could even be evidence of the Self. "Je souffre, donc je suis." "I know my eyes are open," says The Unnamable, "because of the tears that pour from them unceasingly."[4] And Vladimir: "The air is full of our cries." Man is born unto trouble as the sparks fly upwards—but *why*? There is no reason; the pain, the disintegration of the human machine are utterly gratuitous. "What makes me weep so? From time to time. There is nothing saddening here. Perhaps it is liquefied brain"—so speaks The Unnamable again. So intense is Beckett's pity for the gratuitous suffering of man that at times it seems almost intolerable—it is the *angoisse* that runs through all his work. If existence is such suffering, then it were better not to exist. And so, for Beckett's people, the unforgivable sin is to love; for the "music, *music*, MUSIC" which is love is inseparable from the primeval curse—the Calvinistic original sin—of sex. "Love" creates new beings to endure suffering; and, for Molloy, the term "mother" is the obscenest swear-word in his vocabulary. She is "that blind and sordid hag," she is the one "who brought me into the world, through the hole in her arse if my memory is correct. First taste of the shit."[5] Were it not for birth, how much suffering might not be spared—how much absurdity, disaster, futility and death. The decay, the progressive disintegration that Molloy experiences, the whole sordid, malodorous, obscene Calvary-procession from womb to refuse-dump—this is the responsibility of her whom Molloy calls "Mag."

Yet this is only the beginning of the puzzle; for Molloy, having an existence, possesses it only as one member of a series, therefore he is not free. His beginning was determined by another, just as his son's beginning, if he has one, will be determined by him. Molloy hates no one in the world so much as Mag; Moran hates no one so much as his son. Watt's preoccupation with the intolerable determinism of the series is transferred by Molloy into the "chain of generations"—and in addition, Molloy is obsessed with a need for freedom in a way quite foreign to Watt. He feels his freedom threatened on all sides; his very life itself is a sequence of "hypothetical imperatives," and these imperatives, he notes, "nearly all bore on the same question, that of my relations with my mother." He is imprisoned in the chain of life, the three-part sonata-form of beginning-waiting-ending. And there is no escape.

But unlike the sequence of servants in Mr. Knott's house, where the arrival of the third automatically determined the departure of the first, the act of progeniture is not in itself an end. Something has gone wrong here in the sequence—time has got out of step with logic, and seems somehow to be protracting itself quite unwarrantably. There seems to be no end. Molloy is already almost as old as his mother, he notes, and his son, if he had one, would be almost as old as himself. Birth is an irrevocable beginning for him who is born; but it is not, as it should be logically, an irrevocable end for her who gives birth or for him who engenders. There seems to be a rigidly determining enslavement at one end of existence, and a sort of indeterminate and timeless freedom at the other. It is as though the arrival of the number 7 were ruthlessly determined by the number 6, but that, having once begun, 7 could continue indefinitely, regardless of the arrival of 8, 9, 10, etc. In any case, whatever death is, it is not merely the corresponding opposite of birth. There is no conceivable way of reconciling the arbitrary determinism of birth with the freedom of him who is born. But it *is* just possible to think of death as freedom.

Of his own essential freedom, Molloy, despite occasional hesitations, has little real doubt. It is the freedom of the Geulincxian "bodytight mind," the freedom of the Void, the *pour-soi*, of the Self which escapes both reason and the senses: "And once again I am I will not say alone, no, that's not like me, but, how shall I say, I don't know, restored to myself, no, I never left myself, free, yes, I don't know what that means but it's the word I mean to use, free to do what, to do nothing, to know, but what, the laws of the mind perhaps, of my mind. . . ."[6] On the other hand, it is freedom within a deterministic framework, the freedom of the slave to crawl east along the deck of a boat travelling west; and the limiting factor is life. If life is infinite, even if only at one end, then freedom is likewise infinite; but if life is limited by the monstrosity of death as well as by that of birth, and if, within that narrow space, every physical action is arranged beforehand in terms of a Malebranchian or Leibnizian "pre-established harmony," what freedom is there? Merely a thinly-veiled compulsion. "We agents," says Moran, "often amused ourselves with . . . giving ourselves the airs of free men."[7] But then Moran, unlike Molloy, is a rational integer, hemmed in on both sides by the series. His ending is of the same nature as his beginning. Whereas Molloy's ending is the unknown factor, x.

Thus Beckett's people find themselves inextricably involved in problems of beginning and ending, of birth and especially of death. Beckett's very titles reveal his preoccupations: "La Fin," *Fin de partie*, *La Dernière Bande*, and the punning *Comment c'est* ("commencer"). So also does his style: the form of narrative in *Molloy* spirals repeatedly inward around itself, so that it has no beginning and no end; its end is the writer writing the beginning; its beginning—Molloy inexplicably at home in his mother's room—is in fact its end. It is a continuously expanding present, and at the same time an infinite progression: the writer writing about a past which can never catch up with the present moment of writing, because, even as he writes the word "now," or "it is midnight," the instant of "now" has already vanished, and "it was not midnight."[8] About beginnings, Beckett has little to say which is of immediate importance: we cannot *remember* our beginning, so perhaps it never was. We are forced to rely on hearsay. Of Watt he notes tantalisingly, in the Addenda: "never been properly born," and it is interesting that the same phrase recurs in *All That Fall*. But of this we may be certain, that if there *is* a beginning, then it is arbitrary and abrupt. "L' Expulsé" is literally flung down the steps of his house into the gutter. But endings are a different matter altogether. Even $\pi = 3.14159\ldots$ begins abruptly enough: but for its ending you may wait and wait till Doomsday . . . or "for Godot to come . . . or for night to fall."

Thus death becomes the main subject of the *Trilogy*, but not in any ordinary sense. Not one of Beckett's people is afraid of death. Some long for it (Hamm, for instance), but all, without exception, are desperately puzzled about its meaning and its mechanism. All think of life as an exile, a punishment for some unknown crime, perhaps the crime of being born, as Estragon suggests—an exile in time from the reality of themselves, which reality is, and must be, timeless. All think of their essential Self as spatial, yet dimensionless, as "a mote in the dark of absolute freedom" (Murphy), as "a speck in the void, in the dark, for ever" (Hamm), as living out a Belacqua-purgatory before their re-admission to the timelessness of Nothing—but none of them see death itself as really relevant. For either death just simply annihilates—in which case it abolishes the problems of life without solving them; or else life continues indefinitely beyond death, in which case the problems remain unsolved. What is needed to close the exile is an *end*—an end which is a resolution of logical impossibilities and which must therefore be an introduction into a different dimension altogether (the dimension where $\sqrt{2}$ is a rational number), an end which is in the same instant a beginning; and it is extremely improbable that death can offer this. Death itself is a temporal phenomenon, destroying other temporal phenomena—words, memories, bicycles. But how can death destroy, let alone resolve, a Void, a Self? Or time? Or space? Destruction, in fact, is almost as literally inconceivable as survival. There simply are no words: "All I know is what the words know," says Molloy: "and the dead things, and that makes a handsome little sum, with a beginning, a middle and an end, as in the well-built phrase and the long sonata of the dead."[9]

So irrelevant is death, in fact, that Molloy, and Malone after him, are by no means certain that they are not dead already. They cannot recall their birth, so why should they necessarily recall their death? For Beckett's people, the boundary between life and after-life becomes progressively vaguer. Molloy cannot recall whether his mother was dead or not when last he saw her; and of himself, he notes sometimes, with surprise, that he is still alive ("that may come in useful"), at other times that he is dead ("it is only since I ceased to live that I think of these things"), at others again, that both are true at once.

But then, if death is not the end, what is the end? For an end there must be, if this intolerable exile from the Self, the *Nichts*, is ever to conclude. *Comment finir?* is the tormenting question. For Molloy, the problem is insoluble. For, on the one hand, for anything to begin or end, by Watt's "law of series," implies a rigid determinism before and after, and hence a lack of freedom for the Self, which, being a Void, cannot be anything but free. A "total freedom" made to correspond with the Self is only possible in a world (literally) "without end," *i.e.*, without time. But time is inseparable from movement—therefore this freedom is only conceivable in a world without movement either—a world of motionless *waiting*. Or, to look at the same problem from another angle, if the Self *is* totally free, this means that time and movement are illusions, or perhaps just impossibilities—hence the intolerable difficulty that Beckett's people seem to have in going anywhere, or else the terror with which Molloy observes the beginning or ending of anything: "From things about to disappear I turn away in time. To watch them out of sight, no, I can't do it."[10]

To end, therefore, is intolerable, as it immures him for ever in the determinism of the series; and not to end is equally intolerable, for then there is no escape from time. In this *angoisse*, Molloy has two half-comforts. The first is—like the recurring decimal—to envisage an end without ever actually contemplating reaching it. Thus every happening, for Molloy, is "the last but two, perhaps, before the end": "This time, then once more I think, then perhaps a last time, then I think it'll be over. . . ."[11] The second is an expedient, apparently harmless, but full of consequences for Molloy's successors, which consists in reliving, after an interval of time, an event already once lived through, in such a way that the two experiences merge, and in merging, annihilate the interval of time which separated them. For Molloy, the *unique* experience is unbearable; but reiterated experiences superimposed one on top of the other may create an apparently single, yet in fact compound experience, from which the element of time has been abstracted. And as his memory decays and his personality disintegrates, so he includes in his reiterations, experiences which perhaps belonged to other people. Thus step by step he builds up—

by the old Belacqua-process of reliving experiences once lived already—an odd, provisional existence, outside time, a Self which merges with the Selves of others as the first step on the road to the ultimate Self which merges with the Nothing.

Notes

1. *Molloy*, in *Three Novels by Samuel Beckett* (New York: Grove Press, 1965) p. 15.
2. *Molloy*, p. 112.
3. *Molloy*, p. 41.
4. *The Unnamable*, in *Three Novels*, p. 304.
5. *Molloy*, p. 16.
6. *Molloy*, p. 13.
7. *Molloy*, p. 95.
8. *Molloy*, pp. 92, 176.
9. *Molloy*, p. 31.
10. *Molloy*, p. 12.
11. *Molloy*, p. 8.

Myth, Word, and Self in *The Unnamable*

Enrico Garzilli*

It is important to understand the relationship of myth to the structure of the novels of Samuel Beckett as well as of Proust, Joyce, Faulkner, Lawrence, Gide. In Samuel Beckett's *The Unnamable*, critics have found more philosophy at times than mythology and literature. In fact, Susan Sontag makes this statement about Beckett's critics: "Beckett's delicate dramas of the withdrawn consciousness—pared down to essentials, cut off, often represented as physically immobilized—are read as a statement about modern man's alienation from meaning or from God, or as an allegory of psychopathology."[1] She insists that "interpretation, based on the highly dubious theory that a work of art is composed of items of content, violates art."[2] The very valid point Susan Sontag makes concerning the inseparability of form and content suggests that a great work of art perfectly weds form to content and that to divorce them means violation. This does not mean, however, that the work of art does not seek to be understood. . . .

The form of *The Unnamable* seems to be chaos constantly on the verge of cosmos. The "I" of *The Unnamable* is an I who relates to many

*Reprinted from *Circles without Center: Paths to the Discovery and Creation of Self in Modern Literature* (Cambridge: Harvard University Press, 1972) by permission of the publisher.

selves, an I in search of a name, a world. If one is to accept the naming of an object in the mythical sense as the calling into being of the object or the person and the lack of a name as the noncalling into being, *The Unnamable*, with an understanding of the fundamental meaning of the word mythical, is a novel concerned with the search for existence, for being, for definition. Frederick Hoffman, in *The Language of Self*, claims that all Beckett's novels deal with the self: "The basic materials of Beckett's work are selves as inquiring beings, selves as objects, other objects, and the degrees and forms of distance between one of these and another."[3]

From another aspect the novels can be seen as parodies of the creation myth. In the previous treatment of language and mythology it was observed that the word has creative power. In this context the I of *The Unnamable* realizes that his existence depends upon finding the right words which will call the I into being. He has spent so many of his words on others, either his creations or his creators: "All these Murphys, Molloys and Malones do not fool me. They have made me waste my time, suffer for nothing, speak of them when, in order to stop speaking, I should have spoken of me and me alone."[4] The Unnamable is torn between speaking and not speaking. While he craves the silence, he also knows that once the silence begins he has ended his search for existence: "you must go on, I can't go on, you must go on, I'll go on, you must say words, as long as there are any, until they find me" (p. 414). Therefore, all words must be spoken since all are differentiated from, reflectors of, a single unnamable source.

Words are the solution, the creation, the creative material for the I. It is a terrible torment for the I not to know who he is, to want to stop speaking and yet to realize that unless he continues his parodies at creation, he cannot call himself into being. While silence is a torment for the Unnamable, words seem inadequate for his arrival at being: "it's the fault of the pronouns, there is no name for me, no pronoun for me, all the trouble comes from that, that, it's a kind of pronoun too, it isn't that either, I'm not that either" (p. 404). The Unnamable seems to be an "almost" word, alone in the beginning. He parodies all creations in his aloneness. He asks whether Basil, Mahood, and Worm are parts of him or are different from him, or whether they are names with which he confuses himself. In this tension between the names of the others who may have his own name, names of himself, his creations, or his creators, the Unnamable exclaims that he is none of these. Their names don't satisfy him: "Decidedly Basil is becoming important, I'll call him Mahood instead, I prefer that, I'm queer. It was he told me stories about me, lived in my stead, issued forth from me, came back to me, entered back into me, heaped stories on my head. I don't know how it was done. I always liked not knowing, but Mahood said it wasn't right . . . He didn't know either, but it worried him. It was his voice which has often, always, mingled with mine, and sometimes drowned it completely" (p. 309).

These people called Mahood and Basil, the Unnamable claimed, spoke to him, taught him lessons, left him, returned to him again; yet, they remained mysteries to him. The fact that he named them, however, means that he called them into existence, although he doubts their existence at times. "I shall not be alone in the beginning. I am of course alone. Alone" (p. 292). It doesn't really matter whether the Unnamable is alone or not. What does matter is that he does not know who he is and in his attempt to find out who he is he needs words, he needs language, he needs to find a name so that other existences and previous personae can witness his existence. The need for words has an ambivalent attraction in this respect. While they give a name, a definition, and an existence, they also have a way of becoming an obstacle in the path to the self. In this role they become a most pervasive type of witness, perpetrating distinction, multiplying personae, and fixing the person in immobile categories. This is the reason the Unnamable can say he likes the silence before the words.

Actually, it is only the words and language which witness his existence, but none of them are able to give him the definition and identity he needs. While the Unnamable says that he is suffering, he tells his story humorously. He claims that tears are rolling down his face and that is how he knows that he is, that his suffering rather than his thought is his proof of existence and that his name was forgotten by him. He asks himself about Basil, whether it was he who stole his name and took his existence away from him, but receives no answer: "Is he still unsurping my name, the one they foisted on me, up there in their world, patiently, from season to season?" (p. 298).

The oscillation between creating and being created, between having a name and no name, between silence and words, between nonbeing and identity, forms the structure of the novel. The fact that the novel does not have a plot is not important. Its narrative form, its blocks of words, parodies the creation of a self. The style of *The Unnamable* is markedly a humorous one. The tone, in spite of the anxious quest of the narrator, becomes parodic.

In most of the definitions, mythical structure has been characterized by a drive toward the reconciliation of opposites. If the syntax of *The Unnamable* is analyzed from this point of view, the structure that comes to light is primitively mythical in its repetition of polarities struggling for mediation. A typical instance is the insistence with which the Unnamable continues: "I can't go on, I'll go on, you must go on, I'll go on" (p. 414). These contradictions are examples in which the myth seeks some kind of unity. It is through this repetitive contradiction that the structure of the novel takes shape. Since myth, too, is concerned with the origin of things, the Unnamable is concerned with his origin. He wants to recall the stories that he told. Perhaps Murphy, Watt, Molloy, or Malone, his fictions which his word called into existence, could explain him. Yet they seem of little help here, for it is the language of the Unnamable which describes and concretizes the I's search for a self. It is the word, the name, which calls the self into being and separates it from Murphy, Molloy, Malone, Basil, Mahood, and Worm. The Unnamable knows that he must ironically continue in this way to contradict himself, to repeat himself, until he finds the adequate yet imprisoning word which will forever capture his personal being.

The I of the Unnamable sounds at times like the persona of Samuel Beckett, particularly when the I alludes to the other novels of Beckett. With the I as a possible persona, the emphasis on the creator giving himself a name, distinguishing himself from his characters as well as identifying himself with them, becomes very pronounced. While the I of the Unnamable seems to be at times the mask of Beckett, the other characters of the novel are projections and personae of the I whom he accepts and describes. In his attempt to find the real self, the I realizes that he is at the same time all of these characters and none of them. The ironic, humorous and transformed shapes of these people give the search for the self symbolic meaning. This means that all these deformed shapes and characters are not the I, otherwise he would know who he is; rather, they are fictions and names of the I. They are masks and, consequently, creations, or perhaps, creators and namers of the I.

The tension between creation and creator, being alone and with another, silence and words, are all part of the fabric of the mythical structure of *The Unnamable*. In the style of this novel and the continual flow of contradictions and humor, the reality of the creation emerges and becomes the fiction of order and the chief characteristic of the I. In Eliade's terminology the progression from chaos to cosmos is the mythical pattern. Just as this novel is far from a metaphysical treatise, it is also far from a novel in which content is grounded in rational explanation. The reader must almost be hypnotized by the words, by the contradictions, and by the tensions of polarities. He must read the book aloud sometimes to hear for himself a story that seems to be told *in illo tempore*:

> you must go on, that's all I know, they're going to stop me, I know that well, I can feel it, they're going to abandon me, it will be the silence, for a moment, a good few moments, or it will be mine, the lasting one, that didn't last, that still lasts, it will be I, you must go on, I can't go on, you must go on, I'll go on, you must say words, as long as there are any, until they find me, until they say me, strange pain, strange sin, you must go on, perhaps it's done already, perhaps they have said me already, perhaps they have carried me to the threshold of my story, before the door that opens on my story, that would surprise me, if it opens, it will be I, it will be the silence, where I am, I don't know, in the silence you don't know, you must go on, I can't go on, I'll go on. (p. 414)

The "they" as opposed to the "I" who carries the "me" to the threshold of his story, perhaps, is a "they" who could be the words, who are the Basils and the Mahoods and the Worms, the masks of the Unnamable.

They are all those who through words would bring the not yet I into being. The multiplicity of contradictions, the driving force of the words, the constant flow, always produce the effect of a being who is not yet. The Unnamable, therefore, is not yet I or he or me. For, as he said, "if it opens, it will be I, it will be the silence where I am" (p. 414). Silence is identified with the individual world before its creation as well as the I. Words are seen both as an obstacle to the I and as the only way toward being. The Unnamable claims "I don't know, I'll never know, in the silence you don't know" (p. 414). His attempted words include, therefore, contradictions, the search for mediation, the repetition of the story and all the mythical energy needed to progress from chaos to cosmos and allow the not yet I to have a name. They also continually seek the moment immediately preceding the story, the silence at the threshold. Once this name is had, the Unnamable also has a cosmos. The rhythm of the story is persistent, and its search is a process: "you must go on, I can't go on, you must go on, I'll go on" (p. 414). The person in *The Unnamable* is a nondefined person because he has not been named. He has words which function as the product of his mythical consciousness as well as the tools of rational discourse; they are the only aid he has in his pursuit. The "person" in *The Unnamable* is one on a quest, a never-ending quest toward being, toward definition. His reality is always a reality defined in a not yet state. He will continue, however, with the incantation: "I can't go on, I'll go on" (p. 414).

Notes

1. Susan Sontag, *Against Interpretation* (New York: Dell, 1966), p. 8.
2. Sontag, p. 10.
3. Frederick J. Hoffman, *Samuel Beckett: The Language of Self* (New York: Dutton, 1964), p. 80.
4. *The Unnamable*, in *Three Novels by Samuel Beckett* (New York: Grove Press, 1965), p. 303. Further references are cited in the text.

The Later Prose

Conceptions of Inner Landscapes: The Beckettian Narrator of the Sixties and Seventies

Cathleen Culotta-Andonian*

In the prose works written after his Trilogy, Beckett portrays individuals who retreat deeper and deeper into the fantasy worlds they invent, until their awareness does not exceed the boundaries of their own imagination. The narrators' self-centeredness and the inadequacy of their perceptual abilities greatly hinder the creation and development of their stories. Likewise, the improper functioning of their thought processes contributes to the difficulty they experience communicating their imaginary landscapes by affecting the precision, enrichment and even the length of their narratives. Intellectually blank, they cannot always overcome their mental stasis in order to generate images and descriptions to supplement their depleted creative resources. Consequently, they often reexamine the same motifs—themselves, their thoughts, emotions and imaginations.

In order to analyze the conceptual abilities of Beckett's narrators in the recent works, it will be necessary to approach their creative faculties systematically, as they relate to the characters and environments depicted. As the protagonist's physical and mental well-being deteriorates, certain changes in the basic relationship of the narrator to his characters, environment, and narration take place. These alterations in the rapport between author-narrator and fiction correspond to Tzvetan Todorov's classifications of narration presented in his article "Les Catégories du récit littéraire."[1] Each division measures the degree of knowledge the narrator has at his command, which enables him to perceive other characters from a certain vantage point: "par derrière," "avec," or "du dehors." The protagonist's "vision par derrière" indicates that the narrator is well-informed about his characters, frequently knowing more than they do about their own situations, whereas his "vision avec" signifies that his awareness is equal to that of his characters. Finally, his "vision du dehors" denotes that he understands less than his characters and can only describe what he sees at a given moment. In all these stories, the narrators conjure up images and visions from their own imagination. Thus, it is not a

*Reprinted from *Symposium* 36 (Spring 1982) by permission of the journal.

question of how these narrators visually perceive individuals who exist independently of themselves, as in realistic fiction, but rather how active their creative powers are, and to what extent they are capable of conceiving the situations they invent.

Le Dépeupleur and "Autres Foirades, I" illustrate the point of view described by Todorov as "vision par derrière." In both cases the omniscient narrators are more knowledgeable about the condition and fate of their characters than are the characters themselves. As creators of the fantasy worlds they witness, the narrators try to determine the effects certain atmospheric conditions will have on their people. Oddly enough, even though *Le Dépeupleur* is engulfed in a dry, bright atmosphere, and "Autres Foirades, I" reveals a moist, dark environment the final effect seems to be quite similar; the protagonists are mentally confused, devoid of thoughts or emotions, and either frustrated by or indifferent to their confined situations.

In *Le Dépeupleur* the monologuist explains in detail the physical changes that take place in the cylinder and the transformations the inhabitants of that sterile environment will undergo. Since the bewildered creatures are unaware of the continually changing atmosphere of the cylinder, the sporadic alterations in light and temperature, and the inconsistent outbursts of violence, the narrator portrays these individuals in a state of constant fear. He then imagines the myths and the quasi-religious explanations they invent to compensate for their ignorance.

Unconscious of their own feelings and motivations, the inhabitants of the cylinder are divided by the narrator into groups according to their physical traits and movements. External appearances can be misleading to the uninitiated observer: in certain instances, the narrator distinguishes problems that would appear to what he calls an "œil de chair" or a spectator who would have trouble differentiating the three zones of the cylinder (Dé., p. 38)[2] and recognizing the participants in each group who inhabit the various zones. His reference to a possibly incorrect interpretation by an outside observer establishes the narrator as the sole witness to his mental landscape, and as the most knowledgeable, even though he himself may also have doubts about some of the statements he presents. He tentatively posits a description of the future condition of his characters, a condition which they cannot foresee: "Une intelligence serait tenter de voir . . . que tout tôt ou tard chacun à son tour finissent par être des vaincus pour de vrai figés pour de bon chacun à sa place et dans son attitude" (Dé., pp. 29–30). While giving an overall appearance of order and discipline to this created fantasy world, the narrator alone is aware of the extent of the turmoil beneath the surface.

The broken figure who stumbles through the tunnel in "Autres Foirades, I" persists in closing his eyes, thereby remaining ignorant of his physical surroundings. The narrator of the story compensates for his character's imposed blindness by amply describing the conditions of his environment: he analyzes the individual's capabilities and mistakes and tries to imagine what the character would see, should he ever decide to open his eyes. The narrator presents a partial view of the circumstances his hero experiences physically, such as the humidity, the roughness of the stones forming the tunnel or the light at the end of the passage, totally ignoring the character's mental anguish or his personal reactions to his environment.

"Autres Foirades" II and IV and "Au loin un oiseau" illustrate Todorov's category "vision avec," in which the narrator's knowledge is equal to that of his characters. These texts dwell exclusively on the monologuist, his perception of himself and / or his surroundings, yet all three narrators have difficulty concentrating on their stories and know no more about their inner beings, past lives and present environment than their superficial observations reveal. The narrators' descriptions of external beings in "Autres Foirades, II" and "Au loin un oiseau" are nothing but their own fictitious creations, internal fantasies superimposed on their external existence. Not unlike the Unnamable, the monologuists of Beckett's recent stories identify themselves with the heroes they invent, yet, at the same time, persist in retaining their individuality.

The protagonist of "Autres Foirades, II" claims to have complete control of the thoughts and movements of his character and plans to bring about his suicide eventually: "il a mal vécu, à cause de moi, il va se tuer, à cause de moi, je vais raconter ça . . ." (PFE., p. 38). In the end he cannot even predict how his character will die, since he is limited to a direct retelling of the story as it occurs to him. Although the narrator experiences the need to rid himself of this character physically, he in fact never describes his death. More remote from his fiction than the voices in Beckett's Trilogy, the monologuist of "Autres Foirades, II" cannot express his violent fantasy in words, as Moran and Malone have done, and simply terminates his narration.

Likewise the narrator of "Au loin un oiseau" is only aware of his character's actions and desires as they occur, or as he imagines them. The protagonist is surprised to be able to speak through his hero: "il me cherche une voix et je n'en ai pas, il va m'en trouver une, elle m'ira mal, elle fera l'affaire, son affaire . . ." (PFE., p. 48). Dissatisfied with the voice that materializes as he recounts his tale, this narrator, like the Unnamable, is continually restricted to telling someone else's story. Many of the motifs and phrases resemble those of "Autres Foirades, II"; the author-narrator supplies his characters' thoughts, and he undoubtedly will be the cause of his death, although he does not know how or when it will occur.

"Autres Foirades, IV" differs from the other texts in Beckett's collection, because it dwells exclusively on an individual's experiences in a changing environment. The narrator, as the sole protagonist, provides a detailed description of the infestation of his land by May bugs. The destruction he witnesses may be a direct reflection of a mental landscape or his personal desire for annihilation. Even though memories from his childhood interrupt the narrator's thoughts continuously as he stares at the devastation before him, the now barren landscape seems to hinder his creative abilities, to stifle any attempt to develop his visions or to generate new images.

Many of Beckett's recent stories and novels correspond to Todorov's third narrative category, "vision du dehors," defining a narrator who can no longer portray accurately the thoughts and motives of the beings he perceives. As writers of creative fiction, these individuals are not capable of establishing precise characterization or a logical, coherent framework for their narratives. The author-narrators of the remaining works are not as verbose or as flexible as their counterparts in the Trilogy, who frequently deviate from their story to include tedious, long-winded descriptions of their feelings or theories.

Each new fiction manifests a marked decline in the narrator's consistency and succinctness, coinciding to some extent with the chronological order of the texts themselves. This category has been subdivided, and each subgroup will be considered separately, according to the distinctness with which the action, characters and environment are introduced. "Autres Foirades, III" (late fifties or early sixties), "D'un ouvrage abandonné," (1957), *Comment c'est* (1961), and "Assez" (1966) present unusual, fanciful landscapes. The narrator's describe their characters as distinct beings in continuous motion and amply portray their impressions of their environment and monotonous existence. The works "Imagination morte imaginez" (1965), "Immobile" (1970), "Se voir" (sixties) and "Compagnie" (written in 1979, published in 1980) are more abstract, vague, and illusory. The characters are generally unidentifiable, their movements are uncertain and their environment, ambiguous. Even further removed from reality, the short texts "Bing" (1966), "Sans" (1969) and "Pour finir encore" (1976) are so abstract that they are nearly incomprehensible. One is unsure who or what is being portrayed, because the figures are indistinguishable from their backgrounds. The narrators of this last group of texts project scenes that are so vague that they are not illustrated with more than a few simple words and phrases.

In the first group of texts classified as "vision du dehors," which includes "Autres Foirades, III," "D'un ouvrage abandonné," *Comment c'est*, "Assez," and "Compagnie," the narrators are aware of the presence of other individuals, and are quite capable of distinguishing themselves from the additional characters with whom they come in contact. They occasionally lapse into descriptions of the dreams or images they envision, and alternate these fantastic scenes with vignettes recounting their physical progression or adventurous wanderings. Even if these tales represent invented fantasies, they still center around the possible experiences of the monologuists, unlike the abstract portraits which follow these works.

Two distinct individuals are portrayed in "Autres Foirades, II," the narrator and a friend he calls Horn. The monologuist's knowledge of his companion is extremely limited, since their meetings are brief and always take place at night in an unlit room. At the major protagonist's request, Horn lights a match and allows himself to be examined momentarily or takes advantage of the light to contemplate his notes so that he will be able to respond appropriately to the narrator's inquiries. The nature of their exchange is never revealed: the protagonist's major preoccupation at this time is the external appearance of his guest. Failing to discern any enlightening information about his acquaintance, the narrator becomes obsessed, instead, with his own image and the return of his health. The narrator is equally ignorant of his external being and circumstances and those of Horn: darkness is directly responsible for his inadequate perception and also symbolic of his clouded mental state.

The alertness and clarity of the narrator of "D'un ouvrage abandonné" are also subject to question. He watches his mother wave to him from a window, or perhaps it is only his recollection of this scene that is indelibly etched in his memory. He is cognizant of her physical presence and her apparently meaningless gestures, but he is totally ignorant of her intentions and motivations. Unable to rationalize his own bizarre behavior, he is absolutely incapable of even guessing the ulterior motives of the individuals he describes: "Non, ça dépasse l'entendement, tout dépasse, pour un esprit comme moi . . . j'y reviendrai peut-être quant je me sentirai moins faible" (T–M, pp. 14–15). During his three-day journey, many people and images come to mind: his parents, a road worker named Balfe, his dreams of fantastic white animals and imaginary visions of tribes of ermines. Yet all of these fantasies remain vague in his mind, and appear on the same level as the events he describes in his current monologue.

The female monologuist of "Assez" also has difficulty focusing her attention on her partner, and finds it impossible to comprehend his ideas. This narration represents her attempt to document her past wandering with her acquaintance, and her futile efforts to recreate her memories. Given the limited scope of her awareness, it is fitting that the individual she describes so inadequately should be a person who has had an unusual amount of influence on her life. Unable to comprehend the character, or explain his point of view logically, she is forced to restate his opinions by rote, as she remembers them. The reader is faced with a second-hand report: the narration revolves around the couple's explanations of their surroundings, their mutual experiences, and their relationship. In this case, however, the monologuist's memories are too vague to produce more than a sketchy portrait.

The novel *Comment c'est*, published in 1961, is the first of Beckett's works to abstract fictional content one step further. Instead of portraying a hero who reveals his own thoughts and problems directly in a lengthy monologue, Beckett presents a unified account of the creative process. The characters in the novel have a dual role: the narrator perceives these beings as functional elements in the narration and as structural units making up their bizarre habitat. The most important image of the novel is that of the couple depicted in Part II. Pim is the focal point of the story: the narration is reduced to the anticipation, reunion, and regret of the couple. This central figure is intensified by the identical movements of numerous couples imagined by Bom to occupy this bleak landscape. In another sense, Bom's conception of the reunification and separation of the couple may correspond to the movement of his imagination or the development and progression of the words and phrases making up his narration.

Bom's conception of Krim and Kram's role in the text is also related to the redaction of the novel. Bom visualizes these characters as witnesses or scribes who commit the oral narrative to paper, and may correspond to the function of the reader giving life to the author's creation.

Even though these characters represent the imaginary creations of the author-narrator, Bom denies total knowledge of their thought and actions. He forces Pim to speak and to "sing" in answer to his inquiries. The resulting information consists of the terse responses Pim shouts in pain. Bom questions Pim as though he were trying to resolve his own doubts and formulate his own ideas. Yet the monologuist never appears to be satisfied by the responses of his alter ego, and thus demonstrates his incomprehension of the workings of his own imagination which has created this being.

In spite of the fact that Bom's perceptual awareness of his characters often falters, he maintains command of his narration through strict structural control: he may not always be able to describe his partner accurately or his images "from above," but he has no doubts about the major divisions of his story. His detailed mathematical computations occasionally give him a false sense of security and cause him to exaggerate the scope of his fictional world. At this time he generally lapses into the oblivion and ignorance represented by mud and darkness, and denies his previous assertions. Yet it is necessary to submit to the darkness and chaos of the inner world to be able to create images. Once Bom has descended to the depths of his inner consciousness, he rises through the renewed vigor of his creative powers to contemplate images from "above" in the light.

Bom must prod his imagination continually to create his tale, in much the same manner that he jabs or scratches Pim to make him speak. The narrator of *Comment c'est* is able to exhibit the self-discipline and organizational skills necessary for the writing of a full-length novel, because he identifies himself so closely with his work. The still viable perceptual abilities and the structural discipline of the narrator are, more than likely, responsible for the length and coherence of Beckett's last novel. This structural discipline is, in fact, lacking in the subsequent short texts, as the narrators regress to disorder and confusion.

More deeply entrenched in the world of the imagination, the narrators of "Imagination morte imaginez," "Immobile," and "Se voir" attempt to restrict their observations, hoping to create a meaningful portrait through a narrowing of their imaginative field. Even with these self-imposed limitations, their images cannot achieve any significance beyond the flat surface value determined by the protagonists.

The symbol of the author-narrator's failing imagination in "Imagination morte imaginez" is an immobile couple trapped in a circular frame. Their inanimate pose and their blank expression convey the mental apathy of the narrator who struggles to describe their plight adequately. The reader is addressed directly as a witness to judge and imagine the scene depicted by the narrator. "Nulle part trace de vie, dites-vous, pah, la belle affaire, imagination pas morte, si, bon, imagination morte imaginez" (T–M., p. 51).

The specific details of their physical situation are examined, one by one: their appearance, posture, temperature, and respiration. But the initial question of imagination is never repeated—the narrator has recorded what he is capable of imagining and moves on. During his investigation, the author-narrator remains aloof, almost indifferent to his story. The narrator's failure to become a critical observer of his fictional world prevents him from communicating his vision successfully.

The monologuist in "Immobile" is likewise unable to understand the mental landscape he conceives. In fact, he claims he has undertaken the project of describing this individual because he does not comprehend the scene he conjures up: "le mouvement que voici impossible à suivre plus forte raison décrire" (PFE., p. 22). He designates his initial perspective from a safe distance and then moves in for a detailed analysis. No matter how precisely he outlines the anonymous character and his condition, the monologuist cannot clarify the situation and must resort to recounting only what he thinks is happening. The image is abandoned in much the same way that the previous world of "Imagination morte imaginez" disintegrated at the end of the text.

Although written before "Imagination morte imaginez" and "Immobile," the prose piece "Se voir" constitutes a similar approach to the unique subject matter Beckett chooses to depict. The narrator presents a precise image of its physical appearance, but the text ends abruptly without moving beyond a sterile description of the external features of the environment. Unable to perceive the objective world clearly outside his own consciousness, the Beckettian narrator offers vague generalities. The environment greatly resembles that of *Le Dépeupleur*, but the two narrators' perceptions of their created world is quite different. The monologuist of *Le Dépeupleur* is the obvious creator of the cylinder and appears to be quite knowledgeable about the fate of its victims, whereas the narrator of "Se voir" is an uninformed observer of a system he knows little or nothing about. He cannot grasp the significance of what he witnesses and continually dismisses incomprehensible aspects of the scene by stating "ça n'intéresse pas. Ne pas l'imaginer" (PFE., p. 51). Nor is the narrator of "Se voir" so preoccupied with a close inspection of his vision; he is satisfied with a few general remarks and then abruptly terminates his narrative.

In his most recent prose work, "Compagnie," an unidentified protagonist, possibly the narrator himself, lies on his back in the dark listening to a "voice" recount scenes from the past. The portrait is vague and ambiguous, the narration lacks clear characterization, thereby undermining a unified approach to the narrator's vision. Parallels are drawn with many of Beckett's previous heroes, as the narrator refers to his protagonist as M, Unnamable, or "the crawling creator," and to himself as W. Even though the narrator is incapable of accurately portraying the thoughts and emotions of the character he imagines, he is aware of the illusory nature of his tale, "La fable de toi fabulant d'un autre avec toi dans le noir. Et comme quoi mieux vaut tout compte fait peine perdue et toi tel que toujours. / Seul" (Co., p. 88).

The last three texts to be considered here, "Bing," "Sans," and "Pour finir encore" demonstrate a definite departure from coherent conceptual techniques. The narrators of these works imagine vague desert landscapes filled with unidentifiable beings and objects. They are besieged by images, as the repetition of the same fantasies and phrases creates a delirious whirlwind of disconnected thoughts, emotions, and visions around them. The narrators are incapable of ordering their ideas or of controlling the inner chaos they experience. Although the individual monologuists cannot always recognize or describe their visions, their emotions pervade the sterile landscapes they present. Their feelings of loneliness, deprivation, fear, or apathy are obvious from the atmosphere of the texts and the types of images they invent.

The rigidity of the individual described in "Bing" exposes the frustrations of the writer who no longer can create images, or who cannot bring them to life. How can this narrator possibly describe what he has so much difficulty visualizing, when his images are quickly fading into the nondescript background of his mental landscape? The traces of past and present images are either nearly invisible or incomplete. Beckett creates a text struggling to reveal itself, in which all elements of external awareness are stifled. Thanks to the juxtaposition of non-referential concrete images and unidentifiable intuitive images, the reader in the end must form his own impression of the work.

The short text "Sans" repeats many of the motifs presented in "Bing." However, this work is organized around recurring words and themes. The same phrases are then repeated a second time in a different order. The text is impersonal and abstract: Beckett has arbitrarily selected the order of the sentences independent of any notion of point of view. Only the individual sentences can be examined in relation to their context and the clarity or coherence of the images they project. These fleeting mental images and sparse memories of Beckett's narrator are extremely disjointed in "Sans." The increased fragmentation of the character's thoughts, again caused by the random ordering of the sentences in the text, accentuates the impairment of the narrator's perception. Because of the remoteness of the images and the dissolution of the formal context in which they belong, it is obvious that this anonymous protagonist has permanently lost his powers of reasoning and observation.

The lone skull in "Pour finir encore" represents the diminishing mental faculties of a similar narrator who can barely describe the images he envisions. Once again the perception of the third-person narrator is clouded by the uniform grey landscape he creates. This "boîte," the last refuge of the writer, is no longer entirely devoid of action: two midgets scurry across the waves of sand, and the statuesque body falls, yet still contemplates moving forward. The narrator's inventions are perceived more clearly and show more consistency and continuity than those in either "Bing" or "Sans." The images are more numerous, but starker and simpler in nature, and as a result they appear to be slightly more coherent. Each reference to the characters is consistent in content and point of view, even though the narrator's perception of his subject is limited.

In some cases, the narrator's perception of an object or an event is obstructed or at too great a distance for him to clearly identify and characterize his observation; in other instances, his impaired vision or his lack of comprehension prevents him from relating his story. In many of the short prose works, the protagonist is distracted or blinded by the overabundance or lack of light. For example, the individual in "Bing" is confused by the pervading whiteness around him, and focuses on the person he is describing with great difficulty. The figure blends so well with the background that he is almost invisible. Consequently, the perception of the narrator appears distorted, his visual imagery is flat, lacking distinguishing characteristics. Likewise the narrator's impressions in "Sans" and "Pour finir encore" seem vague, because the features of the environment are almost exclusively "blanc sur blanc" (T–M., p. 61). Whereas the protagonist of "Imagination morte imaginez" recognized the fact that "l'inspection est malaisé" and limited his remarks to what he felt he could judge, the narrators of "Sans" and "Pour finir encore" try to enumerate every object and action they can perceive, without questioning the validity or purpose of their remarks. Although there is no indication of movement in the short prose piece "Sans," the protagonist does not hesitate to remark that the exiled figure will move and time will pass, if only in a dream. The individuals in these more recent works by Samuel Beckett in particular recognize the fantastic character of their visions and present them in the dreamlike state in which they appear.

Thus, as the Beckettian protagonist becomes more uncertain about his inner visions, his perception and capacity to describe the figments of his imagination are likewise diminished. This is demonstrated by the fact that the majority of the recent prose pieces correspond to Todorov's third narrative category, "vision du dehors": unable to depict his characters accurately, the protagonist's knowledge decreases to the point where he can only describe what he sees in his mind, without properly situating those images. Explanation of Beckett's latest narratives according to Todorov's categories illustrates the evolution of Beckett's works from omniscient narrators, who seem to be able to comprehend or visualize the situations they present, to anonymous voices reiterating meaningless words and phrases.

Notes

1. *Communications*, 8 (1966).

2. The abbreviations used in this article correspond to the following works: CC. (*Comment c'est*, 1961); T–M. (*Têtes-mortes*, 1967); Dé. (*Le Dépeupleur*, 1970); PFE. (*Pour finir encore et autres foirades*, 1976); and Co. (*Compagnie*, 1980). The quotations have been taken from the texts published by the Editions de Minuit, Paris.

The Voice and Its Words: *How It Is* in Beckett's Canon

Judith Dearlove*

Useful as it otherwise may be, a tripartite division of the Beckettian canon obscures an important shift in the conceptual framework of Beckett's pieces. *How It Is* does not present simply a continuation of the techniques and themes developed in the trilogy. Instead the book marks a turning point in Samuel Beckett's career from an exploration of the limitations of the human mind and an emphasis upon definitions of the self, to an identification of the self with the voice and an acceptance, if not celebration, of the life of the imagination. Indeed, *How It Is* enables Beckett to surmount the attitude of disintegration *L'Innommable* once caused in him[1] by directing attention not to the divorce of the mind from the external world, but rather to the internal worlds the mind creates. *How It Is* reduces everything to a voice speaking in the eternal present creating its own universe. This interior focus in turn makes possible the highly self-conscious and admittedly arbitrary constructions of Beckett's latest fictions.

The works written prior to *How It Is* are concerned with the problems of a mind / body dualism. From Belacqua scoffing "at the idea of a sequitur from his body to his mind,"[2] to Watt discovering the abyss between objects like pots and the words intended to describe them (p. 81

*Reprinted from *Journal of Beckett Studies*, no. 3 (Summer 1978) by permission of Riverrun Press, Inc., New York.

ff.), to the Unnamable trying to say who he is even though there are no names or pronouns for him (p. 404), we see Beckett's characters trying to bridge the gap between the mind, which Murphy describes as a "large hollow sphere, hermetically closed to the universe without," (p. 107) and what Neary refers to as "the big blooming buzzing confusion" (p. 4) of the world. The problem for Beckett's characters, as for the post-Cartesian philosophers to whom Beckett frequently alludes, is that action, speech, identity, and thought become problematic once the mind is isolated from the material world. Ultimately, Murphy's quest to become immersed in the dark flux of his mind's third zone, "where he could love himself" (p. 7), is a self-destructive quest which can be accomplished only by annihilating that physical part of himself "which he hated" (p. 8). Watt's efforts to superimpose the rational constructions of his mind upon the irrational world he encounters meet with no greater success. No matter how many hypotheses he formulates, nor how many generations of "needy local men" he traces to guarantee the feeding of "two famished dogs" (pp. 91–117), Watt never "penetrate[s] the forces at play . . . or even perceive[s] the forms they upheaved, or obtain[s] the least useful information concerning himself, or Mr Knott" (p. 117). Knott cannot be known: the rational mind, incapable of knowing the irrational, can only combine and permute its own limitations. Those limitations are explored further in the trilogy as the first person narrator proffers us a consciousness experiencing itself. From Molloy's inability to recall his name (p. 22) and Moran's contradiction of his own report (p. 176), to Malone's inventory of stories and possessions (p. 181 ff.), to the Unnamable's continuing effort to say the words that will put an end to words (p. 369), we see Beckett's successive narrators struggling to define themselves in relation to the external world and to the words they speak. Even after the Unnamable renounces foreign objects and "vice-existers" as terms in his self-definition, he is still forced to rely on a language learned from others (p. 314). The result is an infinitely repeating pattern in which some larger category is always necessary to encompass the speaker and his definition, to contain the perceiving mind and its self-perceptions.[3] While Beckett's early pieces portray a mind / body dichotomy, his "middle period" works investigate the restrictions that dichotomy imposes upon the mind.

The pieces written after *How It Is*, on the other hand, turn from an emphasis upon the mind's limitations to consideration of its imaginative constructions. References to, and comparisons with an unreachable external reality are replaced by detailed descriptions of objects which exist only in the inner world of the mind's creations. Portrayals of a mind creating stories are omitted in favour of the creations themselves. Moreover, these creations often pay tribute to the imagination.

"Imagination Dead Imagine" is based on a paradox: imagination is necessary to envision a state in which imagination is dead. The envisioned state is that of a solid, white, and silent rotunda containing two figures whose vital signs are reduced to slightly sweating bodies, unblinking eyes, and a misted mirror. Emphasis, however, is placed not upon minimal signs of continuation, but rather upon absence. Without imagination there is no motion, no emotion, no voice, no thought, "no trace anywhere of life" (p. 63). The rotunda must be described through negative propositions. We learn not what it is, but what it is not (p. 63); not what we can say happens, but what we cannot say happens (p. 66).

The identification of colour, movement, sound, and even life with imagination is more subtly continued in "Ping." Instead of entering a rotunda almost at will and observing its inhabitants, "Ping" confines us to a box in which everything keeps fading and disappearing into the shining "white on white invisible" (p. 70). "Ping" becomes, in fact, a catalogue of what is finally over. Significantly, the last element in this catalogue to be alone unover, is not the "heart breath" nor even the blue eyes, but the murmur. More minimal than even the "ah" of "Imagination Dead Imagine," the murmurs are too indistinct to be quoted directly, too fleeting to be recorded. They belong to the world of the imagined, the "never seen," "invisible," "no trace." Yet in a world that increasingly approaches absolute zero, vitality persists in the nonmaterial murmurs and their postulations of what is not: "perhaps [there is] a way out" (p. 69), "perhaps a nature" (p. 70), "perhaps a meaning" (p. 70), "perhaps [the figure is] not alone" (p. 69). Like existence, the piece itself is over only after the final murmur has ended and the last "ping" has faded away.

Just as the imaginative murmurs provide variety and vitality in "Ping," so too those sentences associated with imaginary constructions provide mystery and meaning in "Lessness."[4] Four of the six groups of sentences Beckett wrote in composing "Lessness" are relatively simple: one set describes the "true refuge," another expands the description placing emphasis upon the greyness and / or the endlessness, a third treats the appearance of "the little body," and a fourth set defines the body's intellectual capacities by offering a litany of what is now "all gone from mind." The last two groups of sentences are more difficult to characterize. Whereas the first groups describe setting and body—the known or observable aspects of the present situation—the last groups deal, not with given data, but with the imaginative and mental, with day-dreams and figments. The fifth group postulates things that are not, except in the mind, except in dreams and figments and illusions. The mere mention of these illusions—of passing time, of days and nights, of light, of wild laughter and cries—enriches both this group and the entire work by relieving the grey endlessness. The final group of sentences is similarly suggestive as it deals with future possibilities, with the imagined return of a diverse world in which man can act and speak again "as in the blessed days." But the return to diversity, order, and action is also an implicit return to the false refuge of imagined days and mental containers. By presenting figments and impossible futures, Beckett forces us to see what does not and cannot exist in the "true refuge" except through the imagination.

Although *Fizzles* does not describe self-contained worlds of rotundas, boxes, and cylinders, and although it does return in some sections to first person narration, its stories and images are nonetheless distinct from those of the trilogy. Unlike the narrator of the trilogy, that of *Fizzles* is not obsessed either with defining himself or with labelling, controlling, and hence divorcing himself from his stories. Indeed, the narrator's identity and location are often difficult to determine. Sharp divisions between mind and world are blurred. Moreover, the brevity of the pieces prevents them from self-consciously unmaking themselves or irrepressibly battering the boundaries of human knowledge. Rather than exposing his impotence, the narrator creates images of "stillness" or of "ending yet again." Rather than recording the sounds the mind makes in struggling with its words, the narrator presents prose poems and movements analogous to Sarraute's tropisms. The Unnamable's urgency to say his pensum and to find the correct words is gone. Instead, the words as stated are accepted as adequate. Everything "needed to be known" is known, imagined, and said: there is nothing beyond the world of the fiction: "Closed place. All needed to be known for say is known. There is nothing but what is said. Beyond what is said there is nothing. What goes on in the arena is not said. Did it need to be known it would be. No interest. Not for imagining" (p. 37).

The sense of self-sufficiency suggested in *Fizzles* is central to "Enough." As the title implies, the work is concerned with the moderate and the balanced. Even in a minimal world there can be too much—too much of silence, too much of speech, too much remembered, too much forgotten: "All that goes before forget. Too much at a time is too much . . . Too much silence is too much" (p. 53). The piece, like the weather, deals not with the extremes of storms, but with calm acceptance and the "eternally mild" (p. 59). There are questions one sees, but never asks (p. 53). Desires are no longer manifested (p. 53). Reasoning is a sedative rather than a tool of investigation (p. 58). Emphasis is on the unity and sameness beneath the diversity and flux (p. 58). Parts are fused; "anatomy is a whole" (p. 55); past and present merge (p. 56); entropy is expressed in images, not of decay, but of a spreading calm (p. 60). Instead of the defiance and determination expressed in the claim that "to be an artist is to fail, as no other dare fail,"[5] instead of the commitment to an unending pursuit of futile quests saying, "you must go on, I can't go on, I'll go on" (*The Unnamable*, p. 414); instead of these, 'Enough" hesitantly and tentatively proffers the reconcilation, calm acceptance, and perhaps even the affirmation of a narrator who feels it is enough to have spoken at all, of a narrator who can accept the inevitable failure of his quest saying, "Stony ground but not entirely. Given three or four lives I might have accomplished something" (p. 54). The piece, though a reduced and even minimal literature, is itself enough. When chaos cannot be captured, it is enough to have created an image that fleetingly gestures toward the void. When imagination is divorced from material reality, it is enough to have written words that wipe out everything but a sense of unity with the passing image (p. 60).

The transition from rebellious questing to tentative acceptance, from examination of the mind's limitations to exploration of its creations, from external definitions of the self to internal identifications with the imagination, is first expressed in *How It Is.*[6] By directing the narrator's attention to the self-creating powers of the voice and by eliminating external referents and efforts to locate oneself in opposition to an exterior order, Beckett frees both the voice and his fiction to consider earlier themes and subjects within a new framework. Paradoxically, the more the voice must rely on its own words for both its existence and the wherewithal to endure, the more ambiguous its postulations become. Where everything is produced by, and contained within a speaking voice, nothing need be ultimately affirmed or denied. *How It Is* is bound only by self-imposed limitations. Unencumbered by the problem of sequiturs between body and mind, the voice creates its own space, time, identity, and even style. These creations, in turn, are more meaningful for their metaphysical than their mimetic associations.

The shift in Beckett's framework begins with the reduction of everything to a voice speaking in an eternal present. While *Molloy, Malone Dies,* and even *The Unnamable* contain vestigial characters with bits and scraps of a plot still clinging to them, *How It Is* reduces even those fragmentary characters and plots until there remains only the archetypal elements of the panting, the murmur, the dark, and the mud. Of these elements only the murmur in the mud has the capacity to differentiate, to individuate, to create. This imaginative murmur, then, is the source and substance of the universe—of the Pims and Boms, the sacks and tins, the memories and images. Only through our reading of the voice's whey of words does the narrator assume an identity or existence. Indeed, as the initial and final "stanzas" reveal, the book itself is literally a quotation of the voice's narration. Style and form become content, become surrogate characters and plots. Instead of a three part division of eternity, we have the perpetual present formulation of a voice creating itself in the here and now. When the voice ceases, so does *How It Is*, and our journey through its bizarre world ends.

The structure of *How It Is* intimates the overriding importance of the voice for that work. The presence or absence of the voice distinguishes the journey of part one from the abandon of part three (p. 21). Likewise, the couple of part two is subdivided by the momentous discovery that Pim "can speak then that's the main thing" (p. 56). Repeatedly the narrator anticipates the return of his voice (e.g. p. 60). If it is not with relief, at least it is without objection that he finds this voice "back at last in my mouth" (p. 106). Like Watt seeking to make a pillow of words, the narrator seeks solace in saying something, anything, to himself (p. 43). The flow of words is necessary for without them both the images of life above in the light and existence in the here and now cease (p. 92). Just as the typography of *How It Is* consists of print and spaces, so too the universe consists of words and silences (p. 13). The narrator no longer searches for a "language meet for here" (p. 17); yet only through that language can he live (p. 129).

Although the importance of the voice is emphasized by the structure, its nature remains ambivalent. Indeed, the voice freely contradicts and revises itself. The narrator asks a question, then denies his capability of asking such a question (pp. 92–3); he describes motions he makes to hear Pim's watch, then concludes that "all that beyond my strength" (p. 58); he posits a word, then retracts it as "too strong" (p. 55, p. 115). Uncertainty increases as the voice points out its own faulty transmission. Not only do we depend on some less than assuring witness, but this witness himself depends on a less than definitive narration. Like Sam in *Watt*, the witness is trying to transcribe a story of which he hears only "bits and scraps" (p. 15) and "little blurts midget grammar" (p. 76) which come too fast and end too soon (p. 81). In spite of its ambiguity and uncertainty, however, the voice is consistent in its modes of operation. It remains loyal to the self-imposed limitations of the way the story is told. Reality is not really an issue. Phrases such as "it's one or the other" (p. 11), "I remember . . . or I forget" (p. 8), "it's not said or I don't hear" (p. 18) become refrains. Nothing, not even an ending, need be established irrevocably. The narrator may be engulfed in the mud, may be part of an unending cyclical progression, may be shat into the light. He may be the only figure who exists, or may be diffused into the great collapse of a million Pims and Boms. He may know other figures or may remain isolated. Unlike the trilogy characters, he may even die, "I am not dead to inexistence not irretrievably" (p. 69). The only rule of order for dealing with permutations is that "justice" be maintained. This justice is itself nothing more than the preservation of symmetry. Every Bom must be a Pim for equivalent periods of time (p. 125). Every four yards to the north must be balanced by four yards to the south (p. 47). As in *The Lost Ones* and "Imagination Dead Imagine," the narrator uses his mathematics to create verbal diagrams (p. 47). Ironically, in an uncertain world of undifferentiated mud, we know precisely how the narrator crawls—if he really does crawl. Likewise, the narrator's "dear figures" yield the percentage of words lost (if they are lost) (p. 95), and enable a contrast between Pim's "iso" buttocks (if Pim exists) and the narrator's own "ratio [of] four to one" (p. 37). The voice is thus consistently operating according to the abstract postulations of systems such as "mathematics astronomy and even physics" (p. 41), in an inconsistent world lacking the "history and geography" which gave time and place to mimetic novels.

The ambivalence of the voice is due not only to its uncertainty about the universe it postulates, but also to its ambiguous source. Although the narrator purports to be murmuring in the mud, at the same time he attributes the voice to some external person or thing which he is at best only quoting, "I say it as I hear it" (p. 7). As in *The Unnamable* there is a sense that the words are part of some pensum taught by and belonging to a "them" or "it" (p. 108). But there is no longer any urgency to define "who is speaking that's not said any more it must have ceased to be of interest" (p. 21). Nor are we concerned whether the narrator speaks from obligation, necessity, or desire; whether he uses his speech "freely" or not (p. 18). The narrator accepts without desperation the realization that his words can pass through him and beyond his control. Moreover, he uses the externality of the voice as the first premise in the proof of its divinity. If the voice is other and is the source of words, it may be the source of the murmurings of all Pims and Boms (p. 76). The voice is prime matter and prime mover. Like the Christian God it is creator and trinity, "the voice quaqua from which I get my life . . . of three things one" (p. 113). It is to this "voice quaqua the voice of us all" (p. 138) that the narrator assigns the "minimum of intelligence" required to validate his universe by hearing and noting our murmurings and by filling the "need of one not one of us an intelligence somewhere a love who all along the track at the right places according as we need them deposits our sacks" (pp. 137–8). The tasks are not too difficult since "to hear and note one of our murmurs is to hear and note them all" (p. 138). The external divinity not only creates us by giving us words, but he also confirms us by listening to us repeat them (p. 137). But, just as a rationalist's proofs of God's existence led to agnosticism, so too the narrator's deduction leads to doubt. Given his world, it is unlikely that a voice as powerful and intelligent as his divinity would endure a system whereby it would hear its own story endlessly repeated. Since it is impossible to stop the cycle without causing injustice (p. 139), the voice would be forced rather to formulate a system eliminating himself as divinity and "admitting him to peace at least while rendering me in the same breath sole responsible for this unqualified murmur" (p. 144). The narrator has thus gone full circle. Beginning with a voice which he locates externally, he goes on to construct a universe over which such a voice would be the divine intelligence, only to end by acknowledging the errors of his system and his own responsibility for the voice.

Perhaps it is only in a Beckettian universe that a narrator can without contradiction assume responsibility for an external voice. The consistency, or at least compatibility of such claims is due to the paradoxical nature of the voice. It is both external and internal, archetypal and intimate, universal and individual (p. 7). Internality is emphasized by the soundless voice of the journey (p. 18). No qualitative difference accrues between silent and audible murmurings, between "two cries one mute" (p. 48). The voice and its significance lie beyond mere vocalization. The essential and internal nature of the voice is also supported physiologically. Murmuring and panting are similar processes. An end will not come until both have stopped (pp. 104–5, p. 106). The voice, the pant, and even the fart are all defined by the same elementary description. Foreign matter is brought into the body, it is processed, waste products are expelled: inspiration, respiration, exhalation; ingestion, digestion, excretion. The application of voice to this pattern undercuts western veneration of the mind. In the archetypal world of mud, dark, pant, and murmur, it is the murmur with its ability to invent that must bear the burdens normally associated with the mind, imagination, and thought. With embarrassing ease, principles concerning human understanding can be plugged into the description—perception becomes foreign input, thought becomes processing, and ideas become mere waste products equivalent to the less inspiring and more earthy pant or fart. The voice, the pant, and the fart are the basic life process, are the hiss of air which bestows existence on the little that's left of the narrator:

> escape hiss it's air of the little that's left of the little whereby man continues standing laughing weeping and speaking his mind nothing physical the health is not in jeopardy a word from me and I am again I strain with open mouth so as not to lose a second a fart fraught with meaning issuing through the mouth no sound in the mud.
>
> it comes the word we're talking of words I have some still it would seem at my disposal at this period one is enough aha signifying mamma impossible with open mouth it comes I let it at once or in extremis or between the two there is room to spare aha signifying mamma or some other thing some other sound barely audible signifying some other thing no matter the first to come and restore me to my dignity (p. 26).

On another level, the words restore the narrator to his dignity because they are that dignity. Although there may be an external voice providing the words for the narrator and for thousands of Pims, we hear of that voice and of those thousands only through the narrator's murmurings (p. 87). The voice creates the narrator who in turn embodies that voice or, as the narrator says, "I personify it it personifies itself" (p. 112). He can have no desires beyond those the voice grants him (p. 12). He can make no judgments independent of the voice's evaluations (p. 37). He ceases to exist when the voice leaves him and returns to himself only when the voice returns to him (p. 95). His life is the murmurings in the mud, "my life last state last version ill-said ill-heard ill-recaptured ill-murmured in the mud" (p. 7). Life is presented at its minimal point—the ill-said, ill-heard—nevertheless, a certain dignity inheres in the resiliency and inevitability with which that ill-said continues to speak, to create itself and its fictitious worlds.

In the archetypal world of the ill-said, time is also reduced to its most basic component. Past and future are irrelevant in a world without cause or effect. The three part division of eternity (p. 24) is actually the three part division of a stream of words uttered in the eternal present. Correlation between those three parts and those words is possible if part three is accepted as an accurate description of the present and the book is seen as a version of the traditional flashback. The viewpoint is that of a narrator who has already survived the journey and couple and is recounting them from his current abandoned position. Throughout, the first two stages are consistently referred to by the past tense, while the present is applied to the third, and the future is employed in conjecture about the fourth, "how it *was* I quote before Pim with Pim after Pim how it *is*" (p. 7, my italics). The narrator's decision to follow the "natural order" enables him, like Malone, to tally what he must say in order to make an end (p. 51). His knowledge of the entire cycle enables him to anticipate later stages. In the journey he predicts the discovery and loss of Pim (p. 20) and he knows that the difference between the silent journey and the abandon will be "words like now words not mine before Pim" (p. 21). The narrator's knowledge of the whole order allows—or causes—him to get "the various times mixed up in [his] head all the various times before during after vast tracts of time" (p. 107). Although the images belong to the journey (p. 10), they appear in the couple (p. 85, p. 86, p. 88). Although numbers and "reckoning" are supposed to fade out after part one (p. 51), part three contains elaborate computations (pp. 114–142). The best indication that the whole must be spoken from the part three viewpoint is the existence of the narration itself. The book is dependent upon a voice which is "peculiar to part three or seven or eleven or fifteen so on" (p. 116). The speechless life in the couple can be portrayed only after speech has returned (p. 60).

Unlike the conventional flashback, however, the narration denies the validity of a past and the possibility of a future. As in *Happy Days*, once a state is ended, it is as though it never existed. One "knows one's tormentor only as long as it takes to suffer him and one's victim only as long as it takes to enjoy him if as long" (p. 121). If there is "no more Pim [there] never [was] any Pim" (p. 74). The scenes told of life above in the light are images, not memories (p. 11), because memories imply a past. The narrator is displaced in time, cut off from a causal world, denied an heroic past and a golden age (p. 10, p. 54). The lack of a future denies him any hope or goal. His obligation is "precisely that of fleeing without fear while pursuing without hope" (p. 143). He cannot deal with questions such as what would happen if he were to lose the opener or if the sack were finally empty (p. 9). Nor can he predict that no-one will ever come again to shine a light on him (p. 15). The present formulation undercuts the narrator's entire metaphysics as he is forced to admit that Pim never was and Bom never will be (pp. 86–7), that one cannot present in three episodes "an affair which all things considered involves four" (p. 130). Pim's howl comes when asked how life is (pp. 96–8): the narrator's scream comes when asked how it was (pp. 144). This scream is "good" because it is proof of present life (p. 122). Yet, at the same time, the scream is an acknowledgement that all the descriptions of how it was are false. The narrator is forced to return to the present with its only certainties of the mud, the dark, the panting, and the murmur.

When the voice creates its own material universe out of undifferentiated, soundless, and scentless mud (p. 25), attention no longer need be directed to the height of Cuchulain's statue[7] nor to the location of the Unnamable's jar. Mimetic details are subsumed by their metaphoric and metaphysical implications. Geographic division is less important than perception that the primeval mud (p. 11) is the protoplasm from which all else is derived and to which all things return. The mud is both "humanity restoring" drink and food (p. 27, p. 28) and the excrement of billions (p. 52). It is like that "drop of piss of being" man drinks and "with his last gasp pisses" to the next (p. 132). Although the narrator imposes directions upon the vast plains of mud (p. 47), his compass references are only arbitrary divisions of a purposeless tack. The eastward movement is metaphorically meaningless. It cannot be a movement towards the sunrise with its conventional association of rebirth because birth, sunrise, and even the earth's rotation belong not to the mud, but to life above in the light (p. 123). Nor can it be a journey towards death for "death [is] in the west as a rule" (p. 123). At best the journey from west to east, from left to right, is analogous to the motion of words across the printed page. The voice's geography belongs to its medium of words.

Likewise, objects depend on the voice's narration. The objects presented are purposely simple, few in number, grudgingly given, and rigidly controlled. Unlike the trilogy, where characters, plots, and objects proliferate until they escape control, until for example, Malone does not know why his own character Sapo "was not expelled when he so richly deserved to be" (*Malone Dies*, p. 190), the objects here are contained and carefully labelled (p. 8, p. 9, p. 11, p. 25). They never attain independent existence, but rather always remain subject to the voice's postulations. By revising his description of Pim's watch (p. 58), the narrator calls the materiality of that watch into question. The sack steadily depreciates from one of the early certainties (p. 8), to an incidental object, to one of the "not true" (p. 145). Indeed, the narrator is able to envision himself without sacks or other anomalous objects, "quite tiny," sustained only by the air and the mud (p. 17).

Paradoxically, these problematic objects bear a large burden of meaning. Having stripped away circumstantial reality and external association, Beckett thrusts enormous pressure on the few remaining objects. They must operate on a material level (sack as wet jute sack [p. 8]), on a referential level (sack as penitential shirt [p. 36]), as container of the world's howls and laughter (p. 38), on a symbolic level (sack as lover [p. 44], as body [p. 17]), and on metaphysical and mythic levels. It is the necessity of replacing the sacks which calls into question the narrator's cyclical system and hypothetical divinity. His parallel claims that he will never let go of the sack (p. 10) nor of Pim (p. 55) and the parallel negations of the sack abandoned (p. 46, p. 55) and Pim lost (p. 99) reveal the narrator's ultimate inefficacy. His burst sack and Pim's "not burst" sack raise the problems of justice and human understanding (p. 61). The deposition of sacks becomes a metaphor for the human condition and an image of how it is: ". . . we leave our sacks to those who do not need them we take their sacks from those who soon will need them . . ." (p. 111). Likewise, the tins of tunny tell us more about human existence than they do about the social and material reality of the narrator. They are more important as objects to be counted, opened, thrown away, or returned to the sack half empty (p. 8), than as containers of food. Significantly, the narrator never portrays himself doing anything so lifelike as eating the prawns or a crumb of mouldy tunny (p. 8). Instead, the tins are a crude measure of an approaching end, when it will be possible to count them with one hand (p. 8). The narrator compares himself casting off empty tins to a dealer of cards and to "certain sowers of seed" (p. 11). Unlike the Biblical seed, the narrator's is hollow and exhausted, falling without hope or fertility in the random order of a card game. Even the narrator seeks no harvest from his tins but will, if he sometimes finds a tin, "make haste to throw [it] away again" (p. 11). In a similar fashion Krim and Kram's notebooks function as a paradigm of our three part story. The blue notebook, like part one, is a record of the physical movements of the narrator (pp. 81–2); the yellow notebook, like the presentation in part two of Pim's story, is a record of another's "mutterings verbatim" (p. 82); and the red notebook, like the present state of the abandon, is "for my comments" (p. 82). The attempt to keep distinct in these notebooks what has "up till now all [been] pell-mell in the same" (p. 82) is akin to the narrator's effort to divide his eternity into three. Thus, when "the idea of the three books [is] set aside" as "questionable" (p. 83), the structure of *How It Is* is also challenged. The quest of the narrator, like that of the recorder of the notebooks, is not for a three part history but for an end and a silence.

The quest for an end is itself undermined by the "vast stretch of time" (p. 7) of the eternal present. Before this vastness, any efforts to assign order or to measure segments are as absurd and futile as having "Pim's timepiece . . . and nothing to time" (p. 40). In fact, all of the narrator's chronometric devices are negated by his condition. The diminution of tins as a crude measure of the approaching end is made ineffectual by the loss of both the tins and the need for the tins. Likewise, the alarm-clock, like the breath bag (p. 19), becomes irrelevant when the narrator admits he no longer sleeps (p. 40). Although he may, like Winnie, occasionally speak of time in the "old style" of measurable units like days and weeks, the narrator is aware that such units belong not to his vast, static world but to the revolving world of life above in the light (p. 123). He speaks to fill in the void, discussing things and desires he no longer has in preference to not speaking at all (pp. 12–13, p. 16, p. 18). The whole work becomes his effort to find the "there wherewith to beguile a moment of this vast season" (p. 91).

Denied escape from the "vast season" of the present, the narrator explores the implications of his existence. Like a tree falling in an uninhabited forest, does a voice speaking in the eternal present need some "other" to hear its words and confirm its existence? As in *Film*, the narrator can examine the structural and dramatic convenience of Berkeley's dictum, *Esse est percipi* (to be is to be perceived), without attaching any "truth value" to the idea. The actual reality of a witness is less an issue than are the images and theories resulting from the narrator's felt need for one.

Like the presence or absence of a voice, the presence or absence of another is a major structural device. It is the fact of the couple rather than role of tormentor or victim which is important: part four is unnecessary to our narration because it is essentially a repetition of part two (p. 131). The journey and the abandon are themselves defined in terms of the "other." The journey is a quest without hope and without the "all-important most important" other inhabitant (p. 13). Yet even in that solitude there remains the dream "of a little woman within my reach and dreaming too it's in the dream too of a little man within hers" (p. 13). Or, if that dream is too hopeful, there is an emergency dream of an alpaca llama in whose fleece one may huddle (p. 14). Part three presents not simply man alone, but man abandoned, man rejected, man aware of his lack of the other. The need of another simply for its otherness manifests itself in the narrator's relationship with his sack. During the journey the sack is the only available other. By being an external object against which individuation may occur, the sack becomes the first sign of life (p. 8). More than a thing to be manipulated or an object to be possessed, the sack assumes almost sexual relationships with the narrator, who cradles and caresses it (p. 44), makes a pillow of it to lie "soft in my arms" (p. 46), murmurs endearments to it (p. 17). The narrator clings to the sack not from fear of losing it (p. 10) nor from expectation of any profit from it (p. 66), but because it admits of his own existence.

Like the sack, the narrator's people evolve out of his felt need for a witness. Long before they are named, Krim and Kram appear as listener and scribe. Indeed, the narration technically cannot exist without their recording of the narrator's stream of words (p. 7). Their transcript is the book we hold and read. Yet Krim and Kram are unreliable witnesses. Not only do they "lose the nine-tenths" (p. 81) of what is being said, but their whole capacity for comprehension is made questionable by their inability to determine if the narrator and Pim are alive (p. 93), or to agree if their role permits affording the narrator relief (p. 82). Moreover, the narrator denies them an independent existence, even abandoning his own viewpoint in one scene to speak their thoughts. At one point he tells us there is no witness, no scribe (p. 84). At another, like Watt dealing with the Lynch family, he postulates generations of Krims and Krams to ensure continual observation (p. 80). Pim is similarly undermined. Pim is the necessary other. Only by feeling that Pim is there, can the narrator feel he himself is there still (p. 92). However, Pim's reality is questionable. Just as the book would never be, but for the energy and life the reader invests in it, anything but a pile of paper, so too Pim would "never be but for me [narrator] anything but a dumb limp lump flat for ever in the mud" (p. 52). Like Krim and Kram, Pim may be only a figment of the narration (p. 27). Not only does the narrator, as he says "efface myself behind my creatures when the fit takes me" (p. 52), but he quite blatantly assumes their names (p. 60) and lives (p. 72) and "plays" at being them (p. 57). The hope for another who will penetrate the voice's hermeticism is destroyed.

This failure of the "other" shatters the narrator's most concrete image of the couple. The best the narrator can offer is a melancholic portrayal of an almost couple. Boredom rather than affection induces him to question Pim without hope or desire of an answer (p. 74). The narrator doesn't know if he presses Pim to himself out of love or fear of being abandoned or "a little of each" (p. 66). Emotional overtones of a romantic tradition are gradually stripped away until the couple becomes merely one stop in a meaningless journey "from the next mortal to the next mortal leading nowhere" (p. 62). Part two is a litany of missed opportunities. With a companion the narrator would have been a "more universal" man, another's words could have improved him, he realizes his injunctions could have been communicated by more humane means; but the companion (p. 67), the words (p. 69), and the realization (p. 90) all come "too late too late indisputably" (p. 69). The couple fails to attain certitude, purpose, affection, or vitality. The tragedy of this failure is magnified by the expectations the narrator holds for the conjunction. Not only is it to be the hoped for end to solipsistic solitude, silence, and cosmic loneliness, but it is also to be a source of consolation. The journey is less burdensome when placed in a series of similar sufferings (p. 48). The existence of one other increases the probable existence of a whole universe of others, "the moment there are two there were yes billions of us crawling" (p. 52). An endless progression of "billions of us" makes hearsay knowledge and communication possible (p. 119). Thus the failure of the couple destroys consolation, communication, and knowledge. No one knows another "either personally or otherwise" (p. 123). With the dissolution of the couple and the "other," inevitably comes the dissolution of the self: "at each instant each ceased and was there no more either for himself or for the other vast tracts of time" (p. 122).

Nothing so positive as the hopes from even an improbable couple is left unchallenged in the voice's world. The couple is simultaneously extolled and undermined. Communication and connection are desired and fled. The narrator desires no caller (p. 12) and prefers not to meet even himself. Only after all else has failed will he stop fluttering his hand before his eyes and actually touch it to his face (p. 14). The discovery of Pim's voice which "makes us better acquainted" (p. 55) is the "hitch" that ends the "long peace" of the "beginnings of our life in common" (p. 55). Pim wants the narrator to leave him in peace (p. 98). When conceiving other worlds, the narrator imagines a more merciful one without a couple and thus without an abandonment or journey (p. 143). It is ambiguous whether Pim has been given to the narrator as a reward or as a punishment for his high morale: "the morale at the outset before things got out of hand satisfactory ah the soul I had in those days the equanimity that's why they gave me a companion" (p. 25). Caught in the paradox of his system, the narrator needs the "other" to establish his own identity, yet finds life in the couple yields only false identity. There is no real conjunction and life in common is only an "orgy of false being" (p. 69).

By making the narrator's existence and identity dependent upon a voice whose nature is ambivalent, whose postulations are uncertain, and whose auditor is problematic, Beckett has diffused his work into an intangible, paradoxical vastness. He has gone beyond Proust and Joyce and the problems of temporal identity. As in *Ulysses*, identity is continuous and successive. The narrator is the same ancient voice throughout and he is three figures who cannot recall earlier stages. But Beckett destroys the perimeters of the self in space as well as in time. The narrator is not only the ancient external-internal voice, but he is also the spoken and the heard voice. His existence is contingent upon the other: no sharp divisions separate him from that other. The dispersion of identity yields ambiguous pronouns. The unnamed voice is called "he," "it," and even "I." Often the third person pronoun remains indefinite as "he" refers equally well to the narrator, Pim, Krim, Kram, Pam Prim, or Bom. The absence of individual boundaries results in the conjugation of names (pp. 114–15). In such a schema it is irrelevant whether the narrator is creating Pim or encountering one of a million non-individuating figures all identical to himself: "in other words in simple words I quote on either I am alone and no further problem or else we are innumerable and no further problem either" (p. 124). Each figure is Everyman pursuing the same archetypal cycle through the "warmth of primeval mud impenetrable dark" (p. 11). In his career each plays both Pim's and Bom's role. In fact, there is no real difference between being Pim or Bom, between section two and four. Joy and sorrow, tormentor and victim, "I" and "he" all merge as identity is denied definitive borders and as existence is diffused into spoken and heard, Pim and Bom, I and Other.

Because everything in *How It Is* depends upon the diffuse, narrating voice, the form in which the voice creates its universe is as important as the content of that universe. Style literally is meaning. In a world without past or future, cause or effect, there can be no order, no subordination. The omnipresent now is experienced without punctuation and without the interlocking memories that make the well-made sentence possible. In such a universe the major concern is to pass the time while waiting for an end that will not come. The lack of hope removes urgency from the verbal games the voice plays with itself to fill in the void. But even in these games—even in enumerating what must be said to reach the last at last, in positing resources, or in asking oneself questions and providing the answers—the self-imposed limitations of the voice's universe must still be obeyed. In a world that has rejected traditional time, place, and identity, the voice can no longer ask how it got here, whence come its possessions, or even if it exists (p. 7). Where everything, including identity, is ambiguous, pronouns become indefinite and names generic. Where nothing is certain, language itself begins to dissolve. Not only does the voice begin to contradict itself, but it also finds that its words are too strong (p. 115, p. 127). It has only "the old words back from the dead" (p. 95) from which it must take "bits and scraps" (p. 106), stringing them together to make "phrases more phrases" (pp. 106–7). Where there is no external order, all becomes a free flowing mental construction. The lack of permanent and concrete connections is reflected in everything from the failure of the couple to communicate to the splitting apart of normal syntax groups. In a prose that imitates an entropic universe breaking down in the mud, there can be little imagery. The colours, gestures, near-metaphors, and almost-symbols that survive are few in number and sparingly used. Whereas earlier works are greatly concerned with the degenerating bodies of their characters, *How It Is* is almost amorphous. It is the voice which captures our interest. Its references to eyes, ears, hands, and heads are neither insisted upon nor pursued as physical realities. Indeed, the body fades into surreality (p. 28). Even the eyes become strangely unseeing eyes. The important vision is mental rather than material. Hence the voice's need for two kinds of eyes: the blue to deal with the physical and "the others at the back" (p. 8) for the psychical.

Although *How It Is* does not portray the self-sufficient and hermetic worlds of rotundas, boxes and cylinders, its images are, nevertheless, distinct from those of earlier pieces. Unlike the Unnamable's "delegates" who tell him "about man," provide him with "the low-down on God," give him "courses on love, on intelligence," and teach him "to count, and even to reason" (*The Unnamable*, pp. 297–8), the voice's images create no intellectual or emotional bonds between himself and their "few creatures in the light" (p. 8). Although the narrator begins by saying he has only old dreams, things, and memories (p. 7), he quickly revises this statement. In a world without a definable past or sleep, there can be no memories nor any dreams. Therefore the narrator chooses to call the things he sometimes sees in the mud, "images" (p. 11). Unlike memories, the images are impersonal and independent of an external reality. There is neither recall by the narrator of the life the images portray (p. 8), nor is there any question of, or even desire for returning to such a life (p. 8). Indeed, most of the images in part two ascribed to Pim can also be linked to the narrator. The narrator's brief reference to coming to "in hospital in the dark" (p. 22), is expanded by the image of Pam Prim's hospitalization (p. 77). The scene of the boy praying at his mother's knees (p. 15), reverberates in Pim's description of mamma (p. 78). The setting that leads into the narrator's vision of Jesus (p. 45) reappears in Pim's section. The narrator's concern with slipping and falling to lower levels is fulfilled in the falls that punctuate Pim's life and relationships. The similarities between the two sections invite us to borrow Pim's images to develop a prose context for the narrator. Isolation in the mud seems the inevitable end for one who "tried everything then gave up . . . never any good at anything" (p. 78), who "never knew anyone always ran fled elsewhere some other place" (p. 78), who sought only to "crawl about in corners and sleep" (p. 78) and to find the quickest, safest, darkest way home. The narrator's search for an end seems but a continuation of Pim's struggle to find a hole. However, the details leading up to such a quest are only of secondary importance. We do not need to piece out the birth of love in the twenties nor its decline and the futile "effort to resuscitate" it (p. 82), in order to feel the decay and increasing solitude which inform the narration. In the mud such prose constructions are irrelevant. Everything results in the same voice seeking the same cancellation of itself. As the narrator more graphically says, ". . . what the fuck I quote does it matter who suffers . . . who makes to suffer who cries who to be left in peace in the dark the mud . . ." (pp. 131–2). Just as it is unnecessary to determine if there is only one or three or millions of figures crawling in the mud, so too is it unimportant to distinguish among images or to fill in the gaps in the story they imply.

In an ambivalent world where everything can ultimately be reduced to a voice creating and correcting itself, a refrain of "something wrong there" is inevitable and natural. Inevitable because where nothing is certain, any statement must be only relatively true. Natural because where everything is self-consciously fictive, correction and revision can be flatly announced. Yet at the same time, the refrain is disconcerting as it abruptly destroys any suspension of disbelief we may have willed. The prose demands that we, like the narrator, agonize over and experience the present formulation without the mediation of even the most minimal fictions. Moreover, we are required to draw upon our own resources to discern what is wrong and where. The errors themselves are significant in a work in which "my mistakes are my life" (p. 34). There are three or four basic categories our refrain labels as erroneous. It is used to negate any statements implying a continuity with the past, a predictable future, or a possibility of change. The narrator can say neither that he has steadily gone from bad to worse (p. 9), nor that he crawls toward a ditch which will never come (p. 16), nor that one day he and Pim will travel together (p. 57). The refrain is also appended to any statements granting credence to other bodies or objects. It is wrong to speak of Pim's timepiece (p. 40), of Krim's knowledge of the couple (p. 93), or of the couple itself as "two little old men" (p. 54). We are uncertain one body exists let alone others. A voice may be posited, but a choir of such voices must be undercut (p. 107). The narrator knows only himself, not "[him] who is coming towards me and [him] who is going from me" (p. 116). Indeed, references to the narrator's own body are themselves problematic. Although the hand controls a large amount of the book's imagery, its activities are repeatedly crippled by the refrain. Unsure whether or not the hand is really disintegrating, whether or not the thumb has dropped off (p. 28), we have no assurance that the fingers and thumb do hold a sack (p. 34), that the hand does flesh Pim's buttocks (p. 37) or feel his cheek (p. 56), that a hand ever descends on an arse for the first time (p. 121), or even that the hands exist and can be seen lying "tense in the mud" (p. 43). Finally, the refrain contradicts statements the narrator makes about his own cyclic theory. Unable to determine ultimately if there is eternal recurrence or eternal presence, he finds fault with both systems. In a cyclic world it is incorrect to call anything a first or last member, to say that a clinking tin is the "first respite very first from the silence of this black sap" (pp. 24–5). Likewise, in a cyclic world one is not simultaneously Pim and Bom and the roles should not be equated in the conjugation of their names (p. 115). The "inevitable number 777777" (p. 140) cannot be, at the same time, Bom to 777778 and Pim for 777776. But, if the world is an eternally present now, one cannot alternate roles and be "now Bom now Pim" (p. 115). Everything must stem from the essential present of the abandoned where the narrator has a voice with which to create the other parts. Indeed, it is difficult to imagine any other formulation (p. 129): it is impossible to depict any other order (pp. 116–17). *How It Is* is only a voice speaking in the present and creating a universe of Pims and Boms, sacks and tins, voiced and voiceless. Any statement which tries to ignore or circumvent this essential fact will naturally have "something wrong there" and will inevitably be undermined by the refrain. The prose style of the narration insists upon our facing "how it is present formulation" (p. 129).

Every element in *How It Is*, from typography to time, from "objects" to "others," derives from a voice narrating itself. The imaginary worlds the voice creates assume the ambivalence and uncertainty surrounding that voice. Although everything depends upon a stream of words, the source of those words is ambiguously external and internal just as identity is indistinctly I and Other. Existence and continuation are the present act of speaking. Time is only the now against which words are spoken. The already-mentioned and not-yet-said fade into irrelevance. Murphy's concerns for mimetic details, like the Unnamable's desires for self-definition, are replaced by a voice speaking in the eternal present. Instead of examining the limitations of the mind / body dichotomy, the work explores the fluid universe of the mind and its imagination. The murmurs in the mud mark a shift from exterior orders to internal fabrications. Just as the speaker and his narration intimate the way it is for us, so too the voice and its words suggest how it is in Beckett's canon.

Notes

1. In a *New York Times* interview with Israel Shenker (6 May 1956, Section 2, pp. 1, 3), after describing *L'Innommable* as a work of "complete disintegration," Beckett confided: 'The very last thing I wrote—*Textes pour rien*—was an attempt to get out of the attitude of disintegration, but it failed."

2. Samuel Beckett, *More Pricks Than Kicks* (New York: Grove Press, 1972), p. 29. Other Beckett works referred to in this paper and cited parenthetically will be to the following Grove Press Editions: *Watt* (1959), *Murphy* (1957), *Three Novels by Samuel Beckett: Molloy, Malone Dies, The Unnamable* (1965), *Fizzles* (1976), and "Imagination Dead Imagine," "Ping" and "Enough" in *First Love* and *Other Shorts* (1974).

3. Beckett's infinitely repeating pattern is often observed; for example, see also Hugh Kenner's *Samuel Beckett: A Critical Study* (1973), David H. Hesla's *The Shape of Chaos: An Interpretation of the Art of Samuel Beckett* (1971), and the articles, especially those of David H. Hesla and Edouard Morot-Sir, in *Samuel Beckett and the Art of Rhetoric* (1976).

4. Samuel Beckett, "Lessness," *New Statesman*, 79 (1 May 1970): 635.

5. Samuel Beckett, "Three Dialogues," in *Samuel Beckett: A Collection of Critical Esays*, ed. Martin Esslin (New Jersey: Prentice-Hall Inc., 1965), p. 21.

6. Samuel Beckett, *How It Is* (New York: Grove Press, 1964).

7. In his article, "The Thirties," in *Beckett at 60*, London, Calder and Boyars, 1967, A.J. Leventhal recalls receiving an urgent postcard from Beckett requesting that he "measure the height from the ground of Cuchulain's arse"—referring to the statue in the Dublin General Post Office. As Leventhal points out, Beckett needed this information to be certain Neary actually could "dash his head against [Cuchulain's] buttocks, such as they are" (*Murphy*, p. 42).

Some Ping Understood

David Lodge*

The enigma of Samuel Beckett's *Ping* (*Encounter*, February 1967) derives a special interest from the context of debate, initiated in these pages by Frank Kermode (March–April 1966) and carried on by Ihab Hassan (January 1967) and Bernard Bergonzi (May 1967) concerning the contemporary *avant-garde*. Whether fortuitously or not, *Ping* seems a timely illustrative or testing "case" for such critical speculation.

The speculation is, I take it, concerned basically with such questions as: is contemporary *avant-garde* literature, in common with experimental art in other media, making a much more radical break with "tradition" than did the literature and art of what Kermode calls "paleo-modernism"? Is it, in effect, seeking the extinction of literary culture by denying from

*Reprinted from *Encounter* 30, no. 2 (February 1968) by permission of the journal.

within the epistemological function of the literary medium itself (*i.e.*, language)? Is it, not literature at all, but "anti-literature"? Is it immune to conventional criticism; and if so, does this demonstrate criticism's impotence, or its own?

Of the three critics mentioned above, the one who answers these questions in a spirit most sympathetic to radical discontinuity with tradition is Ihab Hassan. The essential argument of his article "The Literature of Silence" is that today, "Literature, turning against itself, aspires to silence, leaving us with uneasy intimations of outrage and apocalypse. If there is an *avant-garde* in our time, it is probably bent on discovery through suicide." Beckett is one of Hassan's chief examples:

> Writing for Beckett is absurd play. In a certain sense, all his works may be thought of as a parody of Wittgenstein's notion that language is a set of games, akin to the arithmetic of primitive tribes. Beckett's parodies, which are full of self-spite, designate a general tendency in anti-literature. Hugh Kenner brilliantly describes this tendency when he states: "The dominant intellectual analogy of the present age is drawn not from biology, not from psychology . . . but from general number theory." Art in a closed field thus becomes an absurd game of permutations, like Molloy sucking stones at the beach; and "the retreat from the word" (the phrase is George Steiner's) reduces language to pure ratio.
>
> Beckett . . . comes close to reducing literature to a mathematical tautology. The syllogism of Beckett assumes that history has spent itself; we are merely playing an end game. . . . Language has become void; therefore words can only demonstrate their emptiness. . . . Thus literature becomes the inaudible game of a solipsist.

Professor Hassan must have been gratified by the appearance of *Ping* in the very next issue of *Encounter*, for one of its key-words is *silence*, and in other ways it appears to confirm his description of Beckett's art. "Permutation," for instance, seems an appropriate description of the way language is used in *Ping*: that is, an unusually limited number of words are repeated to an unusual extent in various combinations. (By "unusual" I mean unusual for a piece of literary prose of this length.) There are only a few words that occur only once in *Ping: brief, hair, nails, scars, torn, henceforth, unlustrous*. Other words are used at least twice, and most words are used more than twice. The word *white*, which seems to be the most frequently recurring word, is used more than ninety times. Many phrases or word groups are repeated, but rarely an entire sentence. Thus, if the first sentence is divided up into the following word groups: "All known / all white / bare white body fixed / one yard / legs joined like sewn."[1] Each word group recurs later in the piece, but never with all the others in the same order in a single sentence—always with some modification or addition. Typical variations are:

> Bare white body fixed one yard ping fixed elsewhere. (23 / 24)
> Bare white body fixed one yard ping fixed elsewhere white on white

> invisible heart breath no sound. (61 / 63)
> Bare white one yard fixed ping fixed elsewhere no sound legs joined like sewn heels together right angle hands hanging palms front. (99 / 102)

It is this kind of repetition with variation that makes *Ping* so difficult to read, and the label "anti-literature" a plausible one. Repetition is often a key to meaning in literary discourse, but repetition on this scale tends to defeat the pursuit of meaning. That is, a familiar critical strategy in dealing with narrative prose is to look for some significant pattern of repetition hidden in the variegated texture of the discourse: the variegated texture, by which "solidity of specification" is achieved, is woven in a logical, temporal progression, while the pattern of repetition holds the work together in a kind of spatial order and suggests the nature of the overall theme. But in *Ping* this relationship is inverted: the repetition is far from hidden—it overwhelms the reader in its profusion and disrupts the sense of specificity and of logical, temporal progression. It is extraordinarily difficult to read through the entire piece, short as it is, with sustained concentration. After about forty or fifty lines the words begin to slide and blur before the eyes, and to echo bewilderingly in the ear. This is caused not merely by the elaborate repetition, but also by the meagreness of explicit syntax, the drastic reduction of such aids to communication as punctuation, finite verbs, conjunctions, articles, prepositions and subordination.

All this, then, goes to confirm Hassan's comments; and as a general account of what Beckett is up to they are no doubt fair enough. But I must confess to finding something unsatisfactory about this kind of critical response. I don't see, for instance, how it could help us to distinguish between one piece by Beckett and another, except as progressive—or regressive—steps toward silence. If the sole object of the game is to expose the limitations of language by a bewildering permutation of words, it wouldn't matter what particular words were used, or what their referential content was. But I think that the more closely acquainted we become with *Ping* the more certain we become that it does matter what words are used, and that they refer to something more specific than the futility of life or the futility of art. Beckett is telling us "about" something; and if the telling is extraordinarily difficult to follow this is not simply because all experience is difficult to communicate (though this is true) but because this experience is difficult to communicate in *this* particular way.

It would be dishonest to make this assertion without going on to suggest what *Ping* is about. What follows doesn't pretend to be a definitive or exclusive reading, but its tentativeness differs only in degree from the tentativeness imposed on the critic by any complex literary work.

I suggest that *Ping* is the rendering of the consciousness of a person confined in a small, bare, white room, a person who is evidently under extreme duress, and probably at the last gasp of life. He has no freedom of movement: his body is "fixed," the legs are joined together, the heels turning at right angles, the hands hanging palms front; the "heart breath" makes "no sound" (63). "Only the eyes only just . . ."—can we say, *move*? (6 / 7). There are parts of the room he cannot see, and he evidently can't move his head to see them, though he thinks there is "perhaps a way out" there (38 and 76).

The first words of the piece are "all known," and this phrase recurs (17, 31, 46, etc.). But the "all" that is "known" is severely limited and yields "no meaning" (12 and *passim*) though the narrator is reluctant to admit this: "perhaps a meaning" (48 / 49). *Ping* seems to record the struggles of an expiring consciousness to find some meaning in a situation which offers no purchase to the mind or to sensation. The consciousness makes repeated, feeble efforts to assert the possibility of colour, movement, sound, memory, another person's presence, only to fall back hopelessly into the recognition of colourlessness, paralysis, silence, oblivion, solitude. This rhythm of tentative assertion and collapse is marked by the frequently recurring collocation "only just almost never" (16 / 17 and *passim*).

By colourlessness I mean the predominance of white, which is no colour, or at least the "last colour" (112). The shining white planes of walls, floor and ceiling, the whiteness of his own body, make it difficult for the person to see more than "traces, blurs, signs" (11 and *passim*). The attempt to assert colour—black, rose, light blue, light grey—nearly always fades into an admission that it is really "almost white," "white on white," is "invisible," has "no meaning":

> Traces blurs light grey almost white on white. (7 / 8)
> Traces blurs signs no meaning light grey almost white. (11 / 12)
> Traces alone unover given black light grey almost white on white. (20 / 21)
> Traces alone unover given black grey blurs signs no meaning light grey almost white always the same. (77 / 79)

Aural experience is equally meagre. There is "silence within" (16). These words are followed by "Brief murmurs"; but the murmurs are immediately qualified by "only just almost never" (16 / 17). However, the next "murmur" is associated with the speculation "perhaps not alone" (28 / 29). A little later there is another *perhaps* phrase, again associated with "murmur": "Ping murmur perhaps a nature one second almost never that much memory almost never" (42 / 44). This is a particularly interesting and tantalising sentence. What does "a nature" mean? A human nature? His own, or another's? It seems to be associated with memory, anyway, and memory with meaning, for a few lines later we get: "Ping murmur only just almost never one second perhaps a meaning that much memory almost never" (47 / 49).

Towards the close of the piece I think there are more definite indications that the character's search for meaning and grasp on life are connected with some effort of memory, some effort to recall a human image, and thus break out of total impotence and solitude: "Ping perhaps not alone one second with image same time a little less dim eye black and white half closed long lashes imploring that much memory almost never" (105 / 9). "Long lashes imploring" is the most human touch, the most emotive phrase, in the entire piece. It deviates sharply from the linguistic norms which have been set up, and which protect a generally dehumanised version of experience. It therefore has a strong impact, and this is reinforced by other features of the sentence. The "image" is "a little less dim." We have met the phrase "a little less" before, but not with "dim"—it is as if only now can the consciousness complete the phrase it has been struggling to formulate. The eye is "black and white"—it is not black fading into light grey, into almost white, into white on white.

This sentence, then, seems to mark the apex of the character's effort at memory. It is "Afar flash of time," but short-lived: almost immediately it is swamped by the despairing sequence: "all white all over all of old ping flash white walls shining white no trace eyes holes light blue almost white last colour ping white over" (109 / 13). The next two sentences also end with the word *over*, as does the whole piece. *Over*, which makes its first appearance in line 83, seems to echo the curious nonce-word *unover* (20, 27, 56, 65, etc.) which presumably means "not over," and is invariably preceded by the word *alone*, for example: "Traces alone unover given black light grey almost white on white." (20 / 21) Such sentences, which occur mainly in the first half of the text, seem to define the very limited sense in which experience is on-going, "not over"; but after the vision or image of the eye with "long lashes imploring" the emphasis shifts to the idea that experience is finished, over. The formula "that much memory almost never" is changed to "that much memory *henceforth* never" in line 124. The image of the eye recurs unexpectedly in the last two lines of the piece, with the addition of the word *unlustrous*—a word rather striking in itself, and notable for occurring only this once in *Ping*, thus giving a further specificity to the "eye black and white half-closed long lashes imploring." But this seems to be the last effort of the consciousness—the sentence continues and ends, "ping silence ping over." The image or vision is over, consciousness is over, the story is over.

I have implied that the black and white eye (singular) is not one of the character's own eyes, which are, I think, the ones referred to throughout the passage (in the plural) as being light blue or grey, tending to the overall condition of whiteness. This black eye with the lashes is, I suggest, someone else's eye, part of some emotional and human connection which the character is struggling to recall through memory. The effort to do so is only successful to a very limited extent, and exhausts him, perhaps kills him: "ping silence ping over."

I can't offer any confident explanation of the word *ping* itself. On the referential level it might denote the noise emitted by some piece of apparatus, perhaps marking the passage of time (there are repeated references to "one second," though the *pings* do not occur at regular intervals). On the level of connotation, *ping* is a feeble, pathetic, unresonant, irritating, even maddening sound, making it an appropriate enough title for this piece, which it punctuates like the striking of a triangle at intervals in the course of a complicated fugue.

The above commentary is based on some introductory remarks made by the present writer to a discussion of *Ping* by some members of the English Department at Birmingham University.[2] My remarks were followed by the independently prepared comments of a linguist, whose descriptive analysis of the structure of the piece was in general accord with my own (though it corrected some rash assertions I had made). I shall try to do justice to the main points of this linguistic commentary in a general account of the discussion as a whole.

In this discussion there was inevitably a good deal of conflict, but on the whole the measure of agreement was more striking. A minority of the participants were inclined to think that *Ping* was indeed a language game, a verbal construct cunningly devised to yield an infinite number of interpretations—and therefore, in effect, resistant to interpretation. It could be about a man having a bath or a shower or a man under rifle fire or a man being tortured; *ping* might be the sound of a bullet ricochetting, or the sound of water dripping or the sound of a bell, and the bell might be a bicycle bell or a sanctus bell or a typewriter bell (perhaps the writer's own typewriter bell). But the majority were disposed to find *Ping* more specifically meaningful, to see it as the rendering of a certain kind of experience, and as having a perceptible design. While it might not be possible to agree on a formulation of the experience more precise than the effort of a consciousness to assert its identity in the teeth of the void, the verbal medium was operating selectively to induce a much more finely discriminated range of effects than that formulation suggested. Considered as a whole, in isolation, the piece satisfied the traditional aesthetic criteria of *integritas, consonantia,* and *claritas.*[3] At the same time it had an obvious continuity with the rest of Beckett's work, and to consider it in relation to his whole *œuvre* would be the next logical step in interpretation.

The two main points of dispute, and the ones where I feel my own reading of *Ping* to have been most inadequate, concerned the possibility of some allusion to Christ, and the significance of the word *ping* itself.

As to the first, it was pointed out that there are a number of words and phrases reminiscent of the passion and death of Christ: "legs joined like sewn," "hands hanging palms front" are vaguely evocative of the Crucifixion; "seam like sewn invisible" suggests the cloak without a seam. More striking is this passage: "Given rose only just nails fallen white over. Long hair fallen white invisible over. White scars invisible same white as flesh torn of old given rose only just" (82 / 86). The words *nails, hair, scars, flesh, torn*, belong to that (in *Ping*) rare class that occur only once, and their clustering together here might well be designed to alert us to an interpretative clue. For a dizzy moment we entertained the possibility that the whole piece might be a bleakly anti-metaphysical rendering of the consciousness of the dying Christ—Christ in the tomb rather than Christ on the Cross (hence the cramped, cell-like room)—in short, Beckett's version of *The Man Who Died*. But this reading seemed not only to leave much unexplained, but to be impoverishing; for the piece doesn't read like a riddle to which there is a single answer. However, the possibility of some allusion to Christ cannot, I think, be discounted.

Discussion about the significance of the word *ping* polarised around those who, like myself, regarded it as a noise external to the discourse, which it punctuated at arbitrary intervals, a noise so meaningless as not to enter into the murmur / silence dichotomy, the most meaningless item, in fact, in the character's field of perception; and on the other hand those who regarded it as part of the discourse, as having some conceptual content or as being an ironic, or movingly pathetic, substitute or code-word for some concept that cannot be fully and openly entertained, such as God (*cf.* "Godot"). Thus the sentence, "Ping elsewhere always there only known not" (54 / 55) becomes almost lucid if you replace *Ping* with *God*; and it is interesting to note that this is one of the rare sentences that recur in exactly the same form (104 / 5).

Strengthening this case that *ping* is part of the discourse, or stream of consciousness, rather than an arbitrary intrusion from outside, is the fact that it is associated with a selective number of other words and phrases. Thus, going through the piece and noting the words which immediately follow the word *ping*, we get the following pattern:

ping fixed elsewhere
ping fixed elsewhere
ping fixed elsewhere
Ping murmur
ping murmur
ping silence
Ping murmur
Ping murmur
ping elsewhere
Ping elsewhere
ping murmur
ping fixed elsewhere
Ping murmurs
Ping perhaps a nature
ping perhaps way out
ping silence
Ping perhaps not alone
ping silence

Ping image
Ping a nature
ping a meaning
ping silence
ping fixed elsewhere
Ping elsewhere
Ping perhaps not alone
ping flash
ping white over
Ping fixed last elsewhere
ping of old
Ping of old
ping last murmur
ping silence
ping over.

This doesn't look like random occurrence. *Ping* tends to be followed by words or phrases which suggest the possibility of some other presence or place: *fixed elsewhere, murmur, image, perhaps a nature, perhaps a way out, perhaps not alone, etc.* It is natural, I think, to look first at the words and phrases which follow *ping*, for if it has a quasi-grammatical status it would appear to be that of a subject—it is, for instance, often the first word of a sentence. If we look at the words and phrases which immediately precede *ping* we get, in fact, a sequence which is no less patterned, but it is interesting that these words and phrases are mostly of a quite different order; they tend to stress the bleak limitations of the character's situation and field of perception: *bare white body fixed, invisible, never seen, almost never*, are among the most frequently recurring. We might suggest that *ping* marks the intervals between the oscillating movements of the character's consciousness from dull despair to tentative hope; though this leaves open the question of whether it is part of the discourse, or an intrusion from outside which stimulates thought in a mechanical and arbitrary way.

I should note, finally, the ingenious suggestion that *ping* alludes to the parlour game "Ping Pong" which assumes that all words and concepts can be placed in one of two great categories, "Ping" and "Pong." Thus, for example, *white* is Ping and *black* is Pong; and Beckett's piece is the account of a man inhabiting a Ping world, struggling feebly to reach out to recover a Pong world.

The above discussion, needless to say, leaves much unexplained or in doubt (a phrase which particularly puzzles me is "blue and white in the wind" [74, 87, 96, 123]). But it does suggest, I think, that *Ping* is not, as it appears at first sight, totally impenetrable and meaningless. The important point was made in the course of our discussion that the piece *has* got a syntax: it is rudimentary, but it does control the possible range of meaning. It would be perverse, for instance, to read the first sentence grouping the words in this way: "All / known all white bare / white body fixed one / yard legs / joined like / sewn." The piece draws on the principles of a shared language, especially the principle of word order. ("Ping" itself is the most ambiguous word in the text precisely because it is the one least defined by any referential or structural function in ordinary usage.) Though these principles are drastically modified, they are never abandoned. A good deal of logical organisation persists, as can be demonstrated by reading the text backwards and measuring the loss of sense.

If Beckett were really writing anti-literature, it wouldn't matter whether we read the text backwards or forwards, from left to right or from right to left. Of course, terms like "anti-literature" and "literature of silence" are rhetorical paradoxes aimed to suggest a radical degree of innovation: they are not to be taken literally. But they can have the effect of deterring us from engaging closely with a text like *Ping*. To confirm Professor Hassan's comments on Beckett, it is not necessary to give *Ping* more than a quick, superficial glance. If the object of the exercise is merely to baffle our intelligences and cheat our conventional expectations, why should we bother to do more? But if we do bother to do more, the rewards are surprisingly great. *Ping* proves, after all, not to be totally resistant to methods of critical reading derived from conventional literature. Its language is not void; its words do not merely demonstrate their emptiness. It is, like any literary artifact, a marriage of form and meaning.

Notes

1. Line references are to the text printed in *Encounter*, February 1967, pp. 25–6.

2. The other participants were: Miss Vera Adamson, K. M. Green, T. P. Matheson, Mrs. Joan Rees, I. A. Shapiro, T. A. Shippey, G. T. Shepherd, J. M. Sinclair, H. A. Smith, S. W. Wells and M. Wilding. This article is published with their kind permission, but it does not pretend to give a full or faithful record of their contributions to the discussion. It is highly selective and based on imperfect memory, and for this reason I have not attributed opinions to individuals.

3. Using these terms in the senses defined by Graham Hough in his *An Essay on Criticism* (1966), pp. 17–19.

Looking for *The Lost Ones*

Eric P. Levy*

Eliot in his celebrated essay, "Tradition and the Individual Talent," points to the necessity of inclusive perspective in literature; awareness of what has gone before enriches the understanding of what follows, just as the significance of predecessors is completed or even formed by their

*Reprinted from *Beckett and the Voice of Species: A Study of the Prose Fiction* (Totowa: Barnes & Noble, 1980) by permission of the publisher.

followers. Certainly few living writers can match Beckett's sensitivity to a continuous and historical culture, but he goes further. In a magnificent reflexive act, his work embraces its own ancestors, and creates a fully articulated tradition. The more vigorously he advances his own *corpus*, the more strenuously must he eliminate others. Beckett's thrust is not linear, not progressive but circular, revolving around its point of origin, explicating with each orbit what was implicit in the beginning. He is the first to insist upon this. One of his critical pieces on the van Velde brothers written in 1948 emphasises the obligation to repeat the same conviction over and over again: "Fortunately, it's not a question of saying what has not yet been said but of saying again, as often as possible and in the most reduced space, what has already been said.[1]

The Lost Ones demonstrates, as clearly as any of Beckett's longer efforts in prose fiction, how much each successive work depends on what has preceded. This is not simply a matter of treating familiar themes. Beyond these, the text reaches back to earlier works for both the details of the story and its narrative approach. As we shall see, the fundamental problem with which the narrator is grappling concerns his awareness of having always dealt with the same predicament. The best way for us to understand his difficulty is first to consider his story.

The text introduces us to a severely geometric world: the interior of a cylinder where a tribe of naked bodies pursues a barren existence. Crowded into a small space, each body has just enough room to stand. Since each is moved by the need to search "for its lost one"[2] and indeed seems animated by nothing more than this necessity, some order must prevail in the cylinder for motion to be possible. Accordingly, the floor is divided into three different zones. The central one, by far the largest, is called the arena. There bodies circulate clockwise as best they can until the need to search drives them to the second zone, a narrow band where people march in a single file counterclockwise around the arena they circumscribe. From this zone, provided his entry is matched by a corresponding exit, a body may gain access to the third, "a belt about one metre wide" (p. 27) bounded on its outer edge by the cylinder wall. This last area contains fifteen ladders of irregular length used to convey climbers to the niches or tunnels: "These are cavities sunk in that part of the wall which lies above an imaginary line running midway between floor and ceiling and features therefore of its upper half alone" (p. 11). Also in this zone remain "a certain number of sedentary searchers sitting or standing against the wall" (p. 28). Only their eyes still seek relentlessly what they will never find. The zone also harbours four of the five "vanquished"—bodies that, although alive, have lost all will to seek and crouch motionless with heads bowed. Near each ladder are "queues" of bodies waiting their turn to ascend. Once at the head of the line, each has the right to carry his ladder along the narrow zone until reaching an appealing niche.

Conditions in the cylinder are as forbidding as its design. Both temperature and light are in flux, the former oscillating between twenty-five and five degrees centigrade, the latter alternating rapidly between two fixed limits of brightness with almost stroboscopic effect. At rare intervals, both temperature and light suddenly stop changing: "Then all go dead still. It is perhaps the end of all. A few seconds and all begins again" (p. 8). At such moments, the bodies instantly freeze in place, holding their poses until the tumult resumes. A "stridulence" or "murmur" accompanies this flux and, except during the periodic arrests, is the only universally audible sound in the cylinder.

Such rigorous construction admits neither freedom nor purpose. The opening sentences indicate the circularity of the quest: "Abode where lost bodies roam each searching for its lost one. Vast enough for search to be in vain. Narrow enough for flight to be in vain." Lost Ones searching for their lost ones, intent on nothing but the hunt, reacting only when the unchecked momentum of one disturbs the orderly progress of all—this defines a state of collective absence where each, looking for what concerns him alone, helps build a prison that cares for none. In this world of restless movement, waiting becomes the fundamental ordering principle. Ordinarily, waiting, by preceding action, permits everyone in turn to exercise freedom of choice. It is one way of reconciling individual liberty with social control. Here, however, action itself is determined by the need to seek and waiting, holding as its end the resumption of seeking, only confirms necessity.

The Lost Ones are hemmed in as much by necessity as by the cylinder walls, but how can we determine what this necessity is? To every guess we make about the object or end of their seeking, there is always a negation. The text makes it clear that their seeking has no goal but its own continuation. The search is neither for self ("None looks within himself where none can be," p. 30) nor for another ("Whatever it is they are searching for it is not that," p. 36). Seeking, moreover, has nothing to do with eyesight. The eye functions not as an organ but as a symbol either of this need to search or, in the case of the vanquished, of release from such compulsion. We are told that, moved by no impulse other than habit, the vanquished are liable occasionally to resume the motions of seeking. At such times, they wander "unseeing" and are "indistinguishable to the eye of flesh" (p. 31) from those still seeking. Obviously the eye is not what helps the remaining seekers in their search, for they are readily able to distinguish the errant vanquished from their ranks and step aside: "These recognize them and make way" (p. 31). Similarly, the blindness of the vanquished is not a physical handicap, but the result or expression of a complete absence or oblivion where nothing whatsoever, neither self nor object, enters the mind.

A world so severely formulated draws attention to its maker, and a comparison between my earlier summary and the actual text will show that *The Lost Ones* concerns the limitations of narration far more than the torment of bodies in a cylinder. The story becomes a symbol or means of representing the movement of the narrator behind it, and only by remembering this will we discover what necessity drives the Lost Ones. Repeatedly, we are reminded that everything in the story, from the dimensions of the cylinder to the behaviour of its people, exists only as a narrative object at the whims of its narrator. Recurring phrases such as, "for the sake of harmony," "seen from a certain angle," "always assuming," and "if this notion is maintained," clearly subordinate story to narrator. More than once he insists on his omniscience in contrast to the ignorance of his creatures: ". . . to perceive it one must be in the secret of the gods" (p. 19). He leaves no doubt that the customs of the Lost Ones, far from being anthropological relics, derive directly from him. The convention concerning the use of ladders, for example, deals less with the climbers than with the need of the narrative world for harmony. The plight of climbers unable to ascend is less disturbing than the prospect of ladders unable to fulfill a function designated by the narrative: "Not to mention the intolerable presence of properties serving no purpose" (p. 23). The very form of a cylinder has long been associated with Beckett's narrators. Moran, hampered by stiff knees, retrieves his scattered keys by "rolling over and over, like a great cylinder" (*Molloy*, p. 153). Malone describes the precious pencil with which he writes as "a long cylinder" (*Malone*, p. 223), and the narrator in "The Calmative" sees himself reflected in a shop window as "a great cylinder sweeping past as though on rollers on the asphalt."[3] In this context, the phrase "in the cylinder" refers to the narrator's own mind, and indeed *The Lost Ones* strengthens this connection.

The light in the cylinder corresponds perfectly to the narrator's omniscience. It illumines every surface, including the interior of the tunnels: ". . . this light is further unusual in that far from evincing one or more visible or hidden sources it appears to emanate from all sides and to permeate the entire space as though this were uniformly luminous down to its least particle of ambiant air. To the point that the ladders themselves seem rather to shed than to receive light with this slight reserve that light is not the word. No other shadows then than those cast by the bodies pressing on one another wilfully or from necessity . . ." (pp. 3–40). This strange light appears frequently in Beckett's work, and has attracted the attention of critics. The *locus classicus* appears in *Malone Dies* where ". . . all bathes . . . in a kind of leaden light that makes no shadow, so that it is hard to say from what direction it comes, for it seems to come from all directions at once, and with equal force" (*Malone*, p. 220). The similarities between this and the longer passage quoted above are striking; both note the absence of shadows, the lack of a definite source, and the uniformity of illumination. When Malone admits "all that must be half imagination" (p. 185), the link with the cylinder grows clearer, for *The Lost Ones* gives tremendous emphasis to imagination as the power to see what eyesight cannot: "mental or imaginary frontiers invisible to the eye of flesh" (p. 43), "imaginary line" (p. 11), "may be imagined extinguished" (p. 15), "imaginary edge" (p. 29).

This, then, is the light of the imagination. It is uniform because nothing imagined is hidden to the imagination. Everything receives equal emphasis as in the world of dream. For an imaginary being, to be imagined is all there is to being. There are no other angles; the object, unlike those of the real or waking world, is contained by its appearance: "all known," as the narrator, describing a similarly lit interior, says in "Ping."[4]

From Beckett's view of imagination, we can measure just how far his art has moved beyond Romanticism. The Romantic imagination, in recreating Nature by means of projected images, gives the self new scope for expression and expansion through exploring its relation to that recreated world. But with Beckett this function of imagination is no longer possible, for the two poles of self and world have become inaccessible. Imagination now has nothing but its own futility to express, nothing to project but the emptiness of the assumptions that once linked self and world, and gave experience definite meaning by allowing it to unfold in a stable context. This truth is powerfully expressed in "Imagination Dead Imagine" where fluctuates the same light as we found in *The Lost Ones*. Conditions such as light and heat that imagination usually takes for granted are pitted against their contraries, dark and cold. In other ways, too, Beckett eliminates the axioms which nourish imagination. Hence, the faces glimpsed in "Imagination Dead Imagine" entail a number of expectations, such as having two compatible sides: "The faces too, assuming the two sides of a piece, seem to want nothing essential."[5] The voice, despite its careful distance, cannot avoid some ambiguity. Does "want" refer only to a judgement about the correct appearance of the faces or does the word refer to a feeling, a subjective "want"? A kindred ambiguity in *The Lost Ones* gives us a clearer idea of the only kind of want or need still available for imaginative projection. When discussing the light and temperature, the narrator will not consider any change in their respective oscillations: "But that would not answer the need of the cylinder. So all is for the best" (p. 42). The ambiguity of "the needs of the cylinder" emerges near the conclusion where the narrator, projecting "the unthinkable end," observes that, though only one searching body remains, the light and temperature still fluctuate with the old rhythm: "But the persistence of the twofold vibration suggests that all is not yet quite for the best" (p. 61). Here it is obvious that "the needs of the cylinder" concern the narrator and not the inhabitants. All is for the best when the oscillation finally stops forever and his story can end. More precisely, all is for the best when he can turn his hyper-conscious experience of Nothing into an experience of absence such as the vanquished enjoy. That is the narrator's greatest need but one which, as we shall see, can never be satisfied.

The task of imagination, then, in these later works of Beckettian fiction is a little different from that in the previous ones. Where earlier Beckett sought ways to express the experience of Nothing from the inside as it were, as a lived flux with no personal centre, now he tries to express it from the outside by means of images which communicate an experience with less and less content until reaching a state of complete absence. This is the only goal left to imagination and one whose utter impoverishment renders even more vivid the experience of Nothing it tries to escape.[6]

The strategy by which absence is approached in *The Lost Ones* provides a remarkable example of Beckett's consistency. The violent opposition of contraries (light, dark, hot, cold) in the cylinder as well as in "Imagination Dead Imagine" derives from Beckett's early essay on Joyce's *Work in Progress* where he dusts off Vico's doctrine (borrowed from Bruno) of the coincidence of contraries. An analysis of this doctrine will both disclose the nature of the necessity impelling the seekers and connect this necessity with the narrator's own need for absence: "The maxima and minima of particular contraries are one and indifferent. Minimal heat equals minimal cold. Consequently transmutations are circular. The principle (minimum) of one contrary takes its movement from the principle (maximum) of another. Therefore not only do the minima coincide with the minima, the maxima with the maxima, but the minima with the maxima in the succession of transmutations. Maximal speed is a state of rest. The maximum of corruption and the minimum of generation are identical: in principle, corruption is generation."[7] *The Lost Ones* demonstrates this principle. Each contrary generates its opposite (e.g. hot turning cold) with such rapidity that the contraries in "the succession of transmutations" do coincide. The contrary prevailing at any given moment can make no difference to the Lost Ones as it will be cancelled out in the next. If each contrary in turn evokes its opposite so that no given moment is specially significant, then the only thing of "ultimate importance" is the succession itself.

Now, the successions of light, dark, hot, and cold are not the most important ones in the cylinder. That place of honour is reserved for the contraries of "languor" (p. 15) and "fevering" (p. 31) or restless movement of which the others are analogues. The succession here is realised through individuals but its goal is not dependent on any of them. Beckett in the Joyce essay explains: "Thus we have the spectacle of a human progression that depends for its movement on individuals in virtue of what appears to be a preordained cyclicism."[8] As the word "preordained" suggests, the cycle is not purposeless; the end toward which it laboriously tends is contained in its beginning. Beckett quotes with approval Joyce's remarks: "The Vico road goes round and round to meet where terms begin."[9] The cycle is consummated when the contraries causing its revolutions are finally resolved by the dominance of one over the other. Such precisely is described by the last sentence of *The Lost Ones*; the languor in the beginning prevails at the end: "So much roughly speaking for the last state of the cylinder and this little people of searchers one first of whom if a man in some unthinkable past for the first time bowed his head if this notion is maintained." It now becomes clear why the only goal of seeking is to go on seeking. As the contrary of languor or abandonment, seeking seeks only to maintain itself. The fact that it eventually disappears arises not from its own deficiency, but from the cycle in which it occurs.

The protracted cycle involves, beyond the Lost Ones, the endless round of stories through which the Beckettian narrator hopes eventually to earn silence or absence. Beckett's *oeuvre*, consistently developing its own implications, is what Neary in *Murphy* calls "a closed system." The common denominator of the works after *Watt* is the awareness that the fiction is caught in a cycle of repetition. Starting with the Trilogy, this recognition becomes the moving principle of the narrator whose story fundamentally concerns the desire to tell no more. He wishes to escape the necessity that binds him.

The first word of *The Lost Ones*, "abode," applies of course to the cylinder, but refers also to the narrator's wish to place himself inside boundaries so that his story, beginning at its outer limits, can contract more and more tightly upon its own centre and come at last to rest. Both the strategy and the word derive from *The Unnamable*. In trying to establish "my abode" (*Unnamable*, p. 296), as a place from which he cannot stir, The Unnamable hopes to reach himself at the end of his narrative, for no matter how long the description of his abode goes on, he will still be in it at the end. Since he has already decided that he and the abode were created simultaneously (". . . the place was made for me and I for it, at the same instant . . ." [*Unnamable*, p. 296]), it follows that, if he can only remain within the walls, he and the abode will end in the same breath. The Beckettian narrator has no fonder wish than this. In *The Lost Ones*, we can easily determine that the "abode" is built primarily for its narrator, because the cylinder and its inhabitants, he tells us, were created in the same instant, "In the beginning" (p. 34).

Unfortunately, ever since Mr. Knott's house in *Watt*, the Beckettian narrator has not been able to conceal that his abode is merely a patchwork of hypotheses and improvised questions about a meaningless experience. Watt toils with his "series of hypotheses" (*Watt*, p. 78), Molloy admits, "For my part I willingly asked myself questions" (*Molloy*, p. 49), and The Unnamable rattles off a salvo of "Questions, hypotheses, call them that" (*Unnamable*, p. 291). With *The Lost Ones* the narrator feels secure in his abode. As long as he remains inside, the hypotheses by which it is built can be multiplied indefinitely: "To these questions and many more the answers are clear and easy to give" (p. 52). But continuing a story has never been a problem to the Beckettian narrator; to end and never be obliged to begin again, that is his hope. The silent dark at the conclusion of *The Lost Ones* cannot be, however, any less provisional than the narrative hypothesis from which it springs and which the last five words of the story invoke again: ". . . if this notion is maintained."

From this point of view, *The Lost Ones* is a story about the narrator's fabrication and dismissal of yet another narrative hypothesis. The contrary states of seeking and abandonment refer ultimately to the endless narrative cycle of pursuing a theme and discarding it in which he is caught. Each ended story leaves the narrator a little more impoverished, whittles down the range of seeking by increasing the scope of abandonment. The word "abandon" comes directly from the warning written about the entrance to Dante's *Inferno*: "Abandon all hope ye who enter." Mr Conaire, in *Mercier and Camier*, clinches the connection: "I was about to go, said Mr Conaire, all hope abandoned" (*Mercier*, p. 62). The zoned world of the Lost Ones suggests more than simply the Inferno, however. Consider this passage: "Fourthly those who do not search or non-searchers sitting for the most part against the wall in the attitude which wrung from Dante one of his rare wan smiles" (p. 14). Here Beckett alludes wryly to Dante's bemusement at Belacqua's lethargic pose in the Antechamber to Purgatory (*Purgatorio*, Canto IV). Hence, the cylindrical universe of the Lost Ones, with its emphasis on the two concentric circles in the arena bounded in turn by the circular walls, becomes a highly compressed, geometrical version of the purposeless, Dantesque universe inhabited by Mercier and Camier. Just as for that "pseudo-couple" so for the Lost Ones Hell, Purgatory, and Paradise coincide in an empty and meaningless cycle.

This plunging of his narrator ever deeper into an endless and meaningless cycle is one of the chief means by which Beckett transforms his works into a singularly unified tradition whose meaning deepens with each new text. The descent also provides the impetus for Beckett's "minimal art"—expressing the experience of Nothing within increasingly severe limitations, shrinking narration down to the Nothing it tries to reflect. Malone, for example, speaks of abandonment in terms that explicitly anticipate the vocabulary of *The Lost Ones*: "And a little less well endowed with strength and courage he too would have abandoned and despaired of ever knowing what manner of being he was, and how he was going to live, and lived vanquished, blindly, in a mad world, in the midst of strangers" (*Malone*, p. 193). The Unnamable reveals that these strangers are the very words he speaks (". . . I'm all these words, all these strangers . . ," *Unnamable*, p. 386) and then predicts a further descent: ". . . they're going to abandon me" (p. 414). Of course, he is right, for *How It Is*, "Ping," *Lessness*, and *The Lost Ones* all unfold within restrictive verbal boundaries. Yet the situation is even bleaker than this. As long as the dwindling cycle lasts, the law of the coincidence of contraries applies, and thus seeking *is* abandonment. Such, for example, is The Unnamable's position; knowing that he always seeks and that he will never know why: ". . . what do I seek now . . ." (*Unnamable*, p. 387). It is also the case in *The Lost Ones* where the narrator sees his own seeking reflected in a story of abandonment.

The narrator tries to turn this cycle of abandonment to his advantage by running it down to an absolute end. The ploy derives unmistakably from a passage in *The Unnamable*:

> . . . perhaps a whole people is here, and the voice its voice, coming to me fitfully, we would have lived, been free a moment, now we talk about it, each one to himself, each one out loud for himself, and we listen, a whole people, talking and listening, all together, that would ex, no, I'm alone, perhaps the first, or perhaps the last, talking alone, listening alone, alone alone, the others are gone, they have been stilled, their voices stilled, their listening stilled, one by one. . . . I won't be the last, I'll be with the others, I'll be as gone, in the silence . . . it's a lie, I can't stir, I haven't stirred, I launch the voice, I hear a voice . . . (p. 409).

Here The Unnamable tells the story of the Lost Ones in miniature. In narrating a vanquished world, he hopes somehow to enter it. Unfortunately, that world exists only as long as he speaks of it and, if he stops, it can no longer be there for him to enjoy. *The Lost Ones* pursues the same strategy and falls into the same trap—what might be called the law of the excluded narrator, where the many who finally succumb point back to the one voice that can never go silent. Unable to find the peace granted his creatures, he is the true Lost One.

Notes

1. Samuel Beckett, "Peintres de l'empêchement." Reprinted in *L'Herne Beckett*, 67 [my translation].

2. Samuel Beckett, *The Lost Ones*, 7. All quotations are from the 1972 Calder and Boyars edition.

3. Samuel Beckett, "The Calmative," in *Stories and Texts for Nothing*, 35.

4. "Ping," trans. Samuel Beckett, in *First Love and Other Shorts*, New York: Grove 1974, 69.

5. "Imagination Dead Imagine," in *First Love and Other Shorts*, 66.

6. There are plenty of earlier examples of this technique in the Trilogy. The phrase "delicious instants" recurs whenever the narrator refers to a brief experience of absence, a brief experience with no content whatever. Consider this instance (Moran to his son): "Draw the curtains, I said. Delicious instants, before one's eyes get used to the dark" (*Three Novels*, 104).

7. Samuel Beckett, "Dante . . . Bruno. Vico . . Joyce," in *Our Exagmination Round his Factification for Incamination of Work in Progress*, 6. Beckett revives the notion in *More Pricks Than Kicks*, 148: "Indeed he went so far as to hazard a little paradox on his own account, to the effect that between contraries no alternation was possible."

8. *Ibid*, 6.

9. *Ibid*, 8.

A Criticism of Indigence: *Ill Seen Ill Said*

John Pilling*

Though he has rarely said it so explicitly as in his 1938 essay on Denis Devlin, Beckett has always been an apologist for "the art that condenses as inverted spiral of need . . . whose end is its own end in the end and source of need."[1] Indeed his whole writing career is effectively an illustration of how he has tried to free himself of the encumbrances inhibiting the realization of such a programme. For with hindsight it is clear that, though always likely to be regarded as Beckett at his most approachable, *Molloy* and *Godot* can hardly be said to satisfy the conditions expressed in the "Denis Devlin" essay. Though much more "condensed" than the public expected them to be, the works written by Beckett between 1945 and 1950 must quickly have come to seem to him too expansive, too contingent, and too self-indulgent. It was only in the late 1950s that Beckett really began to get close to his self-imposed ideal, notably in the dense and reticulated texture of *Endgame* and above all in the work which has always seemed to me the greatest of his prose writings, *How It Is*.

A writer more easily satisfied than Beckett might have convinced himself that the art of "condensation" had reached a kind of natural limit in these achievements. But Beckett evidently needed to reduce his canvas still further. In 1956 he had told Israel Shenker that, for him, "the area of possibilities gets smaller and smaller,"[2] and it cannot be accidental that Beckett shortly thereafter began the series of monodramas and metafictions which have since occupied him exclusively. Given what I have called his "poetics of indigence"[3] and his belief that "one is a victim of all that one has written," it is clear that there is a kind of inevitable logic in the author of the brilliant and extravagant *Murphy* concluding his career as an ardent, implacable, and austere miniaturist.

It has been the business of Beckett criticism, in the twenty-five years or so of its existence, to trace the lineaments of this logic and, as best it may, account for it. But the monodramas and metafictions have proved much more resistant to conventional critical commentary than what preceded them. Generally speaking—and there are, of course, exceptions to this rule—the more miniaturist Beckett has become, the less his interpreters have found to say about him. It is as if they had gradually and reluctantly been forced to acknowledge that, with an author who believes that "art has nothing to do with clarity, does not dabble in the clear and does not make clear,"[4] criticism—or at least the criticism which is founded upon diametrically opposed beliefs—must confess itself unable to operate and must more or less gracefully retire from the fray. Beckett seems never

*This essay, published here by permission of the author, is the original English version of an essay previously published only in German translation in *Samuel Beckett*, ed. H. Engelhardt (Frankfurt: Suhrkamp Verlag, 1984).

to have concerned himself greatly with the critical problems raised by his work, primarily perhaps because he sees the work of art as aspiring to the condition of "pure interrogation"[5] and therefore inevitably inimical to the necessarily "impure" interrogation to which the critical mind is disposed to subject it.

It seems unlikely, then, that there will ever be a volume of criticism of Beckett's most recent prose "trilogy"—*Company, Ill Seen Ill Said, Worstward Ho*—to compare with that already in existence which deals with *Molloy, Malone Dies* and *The Unnamable*. Of these new, much less minimalist texts *Company* has been more praised than studied, and *Worstward Ho* has only just appeared. Yet familiarity with the former and a lack of it with the latter suggest that the most intractable, for critical purposes, is the central one: *Ill Seen Ill Said*. Of the very few descriptions of this work which have been attempted, much the best is that by Bernard Share, reviewing the French original (*Mal vu mal dit*) for the Irish magazine *Hibernia*:

> The text as a whole—and it is, if nothing else, a whole—is a chimerical balance of appearance and non-appearance, of event and non-event, of immanence and effulgence, producing the effect, for all its stringent calibration, of an almost palpable translucency, as if one were walking straight through the linguistic medium to the thing, or non-thing itself.
>
> But it is a journey from which it is difficult to bring back a cogent report. Beckett's universe has achieved the status of being virtually indescribable except in its own terms: paraphrase conspires with exegesis to make nonsense. *Mal vu mal dit*, for all its meticulously modulated uncertainty, or perhaps because of it, is almost inassailably hermetic. Will we need a new criticism to crack it?

For what Beckett (in his *Lost Ones* vein) would call a "first aperçu"[6] of the text in question this would be difficult to improve upon. And in presuming to proceed beyond it one is bound to admit sooner or later that, in the words of *Company*, "the longer the eye dwells the obscurer it grows."[7] This said, however, it is difficult to agree with Share that "*Company* . . . seemed to point the way, however equivocally, towards a loosening of the rigours," even if one feels that *Company* and *Ill Seen Ill Said*, in spite of what they have in common at the level of motif, method, and incident, are very different works. One needs, I suppose, to be able to see *Company* plain if one is to have any chance at all of saying something significant about *Ill Seen Ill Said*.

Now *Company* is surely primarily concerned, in spite of the reminder that "There is of course the eye" (27),[8] with those issues of "voice" which first became prominent in Beckett's work with *The Unnamable* and its aftermath. *Ill Seen Ill Said*, by contrast, is primarily concerned, in spite of its obsessive quest for the "wrong word," with those issues of vision which were first raised in *All Strange Away* and *Imagination Dead Imagine*. To put it another way, it is clearly a consequence of the fact that a given object is "ill seen" that it must be "ill said," whereas in *Company*, "the truth of what is said" (7), however difficult it may be to verify, is at least partially confirmed by the clear "visions in the dark of light" (84) which, much as in parts one and two of *How It Is*, intermittently occur. This can be regarded as a "loosening of the rigours," in Share's phrase, only in the sense that it permits *Company* to inscribe the trajectory of a "fable." But *Company* is a fable which is ultimately weighed in the balance and found wanting, a "labour lost" (89). Indeed, it is precisely because of the rigour exerted upon the raw material that the consoling notion of "company" is atomized into an infinite regress, very like that in *How It Is*, of creators and created. For the "imagination" in *Company*, much as it may "reason ill" (15), is self-confessedly "reason-ridden" (45). And it is operating, for the most part, "within reason" (43). Quite unlike the faculty operative in *Ill Seen Ill Said*, the creative mind in *Company* is "wearied by [a] stretch of imagining" (59) and therefore cannot help but suffer from what Beckett waspishly describes in the "Denis Devlin" essay as a "morbid dread of sphinxes."

Ill Seen Ill Said, by contrast, is a text written "at wit's end" (17)[9] and "in defiance of reason" (19). In this work the imaginative faculty "makes way for unreason" (23) by conjuring spectral presences from kaleidoscopic adjustments of a kind not found in *Company*. Rational and accredited procedures are such a "fiasco" that "folly takes a hand" (31). In this respect, indeed, without seeking to belabour an otherwise most sensitive critic, it is *Ill Seen Ill Said*, not *Company*, which manifests a "loosening of the rigours." So loosened are the rigors that the classic rationalistic principle of discrimination between one object and another or between one concept and another cannot be applied with any efficacy. The ability to distinguish what is real from what is unreal, a crucial factor in most metafiction (and especially in *Company*), is here conspicuous by its absence. Even more to the point, the loss of this ability is clearly not something to be lamented. There is even a sly joke lurking in the folds of what is arguably the most serious and important single paragraph in the text: "Such the confusion now between real and—how say its contrary? No matter. That old tandem.[10] Such now the confusion between them once so twain. And such the farrago from eye to mind. For it to make what sad sense of it may. No matter how. Such equal liars both. Real and—how ill say its contrary? The counter-poison" (40). Though the "sense" of this is heavily disguised—perhaps wilfully, perhaps as a natural consequence of the "confusion"—it is clear that any appeal to reason or sense will be calamitous, a "farrago," and that it will make the reasoner "sad." As the last words of the text confirm, even the most apparently promising of "decisions"—to reduce confusion to order by rational procedures—must be "revoked" or rather "dispelled," if one is to "Know happiness" (59).

"There is," as Beckett wrote long ago, "at least this to be said for mind, that it can dispel mind."[11] Such "mind" as *Ill Seen Ill Said* manifests—ever alert as it is against lapsing back into conventional ratiocinative positions—is in practice devoted to the act of *dispelling*. Like the dawn which, a "figment" itself, acts as a "dispeller of figments" in *Lessness*,[12] the imagination in *Ill Seen Ill Said* is involved in moving beyond a world that must be rejected as a "figment" in the direction of an "ideal real" similar to that adumbrated by Beckett in the 1930s.[13] This also distinguishes it from *Company*, whose "devised deviser" is presumed to occupy "the same figment dark as his figments" (64, 65). For in the more crystalline world of *Company*, a text which is reluctant to admit "confusion" (however much confusion it may cause its reader), the real and the imaginary are conceived of as belonging to different orders of experience. In *Company* there seems to be no neutral middle-ground in which the separated categories might merge, or of which they might partake. In *Ill Seen Ill Said*, by contrast, all is "confusion," and any given object—a woman's face, for example, or a button-hook—may suddenly take on the lineaments of another—a stone perhaps, or a greatcoat. In either guise the object seems to possess the power of appearing and disappearing at will, "so to say of itself" (53) in the words which the text, in a most helpful locution, invites us to appropriate. All evidence of agency and causality, and hence of an unmoved mover or "devised deviser," has been abolished, and with it all the pressure to establish the identity, or being, or essence of any given object—its *ontology*, as we might say—is dispersed. For perhaps the first time in Beckett's metafiction, the "dream of a way in a space with neither here nor there"[14] begins to seem something more than a mere hope and something other than a compulsive attachment to the mechanics of failure.

Early in *Ill Seen Ill Said* we are confronted by the possibility of a condition of "unalloyed" simplicity in which "all could be pure figment" (20). The "confusion" which prevails throughout most of the text, though a good deal more auspicious than the reasoning of *Company*, cannot single-handedly achieve this curious, though eminently Beckettian, fusion. Weakened as the fabric of the narrative already is by Beckett's utter contempt for "the vulgarities of a plausible concatenation,"[15] it is weakened still further by the intimations of void and absence ("neither be nor been nor by any shift to be," 20) which gradually and apparently gratuitously insinuate themselves into it. A kind of graduated "lessness," nothing like so mechanical as that we find in the text which embodies the notion in its title, begins to offer relief from the "vicissitudes of hardly there and wholly gone" (37–8). Yet this is surely a matter which the critic must leave to the text to articulate. For it is almost impossible to say *why* this miraculous dispensation should be granted. One must suppose it to be part of Beckett's purpose that some questions should be answerable and others not. For whilst there are a number of occasions when questions raised by the text are triumphantly answered (and always within the paragraph in which they occur),[16] there are from the beginning, and without exception in the latter part of the text, questions asked for which no answers are forthcoming. "If there may not be no more questions"—and it is clear that for an artist of "pure interrogation" there may *not* be—"let there at least be no more answers" (43)—and from this point onward there are none. It is as if Beckett, having given way in *Company* to the "morbid dread of sphinxes,"[17] is determined in *Ill Seen Ill Said* to conjure a sphinx, or succession of sphinxes, of which he need not be afraid.

Of the several sphinxes that materialize and immaterialize in *Ill Seen Ill Said*, none are exposed to the "reason-ridden" imagination that was at work in *Company*. Beckett contents himself instead with presenting the raw material which those with a disposition to fear enigmas may make of what they may. Deprived of any of the conventional criteria whereby significances are established—subordination of one element to another and discriminations generally—the reader is continually being reminded that, far from there being a surplus of information available, there are things which "will never be known."[18] The most striking example of this occurs mid-way through *Ill Seen Ill Said* at the point where a scrap of paper is discovered in a coffer: "The coffer. Empty after long nocturnal search. Nothing. Save in the end in a cranny of dust a scrap of paper. Jagged along one edge as if torn from a diary. On its yellowed face in barely legible ink two letters followed by a number. Tu 17. Or Th. Tu or Th 17.[19] Otherwise blank. Otherwise empty" (38). The letters and the number are such as to justify the phrase "as if torn from a diary." Yet they are clearly of a somewhat different status. For although the vagaries of the writing hand (or, it may be, the ravages of time) have left the letters partially obscured, there is no "as if" to undermine them still further. In textual terms they are "a device from the [relative] incontrovertibility of the one to win credence for the other," to borrow a memorable phrase from *Company*.[20] Yet they themselves cannot, in strict terms, command our credence, and their relative incontrovertibility is rendered insignificant when there is no context to which they can be related. This apparently promising scrap of paper is ultimately of as little value as the "sheet" which, near the end of *Ill Seen Ill Said*, is to be "hack[ed] into shreds" (54). One might say of the whole incident what the text itself says at the point where a "trapdoor" occupies the void created by the "coffer fiasco" (40): "Promising the flagrant concern with camouflage. But beware" (41).

Seasoned Beckett readers have grown used to warnings like this; one thinks of the last entry in the addenda to *Watt*—"no symbols where none intended."[21] But *Watt*, strange and difficult though it is, is a much more obliging text than *Ill Seen Ill Said*. In the latter the accredited critical practice of proceeding from the superficies of a text to the hinterland or sub-text encounters almost insuperable difficulties. Beckett obviously wants us, as Share says and as Beckett's own outburst in "Dante . . . Bruno. Vico . . Joyce"[22] tends to confirm, to remain content with "the thing, or non-thing itself." To this end he employs, as Share shrewdly remarks, a language which forces the reader to "take one word at a time, avoiding all resonances." The "beau seul mot" of which Beckett speaks in *Mal vu mal dit*[23] is obviously "beau" in his eyes precisely because it is "seul." Even more attractive to him, however, is "le fin mot enfin"[24] which, the English translation tells us, is "the key" (34). This suggests once again that *Ill Seen Ill Said* is the "last end" which seemed chimerical at the end of *For To End Yet Again*, though of course the publication of *Worstward Ho* might make us want to revise this view. In the French original it is noticeable that the phrase "le fin mot enfin" recurs in a phrase reinforcing in its very form the notion it is conveying: "pour en finir enfin."[25] On translating this into English, however, Beckett seems to have decided, having already perhaps conceived *Worstward Ho*, that it was not so much a matter of *enfin* as *encore*: "pour en finir une dernière fois" is translated "For the last time at last *for to end yet again*."[26] *Ill Seen Ill Said* is hereby aligned more closely with the 1975 text than *Mal vu mal dit*, though as a translator Beckett is self-evidently guilty here of substituting what this text, and indeed this very sentence, would call "the wrong word" (59), neither "beau" nor "fin." This is extremely disconcerting and discomforting for the critic who, recognizing that he must take one word at a time, finds that the French original and the English translation are, despite all appearances to the contrary, at crucial points "so twain." He is left surely in a condition of indigence analogous to that in which his author self-confessedly creates.

In practice, however, as the phrase "for to end yet again" effectively demonstrates, the act of reading is not so much an isolating as a combinative act.[27] Not even *Ill Seen Ill Said* can be said to have rendered reading impossible. Indeed, although its syntax is of the "tattered,"[28] truncated, and elliptical kind which Beckett has favored for more than twenty years, it actually encourages its reader to recognize certain combinations, if not within a given sentence, at least between one sentence and another. This is notably the case with the pervasive alliteration and assonance which are such a striking feature of *Ill Seen Ill Said*. In the last two sentences of the second paragraph of the French original, for example, "cailloux" and "debout"[29] are clearly intended to be combined together across the intervening space between them. Forced to abandon the assonance in translating into English, Beckett has recourse to alliteration: "stones" and "stands" (9). Combinations of this kind testify to Beckett's continuing fascination with what the French call *jeux de mots*. But in this case at least, there is clearly a semantic, as well as a phonetic, element, something which prompts the mind's ear to engage the mind's eye. The connection between the statuesque woman and the "zone of stones" is, after all, something that the text elsewhere insists on; the linguistic devices are designed to make the connection stronger. The text, it is true, grants the "old so dying woman. So dead" (20) a mobility denied to the standing stones or dolmens which encircle her. Yet it is always suggesting an equivalence between them, as if determined to make them synonymous. There are moments when they seem to be "in opposition" (9), to adopt the astronomical metaphor of the second paragraph. But the white stones and the black widow's weeds—each "guardians" of memory in their way—become less and less like polar opposites and more and more like the positive and negative aspects of the same photographic print.

This combinative aspect of the text is especially striking at a point, late in the work, where Beckett dwells on a "beau seul mot" of strange potency: "Forthwith the uncommon common noun collapsion. Reinforced a little later if not enfeebled by the infrequent slumberous. A slumberous collapsion. Two. Then far from the still agonizing eye a gleam of hope. By the grace of these modest beginnings. With in second sight the shack in ruins. To scrute together with the inscrutable face. All curiosity spent" (55).[30] One might pedantically object that "collapsion" is not so much an "uncommon" common noun as an obsolete one,[31] and "slumberous," though certainly "infrequent," might better be called "poetical" or "precious." In tandem, however, they seem to please Beckett, mainly perhaps because they perform the paradoxical role of reinforcing one another and "enfeebl[ing]" one another at the same time. Grammatically speaking, the adjective reinforces, like most adjectives, the noun it accompanies. But semantically speaking, this particular adjective tempers the catastrophic implications of the noun "collapsion." Both words, it must be said, seem very appropriate to a text designed as a "dispeller." Indeed one is invited to consider them as decisively beneficial, creating intimations of "hope," "grace," and the cessation of "curiosity." Only "two mysteries" (56) remain, Beckett tells us at the end. But the mind is in "such abeyance," the condition of *lessness* is now so dominant, that they shed their strangeness instantly. There are not even any "mild shocks" to endure on finding "no trace of all the ado" (56). Except, perhaps, for the reader intent on viewing the "ado" as a weird simulacrum of Christ at Golgotha.[32] Yet even here the text acts as a dispeller. For "Deposition done," despite its association with Christ's descent from the cross, seems to shed its metaphorical potential and to stand as little more than an index of narrative closure. Even the "tenacious trace" of the face—which, like the face in the television play . . . *but the clouds* . . ., cannot quite be dispelled—is not permitted to delay the triumph of the "void" (59). The appetitive instincts[33] are as "spent" as the curiosity that has sustained them. *Ill Seen Ill Said* has accomplished what the "art of condensation" formulated in the essay "Denis Devlin" described: it ends in "the end and source of need," the *fons et origo* of all creation, the void from which it has emerged.

Notes

1. "Denis Devlin," *transition*, no. 27 (April–May 1938):290.
2. "Moody Man of Letters," *New York Times*, 6 May 1956, sec. 2, p. 1.

3. Cf. "A Poetics of Indigence," in James Knowlson and John Pilling, *Frescoes of the Skull: The Later Prose and Drama of Samuel Beckett* (London: John Calder, 1979), pp. 241–56.

4. "Denis Devlin," p. 293.

5. Ibid., p. 289.

6. *The Lost Ones*, in *Six Residua* (London: John Calder, 1978), p. 57.

7. *Company* (London: John Calder, 1980), p. 29.

8. Ibid., p. 27. The other page references in this paragraph are to this edition and are contained within the text.

9. All page references are to *Ill Seen Ill Said* (London: John Calder, 1982), and are contained within the text.

10. The phrase "that old tandem" is susceptible of several readings. The contraries "real" and "unreal" are suggested by the context, which also offers another "old tandem"—eye and mind. But the joke, I take it, is yet another "old tandem," one which summarizes the materialist/immaterialist debate in philosophy in two phrases which, in colloquial English, mean much the same thing: "No matter" (the immaterialist to the materialist) and "Never mind" (the materialist reply).

11. "MacGreevy on Yeats," *Irish Times*, 4 August 1945, p. 2.

12. *Lessness* in: *Six Residua*, p. 49.

13. See my discussion in "A Poetics of Indigence," *Frescoes of the Skull*, p. 248.

14. *For To End Yet Again and Other Fizzles* (London: John Calder, 1976), p. 15.

15. *Proust and Three Dialogues with Georges Duthuit* (London: John Calder, 1965), pp. 81–2.

16. See, for example, pp. 9, 25, 38.

17. "Denis Devlin," p. 293.

18. *Malone Dies* (London: John Calder, 1958), p. 28.

19. The French original reads "Mer ou Mar 17" (*Mal vu mal dit*, Paris: Minuit, p. 48), in "diary" terms obviously *mercredi* and *mardi*. Beckett presumably altered the days in the English text in order to maintain something of the euphony which a strict equivalence would have destroyed. By the same token, "yellowed" and "followed" match "jaunies" and "suivi" (*Mal vu mal dit*, p. 47). In general Beckett has striven to preserve the phonetic values of the original wherever there are instances of "rhyme," e.g. "Yet brunette" (25) and "Fillette brunette" (*Mal vu mal dit*, p. 31).

20. *Company*, p. 8.

21. *Watt* (London: John Calder, 1963), p. 255.

22. "[Joyce's *Work in Progress*] is not about something: *it is that something itself*," *Our Exagmination round his Factification for Incamination of Work in Progress* (Paris: Shakespeare and Company, 1929), p. 14.

23. *Mal vu mal dit*, p. 40.

24. Ibid., p. 43.

25. Ibid., p. 75.

26. My italics.

27. Bernard Share mentions the "almost palindrome" and highly combinate sentence "Hiver elle erre ches elle hiver" (*Mal vu mal dit*, p. 18). It is "erre" and "chez" which prevent a word-palindrome forming, though "chez" is pehaps closer to being a "beau seul mot" insofar as "erre" sounds like an echo of "hiver." The English, though carefully worded and full of echoes, is less palindromic: "Winter in her winter haunts she wanders" (15).

28. *All Strange Away* (London: John Calder, 1979), p. 7.

29. *Mal vu mal dit*, p. 10.

30. Although Beckett elects not to stress the fact, this paragraph also contains the "uncommon," though perfectly accessible, *verb* "to scrute" (*scruter* in the original). The last sentence adapts the last words of Milton's *Samson Agonistes*, an apt choice for an eye "still agonizing."

31. OED offers four illustrative examples, two from the seventeenth century, one from the eighteenth and the latest from a text of 1823.

32. Vladimir in *Waiting for Godot* says: "All my life I've compared myself to [Christ]" (London: Faber and Faber, 1965), p. 87.

33. A forthcoming book on Beckett by Peter Murphy, to be published by the University of Toronto Press, deals fully with the question of the "art of hunger" in Beckett's prose fiction.

The Drama

Beckett's Modernity and Medieval Affinities

Edith Kern*

Because of a circularity that defies customary logic and linearity, critics have often seen in Samuel Beckett's work an absurdity they believe to be modern and expressive of the world we live in. It is true, of course, that the author has given manifold and striking expression to alogical circularity, so that the unassuming ditty (originally a German children's song) hummed by Didi in *Waiting for Godot* may well be considered emblematic of the author's entire work as it teasingly begins again whenever one expects it to end and, indeed, cannot be brought to any logical ending.[1] In *Molloy* the protagonist's assertion that the first lines of his report were its beginning but are now nearly its end conjures up a similar mood of unending circularity bordering on the absurd.[2] In the year of the celebration of Beckett's seventy-fifth birthday, we might do well, however, to ask whether this mood is exclusively modern and meant to reflect merely the chaos known to us. It would seem to me rather that it is informed by a conception of man that Beckett's works and those of other contemporary authors share with the literature preceding both the rediscovery of Aristotle's *Poetics* and the neoclassical emphasis on rationality and individuality. Not unlike authors of the Middle Ages, Beckett conceives of the individual *sub specie aeternitatis*, and in *Waiting for Godot* this vision is brilliantly dramatized when blind old Pozzo, having fallen over decrepit Lucky, is unable to get up. His cries for help are reluctantly answered by Didi and Gogo, whose efforts end in their own loss of balance, though they reply to Pozzo's inquiry as to who they are: "We are men." Nameless and faceless, mankind is groping to get on its feet, and the same medieval notion of the insignificance of the individual is later epitomized by Pozzo when he proclaims: "One day we were born, one day we shall die, the same day, the same second. . . . They give birth astride of a grave, the light gleams an instant, then it's night once more" (57). Such a conception of man does not call for clearly outlined literary protagonists or psychological explanations. Nor is it concerned with personal confron-

*Reprinted from *Samuel Beckett: Humanistic Perspectives*, ed. Morris Beja, S. E. Gontarski, and Pierre Astier (Columbus: Ohio State University Press, 1983) by permission of the publisher.

tations or social problems. The focus is rather on mankind and its unchanging structures and needs within the universe. The individual is but the transitory and ephemeral link in Nature's unending chain of birth, life, and death.

Quite obviously, such a vision of man and the universe affects the function and form of literary dialogue. When it is not employed to develop plot or reveal individual character, dialogue becomes ludic. It is not surprising, therefore, that the verbal exchanges of Beckett's characters often seem absurd to those who approach them with attitudes that conform to neo-classical expectations. But when Didi and Gogo wonder, for instance, whether they should leave, end it all, go on, or come back tomorrow, they engage in conversational patterns of the kind we might encounter in any medieval French farce:

> E: Where shall we go?
> V: Not far.
> E: Oh yes. Let's go far away from here.
> V: We can't.
> E: Why not?
> V: We have to come back tomorrow.
> E: What for?
> V: To wait for Godot. (59)

In his study of French farce, Robert Garapon has referred to such dialogue, which reveals no facts and follows no logical pattern, as "un jeu de paume,"[3] and the verbal exchanges of Beckett's characters resemble, indeed, quite frequently verbal ballgames—although the effect may be, on occasion, highly lyrical and poetic.[4] Beckett's own consciousness of this ballgame effect of dialogue is quite apparent. "In the meantime," Gogo suggests on one occasion, "let us try and converse calmly, since we are incapable of keeping silent" (40). Vladimir—musing why it is that of the four Evangelists "only one speaks of a thief being saved"—prods Estragon, who had remained silent: "Come on, Didi, return the ball." (9) In *Endgame*, of course, Clov's question "What is there to keep me here?" is answered by Hamm with "The dialogue" (58).[5] But in Beckett's work such ludic dialogue may also assume the form of medieval *flyting*, that is, of half-playful, half-serious insults. On one occasion when Didi and Gogo have nothing to do and nowhere to go, as they wait for Godot, they begin to quarrel just to pass the time away. They are close to getting into a fist fight, when Gogo suggests: "That's the idea, let's abuse each other." Stage directions indicate that they turn, move away from each other, and begin to insult each other, one outdoing the other until Didi is utterly vanquished and Gogo calls him "Crritic!" so that Gogo concedes: "Now let's make it up!" (48). In all likelihood, such *flyting* had its origin in more ancient "slanging matches" that, in the view of Johan Huizinga, may well represent the very origin of theater.[6] The exaggerated insults that rival tribes engaged in would have led to violent war, had there not been in existence a tacit understanding that they were meant to be an impersonal game of one-up-manship—a liberation of pent-up emotions in a spirit of make-believe, not unlike that of "playing the dozens" known to black communities. It is interesting in this respect that the *iambos*, the meter of Greek tragedy, is thought by some to have meant *derision*, suggesting that theater and the exchange of insults have been linked from time immemorial.[7] In the commedia dell'arte such slanging matches were standard in the lover's pursuit of his beloved and her playful or serious rejection of him. Eugène Ionesco recently used them with great skill in his play *Macbett* (based on Shakespeare's *Macbeth*) to give expression to the snowballing effect of murder, as he has his conspirators reach the tragicomic frenzy of hatred in the course of their verbal exchanges.[8] Beckett availed himself of such tragicomic playfulness mainly in order to be able to discuss questions as serious as those of man's place in the world and his relationship to God, without sounding pompous or transgressing the limits of theater as entertainment and stage business.

In his early works, ludic dialogue and *flyting* permitted Beckett, above all, to juxtapose the sacred and the profane in a mood of the seeming absurdity known to the Middle Ages. Thus Vladimir and Estragon, wondering whether man is *tied* to God (or is it Godot?), have an answer suggested to them that is as ambivalent as it is ironically farcical when Pozzo appears upon the stage led by Lucky, to whom he is tied (or who is tied to him?) by a rope. In *The Absolute Comic*, I have discussed at some length the significance of medieval parodies that, in similar manner, juxtapose the sacred with the profane and whose popularity is attested to by the large number of Latin manuscripts still extant. Their spirit was caught remarkably well by Nietzsche in *Thus Spake Zarathustra*, which contains a travesty of a Mass, not unlike those celebrated during the medieval Festival of the Ass. A brief sampling of it will convey the flavor of such parody in all its carnivalesque irreverence that laughingly turns the world upside down:

> And the litany sounded thus:
>
> Amen! And glory and honour and wisdom and thanks and praise and strength be to our God, from everlasting to everlasting!
>
> —The ass, however, here brayed Ye-A.
>
> He carrieth our burdens, he hath taken upon him the form of a servant, he is patient of heart and never saith Nay; and he who loveth his God chastiseth him.
>
> —The ass, however, here brayed Ye-A.
>
> He speaketh not: except that he ever saith Yea to the world which he created: thus doth he extol his world. It is his artfulness that speaketh not: thus is he rarely found wrong.
>
> —The ass, however, here brayed Ye-A.
>
> Uncomely goeth he through the world. Grey is the favourite colour in which he wrappeth his virtue. Hath he spirit, then doth he conceal it; every one, however, believeth in his long ears.[9]

Nietzsche's travesty, though used by him in the spirit of satire, would seem to be sacrilegious, unless we recognize that it belongs to that—usually more lighthearted—medieval tradition. It is in this same tradition that James Joyce parodied the litany, the liturgy, and the Lord's Prayer and that his work abounds in ludic travesties such as the following: "Haloed be her eve, her singtime sung, her rill be run, unhemmed as it is uneven." Or: "Oura Vatars that arred in Himmal," with its exuberant fusion of different languages, real as well as invented. Or: "Ouhr Former who erred," a sheer play on sound.[10] Rabelais had indulged in such exuberant and irreverent playfulness in his *Gargantua and Pantagruel*, and in his seminal study *Rabelais and His World*, Mikhail Bakhtin points out that one of the book's protagonists, Panurge, seeking advice from Friar John as to whether he should marry or not, couches his words in praise of the male sexual parts in the form of a litany repeated 153 times.[11] Rabelais used Christ's last words on the cross "sitio" (I thirst) and "consummatum est" (it is finished) in a literal sense as if they referred to food and drink, and such mingling of the sacred and the profane was so readily accepted and enjoyed in the author's time that he did not expunge it from his 1524 edition, which had to pass severe censorship.[12] It would be difficult but also idle to ascertain whether Beckett consciously adopted the spirit of this tradition, or whether it was simply germane to his own concerns. We know, of course, that, like Joyce, he had been a student of Romance literatures and that his early poetry was cast in the Provençal and medieval French forms of the troubadours tradition: the *enueg*, the *planh*, and the *alba*. This "modern minstrel," Harvey wrote, "chooses titles for seven of his thirteen poems directly out of the troubadour tradition. . . ."[13] There can be no doubt, at any rate, that in his theater and fiction Beckett perpetuates or reinvents medieval juxtapositions of the sacred and the profane—both in a sense of playfulness and of profound seriousness.

There is, for instance, the narrator of Beckett's *Watt*, identified as Sam somewhere toward the middle of the novel, who conveys to us that, one day, in the garden of his pavilion (it seems to be part of a mental institution), he espied Watt, whom he had previously and intimately known at another place. Watt was walking toward him but was walking backward. As Watt grotesquely advances—perpetually falling into the thorny shrubbery and painfully extricating himself from it—he turns his face toward Sam, who perceives him both as an image of Christ bearing a crown of thorns and as his own mirror image. The identity thus evoked between a religious image of Christ as painted by Bosch and hanging in London's Trafalgar Square, on the one hand, and the half-crazed representative of mankind Watt, who is the grotesque mirror of Sam himself, on the other, would border on the sacrilegious, were we not conscious of the fact that Watt advancing backward and perpetually falling is also a figure of medieval farce, of carnival, and of what I have designated with the Baudelairean term "the absolute comic."[14] Beckett maintains the ambivalence of that absolute comic so that, through laughter and tears, he can seriously probe the meaning of human existence without assuming the part of the philosopher. Beckett's ability and determination to pursue such serious questions under the guise of farce make themselves felt everywhere in his work and prove themselves perhaps most strikingly in a scene of the second novel of his trilogy, *Malone Dies*. There Macmann (Son of Man) is grotesquely caught in the rain, far from shelter, in an open field. Dressed like a scarecrow, he lies down on the ground in the posture of one crucified as the "rain pelted down on his back with the sound . . . of a drum. . . . The idea of punishment came to his mind, addicted, it is true, to that chimera and probably inpressed by the posture of the body and the fingers clenched as though in torment. And without knowing exactly what his sin was he felt . . . that living was not a sufficient atonement for it. . . ."[15]

But it is above all in Lucky's speech, that torrent of seeming madness, that Beckett's mingling of the sacred and the profane and even the scatological assumes truly medieval aspects. In the manner of participants in medieval farce, Lucky turns traditional patterns of reasoned discourse and theological debate into farce. Yet the seriousness of his concerns becomes apparent when we strip his speech of its carnivalesque elements. He then seems to suggest something like "given the existence . . . of a personal God . . . with white beard . . . outside time . . . who from the heights of divine . . . aphasia loves us dearly with some exceptions for reasons unknown . . . and suffers with those who . . . are plunged in torment . . . it is established beyond all doubt . . . that man . . . fades away" (28–29). A number of critics more or less agree on such a reading. Yet nothing could better illustrate the half-serious, half-playful travesties of medieval carnival and their ridicule of theological and scholarly pomposity that takes itself too seriously than Lucky's speech. It is clearly patterned after a medieval French *sermon joyeux*, a burlesque sermon of the kind preached in churches during carnivalesque celebrations and that later became part of the threesome that made up French traditional theatrical performances: the *sermon*, the *sottie*, and the *mystère* or *farce*. Rhetorically, the *sermon joyeux* was a *coq-à-l'âne*, a discourse defined as disjointedly passing from one subject to another without logical transition of any sort. "Sauter du coq à l'âne" meant literally "to leap from the rooster to the donkey," and the expression may well have its origin in animal debates. Although the sixteenth-century French poet Marot is credited with the invention of a poetic genre by that name, the concept is clearly much older. In the form of a *coq-à-l'âne, sermons joyeux* often travestied sacred texts by speaking of food, drink, and sex as if they were discussing theology or vice versa. The aim of the *sermon joyeux* was, on occasion, satire, but the genre was usually expressive of a sheer joy in verbal fantasy, often starting with Latin invocations, such as "in nomine Patris, et Filii et Spiritus Sancty. Amen."[16] It jumbled together disparate notions and languages and did not hesitate to address itself in the same phrase to Bacchus, Venus, and the Christian God. In its grotesque references and its play on sound rather than meaning, the genre repeated a triumph of carnivalesque fantasy, both in exuberance and in irreverence toward all that was taboo. Unfortunately, the examples extant of such *sermons joyeux* are not easily accessible to the modern reader because of their generous mixture of medieval French with an oddly gallicized Latin, so that the genre is, perhaps, most easily illustrated by a sampling from Molière's *Don Juan*. This is how Don Juan is lectured to by his servant Sganarelle:

> . . . I can keep quiet no longer . . . , but I must open my heart to you and tell you that I think as a faithful servant should. You know, master, the pitcher can go to the well once too often, and . . . men in the world are like the bird on the bough, the bough is part of the tree and whoever holds on to the tree is following sound precepts; sound precepts are better than fine words; the court is the place for fine words; at the court you find courtiers, and courtiers do whatever's the fashion. . . . A good pilot needs prudence; young men have no prudence . . . ; old men love riches; riches make men rich; the rich aren't poor; poor men know necessity and necessity knows no law. Without law men live like animals, which all goes to prove that you'll be damned to all eternity.[17]

Lucky's mock sermon abounds, from its start, in scholarly references to authorities that bear names as grotesque and even obscene as Puncher and Wattman, Testew and Cunard, Fartov and Belcher, Peckham Fulham Clapham, Steinweg and Peterman, and Essy-in-Possy. Lucky's elaborate proof of the existence of God is put in question because it is based on the findings of these authorities. Nor do we derive assurance from the childish picture he evokes of a God with white beard, or from the animal-like sounds—quaquaquaqua—with which he accompanies the word God and which in French pronunciation become obscene references to the body and its elimination. A similarly irreverent effect is achieved by Lucky's stuttering proffering of "Acacacacademy" and "Anthropopopometry." Such phrases as "labors left unfinished," "for reasons unknown," together with heaven, hell, flames, and fire conjure up a world presided over by a god as inscrutable as he is unpredictable, while the phrase "it is established beyond all doubt" ridicules the foolish and arrogant certainties of certain scholars. Like a medieval fool, Lucky truly leaps from topic to topic, as he turns the world mockingly upside down. But while he engages in *fatrasies*, the farcical play with words known to the French Middle Ages, he raises serious questions concerning man and his place in the universe—the same questions, in fact, that were raised by Didi and Gogo at the beginning of the play, namely, whether there is a God who loves man dearly and knows why he saved only one of the two sinners, or whether man's notion that "time will tell" is as absurd as the certainty of some that knowledge can be "established beyond all doubt." Such questions can be dealt with, after all, only in the ludic mode of the *coq-à-l'âne*. For whosoever raises them—be he medieval or modern man—will be listened to only if he plays the role of the fool.

Seen in this light, the play's title cannot but be recognized as one of the half-serious, half-playful bilingual combinations so often encountered in medieval French literature—regardless of what immediate experience might have suggested to Beckett the name Godot. It represents clearly a juxtaposition of the sacred with the profane as it links the Anglo-Saxon word *God* with the French suffix *-ot* that abases and makes laughable any name it is attached to, such as Pierre / Pierrot, Jacques / Jacquot, Charles / Charlot. Such "absurdity" is not an inadvertent reflection in Beckett's work of the chaotic universe we live in but rather a conscious tool in the hand of an author who sees man *sub specie aeternitatis*, who ridicules the desire of most of us, expressed for centuries in literature, to envision himself—not unlike Hamm in *Endgame*—as the center of the universe, of an author realizing that he can speak of what is most serious only in the manner of farce and the absolute comic. I am tempted to impute to Beckett a passage from Plato quoted by Huizinga: "Though human affairs are not worthy of great seriousness it is yet necessary to be serious. . . . God alone is worthy of supreme seriousness, but man is made God's plaything. . . . What then is the right way of living? Life must be lived as play, playing certain games, making sacrifices, singing and dancing, and then a man will be able to propitiate the gods, and defend himself against his enemies, and win in the contest."[18]

Notes

1. Samuel Beckett, *Waiting for Godot* (New York: Grove Press, 1954), p. 37. References to pages of this work will appear henceforth in parentheses in the text. For one of the best discussions of circularity in Beckett's work, see Rolf Breuer, *Die Kunst der Paradoxie* (Munich: Fink Verlag, 1976), passim.

2. Samuel Beckett, *Molloy* (New York: Grove Press, 1955), p. 8.

3. Robert Garapon, *La Fantaisie verbale et le comique dans le théâtre français, du Moyen Age à la fin du XVIIe siècle* (Paris: Colin, 1957), pp. 93ff.

4. See, for instance, *Godot*, p. 40.

5. Samuel Beckett, *Endgame* (New York: Grove Press, 1958).

6. Johan Huizinga, *Homo ludens: A Study of the Play Element in Culture* (Boston: Beacon Press, 1950), pp. 68–69. Cf. Edith Kern, *The Absolute Comic* (New York: Columbia University Press, 1980), pp. 31–32.

7. See *The Absolute Comic*, pp. 33–34.

8. See Eugène Ionesco, *Macbett* (Paris: Gallimard, 1972).

9. Friedrich Nietzsche, *Thus Spake Zarathustra*, trans. Thomas Common (New York: Modern Library, 1929), pp. 350–51.

10. James S. Atherton, *The Books at the Wake* (London: Faber and Faber, 1959), p. 187.

11. Mikhail Bakhtin, *Rabelais and His World*, trans. Helene Iswolsky (Cambridge, Mass.: MIT Press, 1968), pp. 417–18.

12. Ibid., p. 86.

13. Lawrence E. Harvey, *Samuel Beckett, Poet and Critic* (Princeton, N.J.: Princeton University Press, 1970), p. 79.

14. Samuel Beckett, *Watt* (New York: Grove Press, 1959), p. 159. See *The Absolute Comic*, pp. 3 ff.

15. Samuel Beckett, *Malone Dies* (New York: Grove Press, 1956), pp. 66–67.

16. See *The Absolute Comic*, pp. 64, 78.

17. Molière, "Don Juan, or the Statue at the Feast," in *"The Miser" and Other Plays*, trans. John Wood (Harmondsworth, England: Penguin, 1974), p. 245.

18. *Homo ludens*, p. 212.

Waiting

Ruby Cohn*

How describe its initial impact to a generation that has grown up with *Godot*? Now that any serious drama seeks a mythic dimension; now that disjunction is the familiar rhetorical pattern of stage speech; now that tragic depth almost always wears clown costume; now that the gestures of drama border on dance; now that expositions are quainter than soliloquies, and stage presence implies neither past nor future—now it may be hard to recall that it was not always so. *En attendant Godot* brought the curtain down on King Ibsen.

After nearly two decades, my bad memory clings to the warmth of that first *Godot* on a damp winter night. I had never heard of Beckett when I first saw *Godot*. I did not know my Bible well enough to recognize the scriptural kernel of the play. I had not read Hegel's *Phenomenology of Mind* well enough to recognize the archetypical Master-Slave relationship. I was not even a devotee of silent comic films. In short, I came to *Godot* with no background; or with too much background of Broadway problem plays, Comédie Française classics, and verse drama wherever I could find it. And yet I knew almost at once that those two French-speaking tramps were me; more miserable, more lovable, more humorous, more desperate. But me.

Laughter did not ring out through the little Théâtre de Babylone, as in performances I saw later. Rather, chuckles faded into smiles or frowns. I must have been too full of feeling to notice the unusual stage silences through which I fidgeted in later productions. The élan of those aboriginal Beckett tramps carried me right over the silences. But Pozzo and Lucky repelled me, recalling a circus-master and his trained animal. Long a coward about physical pain, I could hardly look at Lucky's neck, for fear of seeing his bruises, and I looked with distaste at Pozzo who supposedly

*Reprinted from *Back to Beckett* (Princeton: Princeton University Press, 1973), 127–39.

caused the bruises I didn't see. Lucky's monologue was so terrible to watch, with Jean Martin's spastic tics, that I thought *that* was the reason I could make no sense of it. I was ashamedly relieved when the other three characters shut Lucky up, and I was not sorry to see what I thought would be the last of him and his master. I can recall none of my intermission questions, but I can still see the Act II leaves on the tree, like shreds of green crêpe-paper. And I caught the point of the dog-song at once. "That's what the play is about." I must have told myself, as I settled back familiarly into the patter of the two tramps. I was surprised by the return of Pozzo and Lucky, no more sympathetic when maimed and subdued. I was even more surprised at the callousness with which the friends treated the unfortunate couple. But I wasn't surprised that Godot didn't come. I was pretty sure that the end of the play *was* the end, but I was pleased to have this confirmed by scattered applause, in which I joined vigorously. I can't remember the number of curtain calls, but there weren't many.

How was *Godot* received by other audiences who did not know that it was to become a classic? It was a running gag in Miami, the American opening city, that taxis could be sure of fares at the end of Act I. Michael Myerberg advertised for (and did not find) an audience of 80,000 intellectuals in New York City. Moving response came from San Quentin prison, but Herbert Blau nearly had a mutiny in his company before he persuaded them to do the play that was so meaningful for prisoners. Several of its first directors returned for another round with *Godot*—Blin, Blau, Schneider. In 1966 Yugoslavian Miodrag Bulatović wrote a sequel, *Godot Came*. Before the death of Bertolt Brecht in 1956, he wanted to adapt Beckett's play, and in 1971 Peter Palitsch, once Brecht's student, produced a Brechtian *Godot*, replete with gestus and estrangement. Though the original reception of *Godot* was unexpectedly good, enthusiasm for it is still far from universal. In 1956 Bert Lahr-Gogo received a letter denouncing the play as "communistic, atheistic, and existential." In May, 1971, an American college professor was forced to resign after directing *Godot*, which was declared "detrimental to the moral fibre of the college community."

Beckett would be the last to defend *Godot*. "I began to write *Godot*," he told Colin Duckworth, "as a relaxation, to get away from the awful prose I was writing at that time." I have tried to show that if the prose of the trilogy is awful, it is in the sense of awe-inspiring, and yet I can guess at what Beckett meant. Malone was unable to stick to his spirit of system; doubt eroded each scene he tried to present. The Unnamable was waiting in the wings or the cellarage. In turning to dramatic form, Beckett may have been seeking an order that he could not honestly impose on his fiction. Later he was to tell Michael Haerdter: "That's the value of theater for me. You place on stage a little world with its own laws." But Beckett's little stage worlds are emblematic of our big real world.

The seed of *Godot* is Luke's account of the crucifixion, as summarized by St. Augustine: "Do not despair: one of the thieves was saved. Do not presume: one of the thieves was damned." The two thieves are Didi and Gogo; the two thieves are Pozzo and Lucky; the two thieves are you and me. And the play is shaped to reflect that fearful symmetry. I am not for a moment suggesting that this was a conscious choice on Beckett's part. Embroiled as he was in the murky lyricism of the trilogy, he sought the repose of order—"cawm," as Gogo would say. The *Godot* manuscript bears evidence of Beckett's sure shaping touch; the handwriting, unusually legible rather than cramped with effort, flows along with few changes. The dialogue rhythm, as Colin Duckworth has shown in careful detail, leans on that of *Mercier et Camier*, but the basic form comes from St. Augustine.

Even before the curtain rises, the program informs us that there will be *two* acts, though we do not know how the second will reflect the first. The set pits the horizontal road on the stage board against the vertical tree. The action will balance four characters falling *down* against their looking *up* at the sky. The very names of the four main characters indicate their pairing: Pozzo and Lucky contain two syllables and five letters each; Estragon and Vladimir contain three syllables and eight letters each, but they address one another only by nicknames—Gogo and Didi, childish four-letter words composed of repeated monosyllables. Even the fifth character, the nameless boy, has a brother, and he says that Godot beats the one but not the other. Godot is as arbitrary as the God of *Matthew* 25:32–33: "And before him shall be gathered all nations: and he shall separate them one from another, as a shepherd divideth his sheep from the goats. And he shall set the sheep on his right hand but the goats on the left." Sheep and goat become saved thief and damned thief of St. Augustine's symmetry.

Didi broods about the two thieves early in the play, as we are getting acquainted with what look like two thieves on stage. Though it is not specified in the text, Beckett's two thieves wear similar clothes in production—the black suit and derby of music-hall or silent film, and we laugh at their antics much of the time that they are constantly before us. (For Roger Blin, the ideal cast would have been Chaplin as Didi, Keaton as Gogo, and Laughton as Pozzo.) Pozzo and Lucky have no nicknames, and we view them formally, externally, during their intermittent presence before us. Their clothes are elaborate but dated, their relationship is repulsive, but it is not really our business. Pozzo seems to want to become our business (through the friends), lush as he is with self-revelation (to the friends), but he himself warns that "there wasn't a word of truth in it." Lucky speaks of his civilization rather than himself in his single long monologue which contains the word "I" only in the mechanical phrase, "I resume." Impersonal Pozzo and Lucky confront personal Gogo and Didi, and for all the many pages that have now been written about the play, *Godot*'s theatricality rests very squarely on this confrontation of two couples. To twist what Beckett said about the two-act structure of *Godot*: one couple would have been too few, and three would have been too many. Pozzo and Lucky alone would have been a caricature of human master-slave tendencies, a caricature of human obsession with moving "On." Caricatures summon no sympathy. Without these contrasting caricatures, however, we would respond less immediately to the concreteness of Didi and Gogo. We appreciate their friendship in the contrapuntal context of Pozzo and Lucky. In the shadow of these compulsive wanderers, who wander into obvious deterioration, Didi and Gogo scintillate with variety. Each couple is more meaningful because of the other, replacing the protagonist and antagonist of dramatic tradition.

None of these symmetries is exact, of course. Act II does not repeat Act I precisely. Each member of each couple is distinctive and individual. And looming asymmetrically offstage is Godot. The very first review suggested that Godot might be "happiness, eternal life, the unattainable quest of all men." And Godot has subsequently been explained as God, a diminutive god, Love, Death, Silence, Hope, De Gaulle, Pozzo, a Balzac character, a bicycle racer, Time Future, a Paris street for call-girls, a distasteful image evoked by French words containing the root *god* (*godailler*, to guzzle; *godenot*, runt; *godelureau*, bumpkin; *godichon*, lout). Beckett told Roger Blin that the name Godot derived from French slang words for boot—*godillot*, *godasse*. A decade after *Godot* was produced, I informed Beckett of a San Francisco mortician's firm, Godeau Inc. Beckett's play tells us plainly who Godot is—the promise that is always awaited and not fulfilled, the expectation that brings two men to the board night after night. The play tells us this dramatically and not discursively.

St. Augustine commented on the crucifixions in Luke's gospel: "Do not despair; one of the thieves was saved. Do not presume: one of the thieves was damned." Fifty per cent may be a reasonable chance, but only one of the four gospels argues for that percentage, so that Didi arrives at a dimmer view: "But all four were there. And only one speaks of a thief being saved." It is no wonder then that Didi and Gogo are more tempted to despair than to presume. And yet they do not despair. Instead, they keep their appointment, and they wait. Night after night, they keep their appointment, and they wait. While they wait, they repeat the activities that add up to a life.

From the beginning of the play Didi and Gogo emphasize the repetitive nature of their activities. Were Beckett to direct the play, he would now begin with their attitude of waiting, which would be periodically repeated throughout the play. In the printed text the play begins when Estragon tries *again* to take off his boots. We read the first example of a frequently repeated scenic direction: "*As before*" (in French, even more pointedly, "*Même jeu*," literally "*Same play*"). In Vladimir's first speech he talks about *resuming* the struggle. He notes that Estragon is there *again*—wherever "there" may be. He is glad that Estragon is *back*—wherever "back" may be. Vladimir wants to celebrate his *re*union with Estragon.

In the first few minutes of playing time each of the friends asks the significant question: "It hurts?" And the other answers: "Hurts! He wants to know if it hurts!" This first of the many repetitions of the dialogue makes pain general, but also musical. Beckett never sacrifices meaning to sound, but as in his complex fiction he often intensifies meaning through sound.

Immediately after the first utterance of the most frequently repeated line in the play—"We're waiting for Godot"—the friends turn their attention to the stage tree. Estragon says: "Looks to me more like a bush." Vladimir counters: "A shrub." But Estragon insists: "A bush." This exchange sets a pattern of poetic variants and refrains, with Estragon always speaking the refrain lines. Throughout the play, phrasal repetition, most naked in Lucky's manic monologue, is reinforced by gestural repetition: Lucky with his luggage, Pozzo with his possessions, Gogo with his shoes, Didi with his hat, and the music-hall routine in which Gogo and Didi juggle three hats (suggested to Beckett by the Marx Brothers' *Duck Soup*). All the characters repeatedly stumble and fall, but in Act I Didi and Gogo set Lucky on his feet, and in Act II they do the same for Pozzo. Repetition is theme and technique of Didi's round-song which reduces man's life to a dog's life—and cruel death.

In the printed text of *En attendant Godot* the most frequent repetitions are two scenic directions: *Silence* and *Pause*. In the theater repeated stillness can reach a point of no return, but Beckett avoids this danger by adroit deployment of his pauses and silences. They act like theatrical punctuation, a pause often marking hesitation or qualification, whereas silence is a brush with despair before making a fresh start. The play never quite negates a fresh start after stillness claims the stage in sudden night. All stage action has to be wrested from the background stillness, the ever-threatening void. Gogo realizes: "There's no lack of void." And he recalls talking about "*nothing* in particular." (The italics are mine; Beckett changes the French "boots" to "nothing" in the English version.) Each of the two acts ends with the stillness after the same lines: "Well? Shall we go?" asks one of the friends, and other replies: "Yes, let's go." In neither act do they move as the curtain falls.

The opening "Nothing to be done" is repeated three times. What distinguishes drama from fiction is that the Nothing has to be done, acted, performed. The body of Beckett's play therefore contains much doing, constantly threatened by Nothing. To open each act, Gogo and Didi enter separately, each in turn first on stage. At least one of them eats, excretes, sleeps, dreams, remembers, plans, refers to sex or suicide. In both acts they comment on their reunion, they complain of their misery, they seek escape into games, they are frightened by offstage menace, they try to remember a past, they stammer a hope for a future, they utter doubts about time, place, and language, they wait for Godot. Beckett's scenic directions show the range of their emotions: irritably, coldly, admiringly, decisively, gloomily, cheerfully, feebly, angrily, musingly, despairingly, very insidiously, looking wildly about, wheedling, voluptuously, gently, highly excited, grotesquely rigid, violently, meditatively, vacuously, timidly, conciliating, hastily, grudgingly, stutteringly, resolute, vehemently, forcibly, tenderly, blankly, indignantly, attentively, sadly, shocked, joyous, indifferent, vexed, suddenly furious, exasperated, sententious, in anguish, sure of himself, controlling himself, triumphantly, stupefied, softly, recoiling, alarmed, laughing noisily, sagging, painfully, feverishly—with violently and despairingly most frequent.

In each act the two friends are diverted by an interlude—the play within the play of Pozzo and Lucky, who enter and exit tied together. Reciting rhetorically and loaded with props, Pozzo and Lucky are cut down to size when they are "done" by Gogo and Didi in Act II. Alone again in each act, the friends are greeted by Godot's messenger, they hear the monotonous message, and the moon rises swiftly. Refrains, repetitions, and pauses camouflage how *much* is happening on stage. Only in retrospect, after viewing it all, do we realize how much is at stake in these hapless happenings.

V. A. Kolve has compared *Godot* to medieval drama: in the Corpus Christi plays, Holy Saturday, the day between Christ's death and resurrection, is the day when nothing can be known or done, when faith is eroded by doubt. Didi and Gogo are to meet Godot on Saturday, but no Easter dawns with its promise of resurrection. The other medieval form, the morality play, portrays Everyman seeking salvation, the medieval human condition. But conditions have changed since the Middle Ages. Didi ponders salvation, but he has to rack his brain before he can think of the opposite of salvation: the damnation that must have been vividly present in the medieval mind, but that is modern everyday reality. Modern man knows no psychomachia; he waits out a life of Holy Saturdays, closer to the passivity of Zen than to redemption. "Doing the tree" of *Godot* is exercise 52 in the yoga series, standing on one leg to pray, but Gogo cannot keep his balance, and there is no evidence that God sees him.

While waiting for Godot, Didi and Gogo act out their condition, together and alone. Gogo, as his name suggests (English "go"), is the more physical in his needs, complaints, perceptions. Didi, as his name suggests (French "dis"), is more voluble and philosophical. They are interdependent, and yet each is a whole man and not an allegorical abstraction. Simply human, each of them suffers while waiting, but they react against suffering by trying to fill or kill the time of waiting. Their activities have an improvisational quality—dancing, juggling, tumbling, miming, falling, and rising—with Gogo the more active of the two. Their dialogue is varied with questions and exclamations, logic and disjunction, incompleteness and alternatives, erudition and obscenity, synonyms and antonyms, paradox and incongruity, tenderness and imprecation—with Didi the more inventive of the two. Their first discussion of Godot is a music-hall routine, and their duet about dead voices is, in Herbert Blau's phrase, "a superb threnody on desire, mortality, and time." Physically and metaphysically, their words and gestures penetrate our own.

Most of us, however, would be reluctant to see ourselves in the doings of Pozzo and Lucky. Pozzo and Lucky of Act I are ready performers, and their flagrant contrast is part of the performance. They dress according to their social station; Pozzo flourishes his props (whip, pipe, atomizer, watch) whereas Lucky bends under burdens. Lucky can dance and think; actor Jack MacGowran has indicated the three threads of Lucky's monologue: the constancy of the divine, the shrinkage of humanity, the petrifaction of the earth. Lucky's monologue displays Western civilization as shards of religion, philosophy, science, art, sport, and modern industry. In that monologue Lucky utters the word "unfinished" seven times; his sentences do not finish, and his monologue is not permitted to finish. Named with devastating irony, Lucky is modern man with his contradictory unfinished fragments.

The Pozzo of Act I needs all eyes on him to answer a simple question. He recites an elocution piece with studied gestures. But though he may be a dilettante, he has meditated on time and life, theory and practice. Physically, he and Lucky lack the friends' gestural variety, and yet they do move about. Lucky carries, and Pozzo sits; both of them fall and shakily rise. Compulsively, they voyage "on," perhaps to perform at another encounter. Both master and servant deliver set-pieces of dialogue, too thoroughly rehearsed. Pozzo resembles a disc jockey or television announcer, and Lucky a broken record. But by Act II, Lucky is dumb, and blind Pozzo speaks only in passion. No longer able to entertain, they present their misery for the friends' diversion. When Didi questions Pozzo, as a journalist might question yesterday's star actor, Pozzo explodes into the most haunting line of the play: "They give birth astride of a grave, the light gleams for an instant, then it's night once more." The night is immeasurably more profound than the twilight of Pozzo's Act I set-piece.

Though less obstreperous than Pozzo and Lucky, Didi and Gogo are also performers. Gogo is a would-be raconteur, and Didi paraphrases the Bible. In Act I Pozzo and perhaps Lucky are aware of being performers, but Didi and perhaps Gogo are aware of being in a play. And they are aware of playing to pass time: "We always find something, eh Didi, to give us the impression we exist?" In giving us that intense impression, the two friends undercut their mockery of their own play. "We are bored to death," complains Didi. Millions of spectators have been entertained by that boredom.

One of the most time-conscious plays ever written, *En attendant Godot* has itself been buffeted by time. In 1971, the same year that it was said to undermine the moral fibre of a college community, *Time* magazine's reporter took a deep breath and pronounced it "no masterpiece" for much the same reason: "*Waiting for Godot* is Beckett's tomb. Need it necessarily be ours?" We seem to have come full circle to some of the early Sunday-supplement reaction to *Godot*. And it is not uncheering that, in spite of the reams that have been written about *Godot*, it can still disturb.

Beyond a very few references, I have said little about these reams. The first book about Beckett focuses largely on *Godot*, and every year brings new interpretations. I have edited a volume that contains theatrical, source, genre, Marxist, Christian, mythic, philosphic, phenomenological, imagistic, linguistic interpretations of *Godot*. Other editors have included other approaches. Many discussions are illuminating, but none is indispensable. It is not even indispensable, or especially helpful, to know Beckett's other works in order to respond to *Godot*. I do not believe that *Godot* is Beckett's greatest work, but it is perhaps his most immediate. As *Malone* presents us with the building-blocks of stories, *Godot* shows us how hard it is to build a play. And since playing is the most direct imitation of living, theater can evoke the most immediate audience response.

I lingered so long on my own first reaction to *Godot* because it is hard today to see *Godot* without ever having heard of it. But if one could, I think one would—as I did—virtually build the play along with the actors. Not in amateur admixtures *à la* "happening," but through absorption in Beckett's scenes. Unlike previous drama that posits a past, Godot's *thereness* unrolls before our perceptions, as Alain Robbe-Grillet understood so early. Only the opening lines are gratuitous in *Godot*. After that each line is uttered on cue. Nor does such sequence contradict what I said earlier about the drama's improvisational quality. Improvisation, as today's actors well know, is hard work. Improvisation is not synonymous with spontaneous effervescence. Stage time has to be played through, and each line, each gesture, takes effort. Combining lines and gestures may result from tedious rehearsal, as in Pozzo's set-piece; or word and motion may remain separate. Even words demanding motion may not attain it. Estragon says "Over there" without gesture. When he says, "I'm going," he goes nowhere. Vladimir offers to give Lucky a handkerchief, but he does not approach him. And each act's curtain-line is, "Yes, let's go," but the two actors "*do not move.*"

All this serves to focus attention on the very elements of drama—entrances, exits, silence, cues, repartee, blocking, and the offstage unknown. Least subtle in *Godot* are the lines that refer to the play as a play: "This is becoming really insignificant." "I've been better entertained." However, the lines embrace more than the particular situation. And it is this extensibility, rooted in particulars, that ultimately makes a classic of *Godot*, as of *Hamlet*. Hamlet's questions—specific questions in the play's dialogue—probe to a depth undreamed of in our revenge plays. *Godot*'s questions—questions, often unanswered, constitute about one quarter of the play's sentences—probe to a metaphysics undreamed of in our physics. The play's opening assertion, "Nothing to be done" (even more casual in the French cliché "Rien à faire"), is spoken by Estragon about his boots. But Vladimir picks it up as a metaphysical generalization: "I'm beginning to come round to that opinion. All my life I've tried to put it from me. . . ." By the end of the play, Vladimir is still living, so he is still trying to put it from him, still only coming round to that opinion. During the course of the play, he has made such metaphysical observations as: "Where are all these corpses from?" "There's no lack of void." "Time has stopped." "But at this place at this moment of time, all mankind is us, whether we like it or not." (The cross-nationality of the names of the four characters reinforces this assertion.) More humorously, Estragon utters comparably cosmic lines: "People are bloody ignorant apes." "Pah! The wind in the reeds" (on a dusty highway). "Everything oozes." "I'm tired breathing." Near the end, Vladimir paraphrases Pozzo's heartrending line: "Astride of a grave and a difficult birth. Down in the hole, lingeringly, the grave-digger puts on the forceps. We have time to grow old. The air is full of our cries." Like other single speeches in the tragicomedy, *that* is what *Godot* is about. "Our cries" compose its dialogue, orchestrated by Beckett, and understood in many languages.

Waiting for Leviathan

Robert Zaller*

Samuel Beckett's affinity to Descartes and the Cartesian tradition has often been remarked.[1] Yet a hitherto unexplored link of perhaps comparable importance exists between Beckett's stage masterpiece, *Waiting for Godot*, and another seventeenth-century philosopher, Thomas Hobbes. A reading of *Godot* beside Hobbes' own masterwork, *Leviathan* (1651), reveals significant thematic and structural parallels.[2]

The bare, or more precisely barren stage that greeted the first audience of *Godot* at the Théâtre de Babylone in January 1953 gave the modern theater its most abiding metaphor: dispossession. Much of the text is preoccupied with the loss of spatial and temporal location, and the vertiginous circularity of the dialogue as a whole is essentially an unfolding of this root dilemma. This is the reductionist world of Descartes' "figure and extension," made punningly literal in the image of two derelicts on an empty stage, and brought to its final human consequences in their unassuageable despair. But the world they occupy is not merely mathematical or metaphysical: it is a social one as well. This world had

*This essay was prepared for this volume and is published here for the first time.

also been descried in the seventeenth century. Thomas Hobbes called it the state of nature, and Beckett's empty, trafficless road and bare, uncultivated tree is its visual metaphor too: "In such condition, there is no place for Industry; because the fruit thereof is uncertain: and consequently no Culture of the Earth, no Navigation, nor use of the commodities that may be imported by Sea; no commodious Building; no Instruments of moving, and removing such things as require much force; no Knowledge of the face of the Earth; no account of Time; no Arts; no Letters; no Society; and which is worst of all, continuall feare, and danger of violent death; And the life of man, solitary, poore, nasty, brutish, and short" (64–65).[3]

Hobbes's own vision grew out of the English Revolution of the 1640s, which resulted in the overthrow of the Stuart dynasty and the execution of the reigning monarch, Charles I. The state of nature was thus not merely a theoretical reconstruction of presocietal life, but a graphic projection of what might befall men in a condition of civil anarchy. It was against such a contingency that government was instituted. The civil population surrendered its natural liberties to a sovereign who forcibly maintained the peace. The sovereign thus wielded an absolute authority based on absolute consent; the commonwealth was the common will united in the person of the ruler. In obeying him, men obeyed themselves; but their obligation to this obedience was total: the sovereign alone might command.

Hobbes's sovereign has one and the same relation with each of his subjects, both individually and as a collective whole. As each individual subject contracts personally with the sovereign, moreover, a commonwealth of two or three persons is theoretically as complete as one of millions. All that is required is the surrender of individual rights and the sovereign's acceptance of lordship. By the same token, an association of millions is nothing more than the multiplication of a relation between two.[4]

With this in mind, we can examine the setting of *Waiting for Godot* and the relationships of its four principal characters. The *mise-en-scène* of the play seems to echo Hobbes's description with almost programmatic exactitude. There are no commodious buildings, indeed none of any sort, nor any evidence of industry or agriculture: Didi and Gogo are apparently subsisting upon legumes (carrots, turnips, radishes), and Godot, their prospective savior, is spoken of as keeping sheep and goats (33v). There are no instruments of moving; even something so simple as a cart has been replaced by a human bearer. Knowledge of the earth, which in the absence of human habitation has reverted to undifferentiated landscape, is so reduced that a tree must serve as a place of assignation. As they are uncertain of place, Didi and Gogo have lost track of time. Night and day flow into each other; even the seasons are no longer distinguished (42v). And certainly there is danger: Gogo is routinely beaten (7r), apparently by roving gangs (39v), though he knows neither who they are nor why he is attacked. This is, indeed, a life that is nasty, brutish, and short; though apparently not short enough, since Didi and Gogo are obliged to attempt suicide to escape it.

At the same time, the two tramps clearly remember better days. They reminisce about the Eiffel Tower, and grape harvesting on the Rhone. Didi is, or has been, an intellectual of some sort, and even Gogo betrays not only a knowledge of the Bible but a seeming acquaintance with Einsteinian physics (42v). If they find themselves in a state of nature, it is not a primitive one, but rather the dystopia of a civil anarchy, in which a previously higher civilization—presumably the West—has been unaccountably degraded.[5]

The state of nature is not necessarily one of solitude, for men seek dominion over one another in it for a variety of reasons (*Leviathan*, chaps. XI and XIII). It may be also that they seek companionship as well, though such relationships are inherently unstable. This instability, Hobbes says, derives from the fact that each man seeks approbation from his fellows without the obligation to reciprocate it, but there is a more fundamental cause. Each man in the state of nature is in a state of absolute freedom with respect to every other man, and so the most necessary bond of association—obligation as such—is lacking. As Hobbes puts it, "men have no pleasure (but on the contrary a great deale of griefe) in keeping company, where there is no power able to overawe them" (64).

Didi and Gogo represent a case in point. Despite their long association, they manifest little apparent commitment to each other. Gogo wanders off periodically, and wonders if he and Didi would not be better off apart: "We weren't made for the same road." This seems a curious conclusion to reach after fifty years of companionship, but Didi replies only, "It isn't certain" (35r–v).[6] Neither takes responsibility for the other, and they seem unable to coordinate their actions for more than a few moments at a time. Their fifty years has been, in fact, nothing more than an accumulation of discrete, particulate experiences which leave them beginning forever anew. Despite a few catches of shared memory, they have no history. Their relationship is epitomized in the brief exchange at the beginning of Act II, when Gogo has returned beaten again from a night on his own:

> VLADIMIR: Did I ever leave you?
>
> ESTRAGON: You let me go. (38r)

That Didi has never left Gogo is beside the fact that he has never been able to keep him from going. At best, moreover, Didi's constancy is a negative virtue. He cannot claim fidelity to the relationship, merely that he has never been the first to desert it. Gogo's reproach is precisely that if Didi were faithful, he would have stayed him; hence, he is responsible for his going. In the state of nature, where force appears to be the final arbiter, nothing can be truly compelled:

> If a Covenant be made, wherein neither of the parties performe presently, but trust one another; in the condition of meer Nature (which is a condition of Warre of every man against every man,) upon any reasonable suspition, it is Voyd. . . . For he that performeth first, has no assurance the other will performe after; because the bonds of words are too weak to bridle mens ambition, avarice, anger, and other Passions, without the feare of some coercive Power; which in the condition of meer Nature, where all men are equall, and judges of the justnesse of their own fears, cannot possibly be supposed. (*Leviathan*, 70–71)

Yet finally there appears to be one project that unites the two tramps: they are waiting for Godot. The identity of Godot is the riddle of the play, of course, but it is a bit of a red herring too: we are never given enough information to base a firm conclusion on. Nonetheless, we may assert that what is known of him is compatible at least with the picture of the Hobbesian sovereign—though a sovereign seen hazily and from afar, not by the author of a philosophical treatise but by two men in a state of confusion, expectation, anxiety, hope and despair.

What do we know about Godot? He is identified as a man (14v), a point worth noting in view of the tendency to interpret him deistically.[7] He employs two boys to tend his sheep and goats who sleep in a hayloft (34r). He himself "does nothing" (59r). A sheepowner who "does nothing" would imply, at any rate, a landed gentleman, though the grounds of inference are admittedly slender. We do not know whether Godot employs anyone else, nor to what use he might contemplate putting two aged tramps.

Didi and Gogo, in turn, appear to have no clear idea of what they want of Godot. The section in which Didi attempts to reconstruct their previous meeting with Godot (12v–13v) contains, in effect, two contradictory accounts. In the first account, Didi represents them as free agents appraising the possible conditions of a contract: "Let's wait and see what he says"; "Let's wait till we know exactly how we stand"; "I'm curious to hear what he has to offer. Then we'll take it or leave it." Godot has, in short, offered nothing. But neither have Didi and Gogo themselves made a request:

> ESTRAGON: What exactly did we ask him for?
> VLADIMIR: Were you not there?
> ESTRAGON: I can't have been listening.
> VLADIMIR: Oh . . . Nothing very definite.
> ESTRAGON: A kind of prayer.
> VLADIMIR: Precisely.
> ESTRAGON: A vague supplication.
> VLADIMIR: Exactly.

In the course of these few lines, Didi's brisk air—the tone of business equals—has become an attitude of "supplication." This transitional passage keys the second account, in which a deal has seemingly been struck:

ESTRAGON: Where do we come in?

. . . .

VLADIMIR: Come in? On our hands and knees.

ESTRAGON: As bad as that?

VLADIMIR: Your Worship wishes to assert his prerogatives?

ESTRAGON: We've no rights any more?

Laugh of Vladimir, stifled as before, less the smile.

VLADIMIR: You'd make me laugh if it wasn't prohibited.

ESTRAGON: We've lost our rights?

VLADIMIR: (*distinctly*). We got rid of them.

Silence. They remain motionless, arms dangling, heads sunk, sagging at the knees.

What is logically necessary to square these two accounts is a second meeting at which Didi and Gogo have made a pledge of complete subordination to Godot, though the text is pointedly silent as to what if anything Godot might have promised in return. But this second meeting cannot have taken place. The dialogue is continuous in real time throughout the scene, and all that occurs between the first and second accounts is a passage of verbal jousting. This jousting, which recurs throughout the text and constitutes a kind of love play between the tramps, is followed by a brief pause before the dialogue resumes. It may be argued that the difference in tone between the two accounts is the difference between the sanguinity that precedes this "love-making" and the depletion and despair that follow it. But this does not enable us to make sense of the two accounts themselves, nor of the contradictions between them.

Again, it is Hobbes who suggests a way to resolve the dilemma. Let us review the difficulties between our two accounts. In the first one, Godot hears a request but makes neither a reply nor a request of his own; in the second, the tramps capitulate completely without receiving anything in return, although there is nothing to indicate that they have been coerced in the least. In short, they have freely bargained away the only thing they possess (their freedom itself) without benefit.

This seems absurd as such. But there is one kind of negotiation it describes exactly: the framing of the social contract that translates men from the equality of the state of nature to the civil subordination of subject to sovereign. This archetypal contract, which forms the basis of all subsequent ones, is unique in its absence of reciprocity. By its very nature, it can impose no obligation on one of its parties, the sovereign,

> Because the Right of bearing the Person of them all, is given to him they make Soveraigne, by Covenant only of one to another, and not of him to any of them; there can happen no breach of Covenant on the part of the Soveraigne; and consequently none of his Subjects, by any pretence of forfeiture, can be freed from his Subjection. That he which is made Soveraigne maketh no Covenant with his Subjects beforehand, is manifest; because either he must make it with the whole multitude, as one party to the Covenant; or he must make a severall Covenant with every man. With the whole, as one party, it is impossible; because as yet they are not one Person: and if he make so many severall Covenants as there be men, those Covenants after he hath the Soveraignty are voyd, because what act soever can be pretended by any one of them for breach thereof, is the act both of himselfe, and of all the rest, because done in the Person, and by the Right of every one of them in particular. (91)[8]

The subject thus engages himself unconditionally to the sovereign. He is full of need, but can make no claim; at best, he can "supplicate" the protection of the civil state. In entering that state, he surrenders his natural rights—specifically his freedom of action—which have become, in the prevailing anarchy, not only a useless but a dangerous burden. While therefore he first approaches the sovereign as one free agent to another—there existing no other relation in the state of nature—the covenant he makes transforms his status. Henceforth, his relation to all other men is determined by the sovereign. He is, in short, at the sovereign's disposal; more bluntly, his slave.

From such a perspective, what appear to be two separate and conflicting accounts can be seen as a single sequential one. In the first part of the sequence, Didi and Gogo approach Godot as free agents preparing to bargain on a plane of equality. They make a "request," which as it is remembered (or repeated?) becomes instead an entreaty, "a kind of prayer," "a vague supplication." This entreaty, as the latter part of the sequence makes clear, is or includes a submission to Godot as sovereign. Godot quite properly makes no reply to the tramps' request, since the sovereign, as we have seen, can make no terms with his subjects. This silence gradually conveys to Didi and Gogo the true nature of their situation, namely that they cannot bargain but only submit. They attempt to disguise this unpalatable truth by "misinterpreting" Godot's silence as a business-like pause in their negotiation (13r, lines 9–24). In reality, however, they have already been reduced from agents to supplicants (lines 5–8); that is, to prospective subjects. It is precisely this realization that constitutes the second part of the sequence, as Didi explains to Gogo their new situation. They will "come in" on their hands and knees," having "got rid of" their rights: as succinct a description of subjects entering a Hobbesian commonwealth as one could wish. Against this, Gogo's baffled responses ("As bad as that?"; "We've lost our rights?") represent not slow-wittedness but the divided consciousness attendant on so radical a change of state. Throughout the scene, Didi "remembers" the encounter with Godot for both partners, while Gogo "forgets" at every crucial point. This role-playing expresses the psychological transition from the status of agent to that of subject, for as one must renounce one's misery in the state of nature (as Didi does), one must also "forget" one's freedom there. The ambivalent nature of the entire process is tersely summarized in the final exchange of the scene:

> ESTRAGON: We've lost our rights?
> VLADIMIR: We got rid of them.[9]

Didi's confirmation of the tramps' new status seems unambiguous enough. But, other than the simple command to wait, they receive no instruction from Godot, and their lives are for all practical purposes unchanged. They are still hungry, still beaten, and still, to all outward appearance, masterless men. Indeed, the assumption of servitude so emphatically asserted by Didi in the covenant scene is undermined a scant two pages later in one of the reversals so typical of Beckett's switchback construction:

> ESTRAGON: I'm asking you if we're tied.
> VLADIMIR: Tied?
> ESTRAGON: Ti-ed.
> VLADIMIR: How do you mean tied?
> ESTRAGON: Down.
> VLADIMIR: But to whom? By whom?
> ESTRAGON: To your man.
> VLADIMIR: To Godot? Tied to Godot! What an idea! No question of it. (*Pause.*) For the moment. (14v)

The attentive reader will note that the key utterance in this exchange, "No question of it," can be read equally as an assertion or a denial. But if throughout the play the convenant with Godot will remain, in Hobbesian terms, a *mariage blanc*, seemingly made but still unconsummated, a perfect Hobbesian couple soon make their appearance:

> *Enter Pozzo and Lucky. Pozzo drives Lucky by means of a rope passed around his neck, so that Lucky is the first to enter, followed by the rope which is long enough to let him reach the middle of the stage before Pozzo appears. Lucky carries a heavy bag, a folding stool, a picnic basket and a greatcoat, Pozzo a whip.* (15r)

A rope, a whip, and a picnic for one: the relation between sovereign and subject could not be more perfectly epitomized. Lucky has been reduced to a beast of burden, and the twin epithets by which Pozzo addresses him ("pig," "hog") degrade him still further. Pozzo utters only words of command to him ("On," "Up," "Back," etc.); Lucky responds only by action.

Yet the relationship between Pozzo and Lucky has not always been thus. Pozzo reveals that he has appropriated (and apparently memorized) all his finer sentiments from Lucky, the vestiges of whose eloquence are horrifically displayed in his monologue (28v–29v). Nor is Lucky without rights. Though Pozzo feasts on chicken, the bones belong to Lucky, and cannot be given away without his consent (18v). When Gogo asks why he does not put down his burden, Pozzo is at pains to clarify the matter: "Why doesn't he make himself comfortable? Let's try and get this clear. Has he not the right to? Certainly he has. It follows that he doesn't want to. There's reasoning for you" (21v).

The "right" Lucky possesses is a civil, not a natural, one. In the civil state, whatever is not commanded or forbidden may be considered as permitted. Sometimes these rights are spelled out as positive law ("the bones go to the carrier"); sometimes they are merely at discretion. Thus, while Lucky may not sleep (16r), he is free to rest: free, that is, until the next command is issued: "Leave him in peace! Can't you see he wants to rest? Basket!" (18r).

In contrast, Pozzo treats Didi and Gogo with a politeness that appears comically disproportionate to their station. He presents himself formally, addresses them as "gentlemen," seeks anxiously for their approval, reproaches himself for impertinence in asking a personal question, and thanks them for their "society" (15v, 21v, 25v, 19r). For their part, Didi and Gogo are at once deferential. Gogo takes Pozzo for Godot, and Didi "sirs" him obsequiously at the first hint of command in his voice (15v, 16r). Once assured that he does not threaten them, however, they become bold and even, as Pozzo notes ruefully, rude (20r). Finally they enter into what they take to be the spirit of the occasion, exchanging elaborate courtesies with him (24r–v, 25v, 31r). But Pozzo is not at all ironic and, apart from a few lapses when the habit of command overcomes him, remains fully consistent in tone. He treats the tramps, in short, as equals. Only when Gogo approaches Lucky for the chicken bones is he as amused by their manners as they are by his:

ESTRAGON: Mister . . . excuse me, Mister . . .

POZZO: You're being spoken to, pig! Reply!
(*To Estragon.*) Try him again.

ESTRAGON: Excuse me, Mister, the bones, you won't be wanting the bones?
Lucky looks long at Estragon.

POZZO: (*in raptures*). Mister! (*Lucky bows his head.*) (18v)

What throws Pozzo into "raptures" is the idea of anyone approaching Lucky as an equal. But this is precisely what the reader or spectator of

Godot finds humorous in Pozzo's own demeanor toward the tramps. In fact, both Gogo and Pozzo behave appropriately. Gogo has just been informed that Lucky is the rightful owner of the bones. He therefore quite properly asks Lucky's permission to have them. Similarly, Pozzo has no grounds for presumption against Didi and Gogo. Though Pozzo is the master of Lucky, and Didi and Gogo may possibly be the servants of Godot, Pozzo, Didi and Gogo are all in the state of nature with respect to each other. This may be summarized graphically (where SN = the state of nature and C = commonwealth):

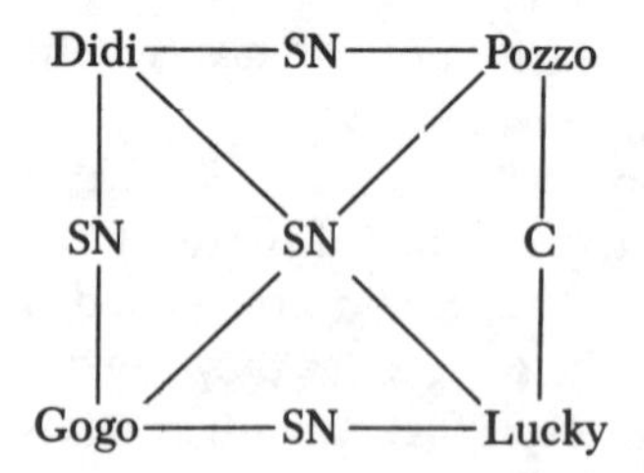

The relationships between the four characters are inherently fortuitous and unstable. In the state of nature, they are governed by calculations of immediate interest; in the commonwealth, they are founded on the artificial creation of the sovereign. As Pozzo remarks, it is only by "chance" that he is Lucky's master rather than vice versa (21v). By the same token, all four are potentially masters or slaves of each other. Didi and Gogo begin by mistaking Pozzo for Godot, and there is no reason why he cannot become Godot if he and they wish it. All roles are reversible, all identities are arbitrarily defined. "Godot" can be anyone who is willing to play the part.

Beckett demonstrates this interchangeability in a variety of ways. He undermines the stability of character by reversal and self-contradiction. Lucky, who is mute, unleashes a torrent of words. Gogo, who cannot identify Christ at the beginning of the play, claims to have imitated him all his life. Pozzo, who prides himself on punctuality, declares he has "no notion of time." In effect, anyone's statement or action—Lucky excepted—can be anyone else's. The exchange of roles between Didi and Gogo is symbolized by the furious exchange of hats (46r–v).[10] Names themselves are subversive of identity. "Pozzo" becomes Bozzo, Gozzo, Godot; "Godot" is Godin or Godet. Gogo proposes to "try" Pozzo with names (53v). In the end, all the protagonists become Everyman. Gogo reflects on the blind Pozzo that he is "all humanity," a statement that echoes Didi's "at this moment of time, all mankind is us" (54r, 51r).

This levelling process prepares us for the great "event" of Act II, Pozzo's downfall. He appears blind and helpless, led by Lucky. Lucky too is changed. He is still burdened "as before," but wears a different hat (49v). He has also lost the power of speech, a power which, it will be recalled, he exercised only at Pozzo's bidding. Both master and slave have suffered disablements, though Pozzo's appears the more serious one. Yet Pozzo is still the master, and Lucky still responds to the single command he gives him: "On!"

We are left with few clues to account for this transformation. Pozzo himself shakes off all inquiry:

> POZZO: When! When! One day, is that not enough for you, one day he went dumb, one day I went blind, one day we'll go deaf, one day we were born, one day we shall die, the same day, the same second, is that not enough for you? (57v)[11]

Pozzo's repudiation of time signifies the collapse of the commonwealth, of the socially ordered sequence of *chronos*, of hierarchy and meaning. He is "all humanity," a blind wanderer-king like Lear or Oedipus, helpless and stricken, yet greater naked than in his shabby pomp. Gogo sees only the fallen despot, but for Didi, and for us, the nature of that fall is critical:

> VLADIMIR: You were bringing him to the fair to sell him. You spoke to us. He danced. He thought. You had your sight. (57r)

The answers that Pozzo cannot or will not give are locked up between him and the now forever mute Lucky. They cannot lie anywhere else. Lucky, as Act I demonstrates, is not merely passive; he surprises Pozzo by refusing to claim his bones, is dilatory in his response to commands, and kicks Gogo in the shins (21v). Pozzo reveals that he once refused an order—in the Hobbesian state, the equivalent of lèse-majesté—but when Didi questions him about it, he receives no answer (26v, 27r). Has a far greater, a fatal act of disobedience occurred? It may be noted that Pozzo, while repudiating time, nonetheless places Lucky's "loss" of speech before his own loss of sight. Gogo, inspecting the fallen pair, addresses Pozzo as "Abel" and Lucky as "Cain" (53v). Beckett is not idle in his choice of names; Lucky has been designated as the slayer, if not of Pozzo the man, then of that artificial person and social hero, the sovereign. Yet rebellion has not severed the bond between master and man, only rendered it inefficacious. Lucky, who is free to abandon his blind master, does not do so; nor does Pozzo, though helpless, forsake command. Unlike Didi and Gogo, who can exchange roles at will, they are chained to one another until death. Rebellion cannot liberate either one, but only circumscribe them both more closely; for those who have taken up the burden of society, there is no return to the state of nature.

The second act of the play takes place in a subtly but profoundly altered environment, symbolized by the flowering of the bare tree. Vivian Mercier has noted Beckett's predilection for the dialectic of paired opposites.[12] This is a perfect description of the four protagonists of *Waiting for Godot*, but it is also a description of the play's general structure. Act II is a dialectical opposite of Act I, in which the "same thing" happens— the tramps wait for Godot, are interrupted by Pozzo and Lucky, and wait again—but in a different key. The same kind of parallel structure occurs in *Leviathan*, and to much the same effect. In the first part of Hobbes's treatise, man is described in purely secular terms as a creature of interest, and the commonwealth as an artifact necessitated by the clash of that interest. In the second part, human institutions are seen under the aspect of a divine dispensation, and the commonwealth is validated by the lordship of God over the Jews and the legitimation of secular authority by Christ. In homiletic terms, the first part of *Leviathan* is a description of the *chronos*, the ordinary sequential time in which the events of the secular order take place, and the second of the *kairos*, those moments of divine intervention which transform the saeculum and form the basis of millenial expectation, in a word of hope.

Waiting for Godot also takes place in two frames of temporal reference. In Act I, the clock time of the *chronos* predominates, in which the tramps wait for the secular savior, Godot, who is to arrive on "Saturday," and whose type is Pozzo. In this clock time, men may have (under the dispensation of the commonwealth) a rational expectation of contract, i.e., that appointments will be kept and promises met. This certitude is undermined by Gogo, who questions the date of the appointment (11r), cannot keep track of time, and "forgets" events, including the meeting with Godot itself, that he might be presumed to easily remember. Didi's faltering sense of *chronos* is however reinforced by Pozzo, who, with his schedule and his watch, might almost be Time personified.

In Act II, *chronos* breaks down. Beckett's stage direction for the act is that it takes place "next day." Didi anxiously seeks to confirm this, rehearsing what he takes to have been the events of the previous day: the encounter with Pozzo and Lucky, the wait for Godot, etc. But he cannot account for the sudden blossoming of the tree, and Pozzo, when he returns, cannot remember either their meeting or his own blinding (55v; 56v–57r). He is, in fact, no longer troubled by memory at all: "I don't remember having met anyone yesterday. But to-morrow I won't remember having met anyone to-day." Gogo says something similar: "That's the way I am. Either I forget immediately or I never forget" (39r). To forget nothing or everything is to live in a condition of perpetual simultaneity, acausal and ahistorical, and indeed Gogo declares, "I'm not a historian" (42r). Another day might as well be another life, and vice versa: when Didi asks Gogo where he thinks he spent the previous evening, he replies: "How would I know? In another compartment. There's no lack of void" (42v).

The reappearance of Pozzo, and specifically his denial of time, plays a crucial role in the breakdown of the *chronos*. At his return, he is once more taken for Godot, first by Didi and then by Gogo (47v, 50r). In a sense they are right; Pozzo *is* a Godot as he is defined in Act I, that is, as a Hobbesian sovereign. So might Didi or Gogo be as well if they wish it, a point Beckett underscores when Didi suggests to Gogo that they "play at" Pozzo and Lucky (47r). But if Pozzo's behavior in Act I shows what a Hobbesian sovereign can be like, his collapse in Act II demonstrates a more fatal defect: instability. The secular sovereign can no longer guarantee what, in the French version of the play, Didi hopes to find with Godot: "Ce soir on couchera peut-être chez lui, au chaud, au sec, le ventre plein, sur la paille": a bed of warm, dry straw and a full belly.[13] The wait for Godot then becomes an eschatological one, like the wait upon the Christian redeemer in the Hobbesian commonwealth itself. But in Beckett, unlike Hobbes (who was in his own time accused of atheism), there is no real expectation of the *kairos*, no hope of Providence. If in the last analysis Godot is to be taken as the substance of things hoped for, then he will not come.[14]

At one point, Didi attempts to comfort himself with the reflection that "We have kept our appointment and that's an end to that" (51v). It is by no means clear however that there has ever been an appointment, either in the secular or the eschatological sense. Didi affirms it, Gogo "forgets" it, and Beckett, with a neutrality more devastating than any overt skepticism, refuses to choose between them. In the end, they decide to hang themselves from the tree whose blossoming had once offered, if nothing else, at least hope of change. But Beckett is not to be denied his last joke. The tree he has planted is not the sturdy fig of Judas, but a willow that will bear no weight, like the rotten cord of Gogo's trousers. Deliverance in every sense is forever just out of reach. Like the hero of Beckett's *The Unnamable*, whose last words echo the last words and action of *Godot*, the tramps are left finally with the paralyzing equality of all choices, a world in which, because all things are possible, nothing is.

Notes

1. See, for example, Richard Coe, *Samuel Beckett* (New York: Grove Press, 1964); Michael Robinson, *The Long Sonata of the Dead* (New York: Grove Press, 1969); and Hugh Kenner, "The Cartesian Centaur," in Martin Esslin, ed., *Samuel Beckett: A Collection of Critical Essays* (Englewood Cliffs, N.J.: Prentice-Hall, 1965), 52–61.

2. The neglect of Hobbes as a possible influence on Beckett is puzzling, since Hobbes himself was one of the early disciples of Descartes's materialism, and there have been few major Western philosophers who have not been mentioned in connection with Beckett at one time or another (see the brief and only partial overview in Ruby Cohn's "Philosophical Fragments in the Works of Samuel Beckett," in Esslin, *op. cit.*, 169–77). Darko Suvin comes closest to perceiving the link from a Marxist perspective in his "Preparing for Godot—or the Purgatory of Individualism" (in Ruby Cohn, ed., *Casebook on Waiting for Godot* [New York: Grove Press, 1967], 121–32), where, commenting on the relationship between Cartesian thought and bourgeois rationalism, he remarks, "When Man is a Hobbesian wolf to Man, the realistic result is a ruthless defense of the Self and a denial of human solidarity. . . . The dehumanized Leviathans of economics, society, State, correspond to a reified Man" (p. 127).

But Suvin uses Hobbes only as a metaphor; he never cites him by name. Cf. C. B. Macpherson, *The Political Theory of Possessive Individualism* (Oxford: Oxford University Press, 1962), on the links between Hobbes and the development of political and economic liberalism. There is no attempt here to argue against any of the other interpretations advanced about Beckett, whose project in fact engages the whole of Western philosophy and whose work is consequently as overdetermined as any in modern literature, but simply to point out structural and thematic congruities between *Godot* and *Leviathan* that cannot, I believe, be viewed as merely coincidental.

3. All internal page references are to Thomas Hobbes, *Leviathan* (New York, 1975, reprint of the Everyman Edition, London, 1914), and Samuel Beckett, *Waiting for Godot* (New York: Grove Press, 1977). *Leviathan* was first published in 1651.

4. Hobbes envisions a series of bilateral agreements between prospective subjects to acknowledge the same sovereign, "as if every man should say to every man, *I Authorise and give up my Right of Governing my selfe, to this Man, or to this Assembly of men, on this condition, that thou give up thy Right to him, and Authorise all his Actions in like manner*" (*Leviathan*, p. 89). Hobbes would not, obviously, have conceived of a commonwealth of two, since he was interested in describing the genesis of civil society, but his model—unlike that of even small utopian commonwealths such as those of Plato and Aristotle—is theoretically applicable on any scale. It was the genius of Beckett to recognize this, and to create the theatrical environment to realize it.

5. Among other things, *Waiting for Godot* must be regarded as one of the first major works of the postwar period to respond to the implications of a nuclear apocalypse. Unlike Orwell's *1984*, that response is indirect, but its pressure can be felt:

> ESTRAGON: The best thing would be to kill me, like the other.
> VLADIMIR: What other? . . .
> ESTRAGON: Like billions of others. (40r)

In one sense, the division between the pairs of protagonists may be taken as a distinction between the "real" situation created by the nuclear age, which makes all previous political calculations obsolete, and the illusion of normality kept up by Pozzo and Lucky. In any case, the historical context in which the play was written is part at least of the wasteland in which it takes place, and deserves more attention than it has received.

6. Beckett directs that this line be delivered "without anger." There can be in fact neither anger nor recrimination where there is no basis for obligation.

7. This view is most simplistically stated in Hélène L. Baldwin's *Samuel Beckett's Real Silence* (University Park: Pennsylvania State University Press, 1981): ". . . with our present knowledge of Beckett as an artist who relishes the metaphysical search, it appears that Godot is God" (p. 107). Alain Robbe-Grillet is even more straightforward: "Godot is God." But he goes on to add in the same breath that he is also "death," "silence," "the inaccessible self," etc., in short everything *but* a man (Esslin, p. 140).

8. For Hobbes's definition of "person," see *ibid.*, Chapter XVI. The sovereign is, in effect, he whose words and actions are deemed to represent the collective "person" of the commonwealth, united in (and only by) him.

9. The talk of "rights" makes the reference to contract theory plain, and the anachronism of Didi's gibe at Gogo, "Your Worship wishes to assert his prerogatives?" underlines the seventeenth-century context. "Prerogative," in pre-Hobbesian political thought, meant specifically that portion of royal authority exercised at discretion. See Francis D. Wormuth, *The Royal Prerogative 1603–1649* (Ithaca: Cornell University Press, 1949).

10. In Act I, all four protagonists "wear bowlers," a fact that implies both degraded hierarchy and the radical equality of the state of nature in which they find themselves vis-a-vis one another. Curiously, Beckett inserts this direction only midway into Act I (22v). The hat the tramps exchange is Lucky's, an action that presages Didi's suggestion that they "play at"

being Pozzo and Lucky. Lucky, when he reappears, wears "a different hat" (not a bowler?). Beckett's use of hats and boots in general requires more comment.

11. The end of this speech is the famous line, "They give birth astride of a grave, the light gleams an instant, then it's night once more." This Lear-like insight, usually considered out of context, can only be fully appreciated as the utterance of a fallen king.

12. In *Beckett / Beckett* (New York: Oxford University, Press, 1977).

13. Cited by Mercier, *ibid.*, p. 13.

14. Suvin finds grounds for at least guarded optimism in Beckett's refusal to specify Godot: "Godot is and is not God; consequently, the universe is and is not a closed one" (Esslin, p. 130). I wonder if that is not precisely the ground of Beckett's despair.

[Metaphor in *Endgame*]

David H. Hesla*

[Endgame] is difficult, but by no means impossible, provided that we respect its elliptical quality and its multifaceted character. Richard M. Eastman has pointed out how *Endgame* operates on several "planes of reality": the characters inhabit a kind of limbo; they are pieces in a chess game; and they are actors who call attention to the fact that they are only actors.[1] Ruby Cohn notes the several correspondences between the play and the Gospel of John and Revelation.[2] Hugh Kenner says of the opening moments of the work that this is "so plainly a metaphor for waking up that we fancy the stage, with its high peepholes, to be the inside of an immense skull."[3] There are still others. Instead of referring to these several facets of the play as "planes of reality," however, I should prefer to call them dramatized metaphors for human existence. We may briefly describe five of the most important of these metaphors.

The stage set represents a portion of the board on which the last stage (endgame) of a game of chess is being played. Hamm is king, Clov a more mobile piece (knight, perhaps—he sometimes inspected Hamm's paupers [pawns] "on horse"), and Nagg and Nell two enemy pieces which have been taken and put out of the action (their faces are "very white" whereas Hamm's and Clov's are "very red"). (Parenthetically, we may note the language of other games. "Deuce": existence is like that point in tennis where advantage is to neither player and the game is at a stalemate. "Discard. . . . A few more squirms like that and I'll call": existence is like a hand of poker—you can't know if you are a winner unless you take the chance ["I'll call"] that you are a loser.) The chess metaphor concludes the play, for Hamm "remains motionless" in the brief tableau at the end: having sacrificed every piece in his own defense—pain-killer, coffins, bicycle wheels—he is now in check.

Checkmate (from Arab., shāh mātah, "the king is dead") reminds us

*Reprinted from *The Shape of Chaos: An Interpretation of the Art of Samuel Beckett* (Minneapolis: University of Minnesota Press, 1971) by permission of the publisher.

of the second metaphor. The stage represents a throne room, Hamm a king, Clov a courtier (prince?). Kenner tentatively compares Hamm with Hamlet, Richard III ("My kingdom for a nightman"), and Richard II.[4] But Hamm is ruler over an empty and dying kingdom, his authority absolute and meaningless. He knows it, and quotes another king to show he knows it: "Our revels now are ended." The metaphor now attaches king to actor. The stage set represents a stage set, Hamm is a star actor, Clov has a supporting role. Existence—we have heard this before—is a game, like chess or tennis or poker, or like a play; and Hamm and Clov would agree with Jacques that

> All the world's a stage
> And all the men and women merely players:
> They have their exits and their entrances,
> And one man in his time plays many parts,
> His acts being seven ages. . . .[5]

The last of the seven scenes that Jacques describes is "second childishness"—when for example, one plays with toys again (Hamm: "Is my dog ready?")—and "mere oblivion, / Sans teeth, sans eyes, sans taste, sans everything." From this, Hamm's catalog of losses varies a little: "We lose our hair, our teeth! Our bloom! Our ideals!"

Prospero's speech too is apposite to the metaphor, but the last lines seem especially applicable to the world described by *Endgame*:

> the great globe itself,
> Yes, all which it inherit, shall dissolve
> And, like this insubstantial pageant faded,
> Leave not a rack behind.[6]

It would seem reasonable that of clouds too it must be said, "There are no more."

The human being who plays Hamm plays the role of a man who believes that to exist is to play a role, or several roles—one of which is that of storyteller. Hamm tells himself—and Nagg—the story of a man who once appeared to Hamm to beg a favor. Hamm is narrator, plays the role of the beggar, plays the role of Hamm. He drops his roles and says to himself that he will soon be done with this story unless he finds other characters.

> HAMM:. . . But where would I find them?
> (*Pause.*)
> Where would I look for them?
> (*Pause. He whistles. Enter Clov.*)
> Let us pray to God. (54)[7]

The stage set now represents the narrator-writer's study, his "scriptorium." Hamm is a writer, Clov a character created by the writer (Hamm to Clov:

"It was I was a father to you. . . . My house a home for you"), Nagg and Nell characters who once were alive for the writer but now are useless, manuscripts chucked into the wastebasket. Time was when the writer had only to whistle and out would pop a character ready to "play." Malone, in the trilogy, suffered the same decline of powers. "All went well at first, they all came to me, pleased that someone should want to play with them. If I said, Now I need a hunchback, immediately one came running, proud as punch of his fine hunch that was going to perform. . . . But it was not long before I found myself alone, in the dark." . . . So it is with Hamm. His "character," the man begging, is the last to be created in the imagination. He can whistle Clov out of the kitchen as he used to be able to whistle a character out of nowhere, but now "There are no more characters," or if there are, they will have to be supplied out of the grace of the Divine. Hence Hamm's behest, "Let us pray to God." Worse yet, even the one character who remains obedient to his master's every wish is now getting very tired of the "goings-on."

> CLOV: (*imploringly*) Let's stop playing!
> HAMM: Never!

The writer, we may recall, is bereft of everything but the "obligation to express." It is the act of ultimate desperation, then, when Hamm discards his gaff, for in *Endgame* as in *Malone Dies*, the gaff (equivalent to Malone's stick, later, his axe-pencil) is the author's instrument for expressing whatever he has left to express.

Already at the beginning of the work Clov-as-character displays the qualities of recalcitrance and uncooperativeness which will result in his being quite unavailable to Hamm-as-artist at the end of the work.

> HAMM: All right, be off.
> (*He leans back in his chair, remains motionless. Clov does not move, heaves a great groaning sigh. Hamm sits up.*)
> I thought I told you to be off.
> CLOV: I'm trying.
> (*He goes to door, halts.*)
> Ever since I was whelped.
> (*Exit Clov.*) (14)

But in this multifaceted work, Character is to Author as Body is to Mind, and Clov carries out his master's orders with all the verve and dispatch we have been led to expect from bifurcated Cartesian man. And now the stage set represents, as Kenner suggests, the interior of a skull, Hamm being unextended thinking substance, Clov the Body-Sensory apparatus which is extended and unthinking. Hamm knows of the "without" (the term used in *Murphy* to apply to extramental reality) only what Clov tells him; Clov, as Body, can initiate no action on his own but can only obey his master. Neither can exist without the other, but neither one can abide the other.

HAMM: . . . Why do you stay with me?

CLOV: Why do you keep me?

HAMM: There's no one else.

CLOV: There's nowhere else.
(*Pause.*)

HAMM: You're leaving me all the same.

CLOV: I'm trying.

HAMM: You don't love me.

CLOV: No. (6)

Despite his pretensions to casualness, Hamm is very concerned about his location in the room. His chair must be placed ever so carefully ("Put me right in the center! . . . Bang in the center!"). The maneuver is a delicate one ("I feel a little too far to the left . . . to the right . . . a little too far forward . . . too far back . . .") since Hamm must be located such that "the animal spirits in its [the brain's] anterior cavities have communication with those in the posterior, . . ." and so on. Hamm's seat is the pineal gland, the mediator in Descartes' system between mind and body; and the fact that Hamm is paralyzed from the waist down is symptomatic of advanced atrophy of the conarium. The fate suffered by Murphy is close at hand, for Hamm.

At least these five metaphors are to be discerned in the structure of *Endgame*. The stage set represents a chess board in the last moments of play, the throne room of a dying king, a stage set on which the last scene of a drama is being enacted, the study of a writer who no longer is able to create, and the interior of the skull of a man who is dying of dichotomy. Moreover, Ruby Cohn is surely correct in urging that the stage also represents a Golgotha; and we may perhaps also see in it a prison and a man condemned to die in a gas chamber or an electric chair.[8]

It takes nothing more than a recitation of these metaphorical dimensions of the play to indicate their common theme. The world is coming to an end: ". . . time is over, reckoning closed and story ended." Time is over for kings and actors and writers and all who play the game of human existence. It is the end of the Self whose body and mind we may have seen continually abrading each other. It is the end of the World which lies on the other side of those hollow bricks which represent Skull. The final tableau ends in stillness and motionlessness. Nagg and Nell are locked in their ashbins, Clov has stood through the last minutes "impassive and motionless," Hamm's last act is to lower his arms to the armrests of the wheelchair, whereafter he "remains motionless." Clov's dream has come true.

HAMM: . . . What are you doing?

CLOV: Putting things in order.

(*He straightens up. Fervently.*)
I'm going to clear everything away!
(*He starts picking up again.*)

HAMM: Order!

CLOV: (*straightening up*). I love order. It's my dream. A world where all would be silent and still and each thing in its last place, under the last dust. (57)

The final tableau shows exactly this—each thing in its last place. To the long list of things of which there are no more, we add the two last: there is no more speech; there is no more motion. It is the condition of maximum entropy.

I realize, of course, that I have just used "entropy" as a synonym of "order," whereas in fact the term ought to be used of its opposite, "disorder" or "randomness." But in connection with Clov's speech it makes sense to use the term in this way, for by "order" Clov means the disposition of things in such a way that they will not interact with one another. This, roughly, is what entropy means as well, for entropy is the unavailability of energy for work. Anatol Rapoport supplies a clear example.

> For instance, if we have two bodies at different temperatures, we can rig up a heat engine between them. . . . But if the bodies are left alone, say in contact with each other, eventually the hotter one will cool off and the cooler one warm up, and they will settle down to the same temperature. Then no heat engine can be rigged up between them because a heat engine must work between two temperatures. No heat has disappeared; it was only redistributed. But now no heat is available for doing work, because of this distribution. The physicist says, "The entropy of the system has increased. . . ."[9]

In a heat engine (automobile engine, steam locomotive engine) a fuel—gasoline, diesel oil, coal—is converted into heat in the form of a gas or steam which expands and drives a piston which turns a wheel. In a perfect engine, the amount of work done is equal to the amount of energy expended, in accordance with the First Law of Thermodynamics (the conservation of energy). But the Second Law of Thermodynamics qualifies this by saying that in any such system a certain amount of energy is "degraded," made unavailable for work. This energy is not lost or destroyed; it is simply shunted off, useless. The cosmological implication is obvious. The universe itself is an energy system, and in the course of time will gradually have less and less "useful energy" available to do work. Entropy—energy unavailable for work—will increase, and the universe itself will finally "run down."

Moreover, the process whereby entropy increases in any given energy system is a process that is unidirectional and irreversible. As Rudolph Clausius put it in one of the early formulations of the Second Law of Thermodynamics, "Heat cannot, of itself, pass from a colder to a hotter body." The only "direction" is from hot to cold, from energy to work. The cold body cannot pass whatever little heat it retains to the hot body. (If it could, a "perpetual motion" machine could be constructed.) Hence, time's arrow is pointed at the bullseye of cosmic stasis. History is running downhill to the point where the original impetus peters out and everything takes its last place under the last dust. The universe itself will eventually come to its rest, its own *apatheia*, its own peace.

Man too is an energy system, fueled by the food he eats, converting this to work, doomed eventually to the condition of maximum entropy called death. So is a society a heat engine, for they are "hot" who command, and they are "cold" who obey. By his orders to Clov, Hamm "drives" him as steam drives a piston. Exactly the same holds for the relationship between Pozzo and Lucky. If we generalize, we may call it the "master-slave" relationship, where master is heat or energy, slave is cold or work. In good time, and with the increase of entropy, "master" will run down: Pozzo loses all his paraphernalia; Hamm loses the little enthusiasm or drive that he has left at the opening of the play. Again, the two units in a system, hot and cold, if left "touching" one another will gradually become the same temperature, colder than the "hot" unit, warmer than the "cold" unit, for the heat of the "hot" unit will "of itself" pass over into the "cold" unit. In terms of capacity for work, however, the system will have achieved a high degree of entropy, and will be wholly dead, wholly cold.

Nagg and Nell, of course, in their ashbins. Their faces are "very white," not simply because they are pieces in a chess game, but because they at one time composed an energy system which was a going concern, but is now dead, or nearly dead, their faces white and cold as ice. (Lucky's hair is white, too.) As befits energy systems which are younger, Hamm's face and Clov's face are "very red." They are still active, each after his fashion; though it is clear that the metaphor of the chess game here takes precedence of the metaphor drawn from thermodynamics, else their faces would be described rather as a fading pink in token of their subsidence of their late strengths.

Man, society, the universe itself are all heat engines, obedient to the laws of thermodynamics. But even the life of the spirit may be comprehended in this fashion. The heat of hope may cool to tepid doubt, and doubt may become the ice of despair. Courage may decline to policy, and this to cowardice and fear. Love may become toleration, then hatred. In all other realms this decline is irreversible. Is it possible that in the realm of the spirit it is *not* irreversible? Is it possible that the source of a man's spiritual energy can be renewed? Perhaps so. It is just possible, it is barely but really conceivable, that when the heat of life in a man is dying, it may be restored to him.

HAMM: . . . Give me a rug, I'm freezing.

CLOV: There are no more rugs.
(*Pause.*)

HAMM: Kiss me.
(*Pause.*)
Will you not kiss me?

CLOV: No.

HAMM: On the forehead.

CLOV: I won't kiss you anywhere.
(*Pause.*)

HAMM: (*holding out his hand*). Give me your hand at least.
(*Pause.*)
Will you not give me your hand?

CLOV: I won't touch you. (67)

Significantly, Hamm asks first for a rug, in the expectation that he will be able to insulate himself and prevent what warmth he has from escaping. Only after he learns that there are no more rugs does this thermodynamical solipsist turn to his fellow man to be "recharged," as it were, with the warmth of human compassion—and then it is an act of the utmost selfishness. Equally selfish, Clov denies Hamm even this one gesture of friendship.

So it is natural that only a few lines later Hamm should speak in direct address to the audience which is attending the death-by-freezing of this actor-king-author-energy system: "Get out of here and love one another! Lick your neighbor as yourself!" It is the proclamation of one who has learned too late that the decline of the world of men into a frozen wasteland of the spirit can be restrained only if man will reach out to touch the hand of his neighbor—if, indeed, he will permit himself the sympathy which dogs show to one another when they lick one another's wounds.

So in *All That Fall*:

MISS FITT: Is it my arm you want then [as support in climbing stairs]? (*Pause. Impatiently.*) Is it my arm you want, Mrs. Rooney, or what is it?

MRS. ROONEY: (*exploding*). Your arm! Any arm! A helping hand! For five seconds! Christ, what a planet!

....

MISS FITT: (resignedly). Well, I suppose it is the Protestant thing to do.

MRS. ROONEY: Pismires do it for one another. (*Pause.*) I have seen slugs do it.

Halfway through the play, Hamm prophesies to Clov—though coming from the mouth of the one who takes obvious delight in the story about the man who came pleading on behalf of his starving son, Hamm's prophecy is intolerably hypocritical; but even hypocrites can speak the truth: "Infinite emptiness will be all around you, all the resurrected dead of all the ages wouldn't fill it, and there you'll be like a little bit of grit in the middle of the steppe. (*Pause.*) Yes, one day you'll know what it is, you'll be like me, except that you won't have anyone with you, because you won't have had pity on anyone and because there won't be anyone left to have pity on" (36). It is an accurate picture of the man who in lovelessness and pitilessness has isolated himself from those sources of spiritual heat and energy and life which are available to him in the relationship of compassion between one man and another. Martin Buber once wrote: "A newly-created concrete reality has been laid in our arms; we answer for it. A dog has looked at you, you answer for its glance, a child has clutched your hand, you answer for its touch, a host of men moves about you, you answer for their need. . . ."[10] You either answer for it, in love and pity and respect, or you end up a "little bit of grit in the middle of the steppe," remembering and forgetting and forgotten in an ashcan, dying from the unavailability of life, alone on a planet as cold and white and silent as the moon.

Notes

1. Richard M. Eastman, "The Strategy of Samuel Beckett's *Endgame*," *Modern Drama* 2 (May 1959):36–44.
2. Ruby Cohn, *Samuel Beckett: The Comic Gamut* (New Brunswick, NJ: Rutgers University Press, 1962), pp. 226–42.
3. Hugh Kenner, *Samuel Beckett: A Critical Study* (New York: Grove Press, 1961), p. 155.
4. Kenner, p. 160.
5. *As You Like It*, II.vii.139–43.
6. *The Tempest*, IV.i.153–56.
7. Page references for *Endgame* (New York: Grove Press, 1958) are included in the text.
8. Cohn, p. 239.
9. Anatol Rapoport, *Operational Philosophy: Integrating Knowledge and Power* (New York: Harper and Brothers, 1954), p. 181.
10. Martin Buber, *Between Man and Man* (Boston: Beacon Press, 1961), p. 17.

Chess with the Audience: Samuel Beckett's *Endgame*

James Acheson*

In *Samuel Beckett: a Biography*, Deirdre Bair reveals that, shortly after he had completed the original French version of *Endgame* (*Fin de Partie*) in 1957, Beckett mentioned the play to friends and corrected them when they translated the title as "End of the Game." "No," she quotes him as emphasising, "[it] is *Endgame*, as in chess."[1]

This comment of Beckett's, unknown to most critics until recently, serves as retrospective justification for the many articles and book chapters written in the past twenty years claiming that *Endgame* is, in effect, the last part of an on-stage game of chess. In general, their authors agree that Hamm should be viewed as a king threatened by checkmate, Clov as a knight, and Nagg and Nell as either rooks or pawns. Disagreement arises only over the identity of the side seeking to checkmate Hamm. On the basis that Hamm and Clov have "*very red*" (*E*, pp. 11, 12)[2] faces, while Nagg's and Nell's are "*very white*" (*E*, pp. 15, 18), David Hesla argues that the latter are "two enemy pieces which have been taken and put out of the action."[3] But Francis Doherty reminds us that red and white are the same side in chess,[4] and thereby implies that Hamm, Clov, Nagg and Nell have a common opponent—a traditionally black opponent—in death.

It is certainly true that *one* of the play's chess games takes place between the ostensibly mortal characters on the one hand and the immortal universe on the other. But while this game is being played, another is also in progress—a game in which Beckett pits his four red- or white-faced characters against the darkened faces of the theatre audience. The second game's purpose is to frustrate our attempts to interpret *Endgame* definitively; checkmate occurs when we recognise that the play is deliberately designed to resist even the most ingenious of explications.

Throughout this game, Beckett as White is on the offensive, and thus requires us to develop defences against his attack. The most obvious defence is to assume that *Endgame* is essentially naturalistic—that it presents us with ostensibly real people enacting a real-life situation. Initially, the action might seem to take place in a bomb shelter in the aftermath of a nuclear war. Yet there is no *explicit* evidence that this is the situation the play presents; moreover, comments in the dialogue to the effect that there is "no more nature" (*E*, p. 16), that there are "no more tide[s]" (*E*, p. 17) suggest that a disaster of a quite different kind has taken place. Ruby Cohn has pointed out that in earlier drafts of *Endgame*, Beckett makes repeated references to the Flood, and even has Clov read out a passage from Genesis.[5] But our sense that the play dramatises some

*Reprinted from *Critical Quarterly* 22, no. 2 (Summer 1980) by permission of the author.

latter-day judgement on man is undermined by the prayer scene in the final version, where God is said to be a "bastard" who "doesn't exist" (*E*, p. 38).

Moreover, if *Endgame* is meant to be a condemnation of the wickedness of our times, its effect is diffuse. "Why," F.N. Lees has asked, "is it at Sedan that Hamm's parents lost their legs?—Sedan where the 'Second Empire' ended? Is it only a freak that Napoleon III was a prisoner at Ham? . . . [Is] there a clue here to a political face to the paradigm?"[6] Lees is right to advance these suggestions as rhetorical questions, rather than as dogmatic statements, because the name "Sedan," for example, raises as many interpretive problems as it solves. Sedan was indeed the place where the Second Empire ended; yet it was also the site of a major battle at the beginning of the Second World War.[7] If, as audience, we begin to suppose that *Endgame* is a condemnation of life in nineteenth- or twentieth-century France, we must, in addition, contend with the fact that "Clov" is a possible reference to Clovis, the famous early medieval king of Gaul. The allusion expands in significance when we remember that the royal name "Clovis" was eventually softened to "Louis":[8] *Endgame* now seems more probably a comment on French history generally, than on France of the last hundred years. On the other hand, there is no definitive evidence that the play is either set in France or exclusively about that country: Sedan is mentioned, but so are Kov (*E*, p. 36; a possible reference to Kovno, Lithuania), and Lake Como (*E*, p. 21), which is in Italy.

Beckett is vague not only about the setting of *Endgame* but about the identity and relationships of its characters. Their names (all first names, apparently) suggest a bewildering array of nationalities in a family in which it is clear that Nagg and Nell are Hamm's parents, but only implied that Clov is Hamm's adoptive son. We learn next to nothing about the characters' past—about their occupations and living conditions prior to entering the shelter—and are never quite certain about the factors that motivate their behaviour. Why Clov continues to serve Hamm, for example, is a question the play never answers definitively. One explanation seems to be that Hamm is the only character who knows the combination to the food cupboard, and that he retains Clov's loyalty by threatening him with starvation. Yet Hamm is blind: Beckett perplexes us with the question of how it is possible for a blind man to operate a combination lock.[9] Moreover, we are told time and again that things are running out, the implication being that all four characters are living in any case on a starvation diet. Why, then, does Clov stay? Where does he get the energy to climb up and down ladders, and to push Hamm around the stage? Why do he and the other characters not show more signs of increasing physical decrepitude?

All these questions and more would be answered by a conventional naturalist in order to create and maintain an illusion of reality. It is, however, part of Beckett's strategy in his chess game against the audience that they be left unanswered. Beckett not only fails to create an illusion of reality through his vagueness about details; he undermines, in Brechtian fashion, whatever illusion the play might fortuitously create, by insisting on *Endgame* as theatre. Thus, in answer to Clov's repeated question, "What is there to keep me here?", Hamm at one point says, "The dialogue" (*E*, p. 39); elsewhere, he speaks of delivering both "an aside" and his "last soliloquy" (*E*, p. 49). These insistent disruptions of our suspension of disbelief are not just playful bits of comedy; they are deliberately included to make us abandon our attempts to interpret *Endgame* naturalistically.

An alternative defence to Beckett's attack is the symbolic, or allegorical. Given the episode in which Hamm lays a hand on the wall of the shelter and says, "Old wall! (*Pause.*) Beyond is the . . . other hell" (*E*, p. 23), we might suppose that *Endgame* is mean to depict a timeless, punitive afterlife. Our sense of this is reinforced by Clov's comment that the time is always the same—"Zero" (*E*, p. 13)—suggesting that the shelter is a place where time stands still. For Nagg and Nell, significantly, "yesterday" is a meaningless term: it applies not to any previous day in the shelter, but to a life they remember living much earlier. Moreover, Clov's comment that "something is taking its course" (*E*, p. 17) suggests that all four characters are being punished like Sisyphus, in having to play the "endgame" endlessly.

In another depiction of hell, Dante's *Inferno*, a work Beckett is known to admire, many of the sufferers are people who lived with Dante in Florence. *Endgame*'s characters, on the other hand, seem all to derive from earlier works of literature. Hamm has often been said to be based on the Ham of Genesis, Noah's son; yet he also recalls the Ham of *David Copperfield*, just as old Mother Pegg recalls Peggotty. Nell, too, may be Dickensian: her apparent death in the play calls to mind the famous death of Little Nell in *The Old Curiosity Shop*. Dickens and the Bible are not Beckett's only sources, however. Hamm reminds us also of Hamlet, and Hamm and Clov of Proust's Charlus and Jupien, respectively.[10] In addition, the name "Hamm" may, as various critics have said, be a shortened form of "hammer," where the other characters are nails.[11]

Obviously, all these possibilities lead in different symbolic directions. If Hamm is a hammer and the others are nails, *Endgame* would seem to be making the same point as Sartre's *Huis Clos*: that hell is other people. But if Hamm is the Ham of Genesis, the play is, arguably, about God's (or, in His absence, Beckett's) displeasure at the existence of filial impiety; or, if he is Dickens's Ham, displeasure with Victorian sentimentality. Alternatively, if Hamm is based on Charlus and Clov on Jupien, the play could be a condemnation of homosexuality; and if Hamm reminds us of Hamlet, a condemnation of vacillation. *Endgame* might also be regarded, however, as an expression of Beckett's sympathy for human weakness—as a comment that life is hell for homosexuals, for the naive and sentimental, and for those who procrastinate or feel contempt for their fathers. Frustrated by this surfeit of symbolic possibility, we are obliged to concede that, like the naturalistic, the symbolic defence against Beckett's attack is unsatisfactory.

The next defence that suggests itself, the expressionistic, is based on the assumption that the set of *Endgame* is a reflection not of the world at large, but of the interior of a skull. The play's allusions again suggest a number of different interpretive possibilities. David Hesla and Ross Chambers, for example, find in Hamm's desire to be at the centre of the skull-like set evidence for a Cartesian interpretation:[12] Hamm, says Hesla, is meant to be "unextended thinking substance, [and] Clov the Body-Sensory apparatus which is extended and unthinking."[13] Similarly, Martin Esslin suggests that *Endgame* may allude as a whole to Evreinov's *Theatre of the Soul*, in which, as in Beckett's play, one of the characters represents the rational half of a personality, and the other the emotional.[14] Colin Duckworth sees in the play's relationship to the story of the Flood the possibility of a Jungian interpretation: Jung, he reminds us, considers Noah's ark to be "a kind of giant uterus." Hamm, having attained in his womb-like rotunda something resembling the timeless peace of the embyonic existence, refuses to be reborn, to go out."[15] Like G.C. Barnard before him, Duckworth regards Hamm and Clov as two halves of a schizophrenic personality.[16]

Each of these expressionistic interpretations can be faulted on points of detail[17]—the one fault they all have in common being that they do not take sufficient account of Nagg and Nell. Much more satisfactory (from this point of view) than any other expressionistic interpretation advanced so far is one no critic has yet attempted: an interpretation based on the observation that *Endgame* alludes extensively to Freud's essay, "The Ego and the Id" (1923).[18]

In his essay, Freud posits the existence of three mental components—the ego, the id and the super-ego—and attempts a diagrammatic representation of the mind. The diagram is important, because it bears an uncanny resemblance to the set of *Endgame*, as seen from above.[19] It is a rounded figure with a small box on its circumference in exactly the position of Clov's kitchen, marked "Acoust.," with an area next to it, in the same position as the windows, designated "Pcpt.-Cs." By "Pcpt.-Cs.," Freud means the part of the mind that deals with the immediate experience of sense-data—with the data afforded by four of our senses, including our sense of sight. This is significant, since the two windows have often been interpreted expressionistically as eyes. The mind's experience of auditory data is for Freud a thing apart: he gives special emphasis to our assimilation of the aural on the grounds that it is the means by which we learn language. It is appropriate, then, that "Acoust."—the part of the mind that deals with aural data—appears in the place occupied by Clov's kitchen, since Clov often reminds us that he has learned to use language from listening to Hamm.[20]

Clov himself can be identified with the ego, the part of the mind which orders our conscious thoughts. Significantly, Clov "love[s] order" (*E*, p. 39), and is responsible for the storage and dispensation of supplies. Hamm in turn can be identified with the id, which, in contrast to the ego, is not an ordered and ordering mental constituent, but is instead a welter of passions, instincts and repressed memories. Just as Hamm is blind, and often acts cruelly and thoughtlessly, so the id blindly strives to satisfy its desires; in itself, it is completely without conscience. Freud tells us, however, that "in its relation to the id, [the ego] is like a man on horseback, who has to hold in check the superior strength of the horse; with this difference, that the rider tries to do so with his own strength while the ego uses borrowed forces. The analogy may be carried a little further. Often a rider, if he is not to be parted from his horse, is obliged to guide it where it wants to go; so in the same way the ego is in the habit of transforming the id's will into action as if it were its own" (*EI*, p. 25). Significantly, Clov has sometimes inspected Hamm's paupers on horseback, and is often also seen transforming Hamm's will into action to suit his own purposes. A good example occurs in the exchange following Hamm's narration of his chronicle where he apparently bullies Clov into commenting on it:

> HAMM: I've got on with my story . . . (*Pause. Irritably*). Ask me where I've got to.
>
> CLOV: Oh, by the way, your story?
>
> HAMM: (*surprised*). What story?
>
> CLOV: The one you've been telling yourself all your . . . days.
>
> HAMM: Ah you mean my chronicle?
>
> CLOV: That's the one.
> *Pause.*
>
> HAMM: (*angrily*). Keep going, can't you, keep going! (*E*, pp. 39–40)

When only a few moments later, the conversation begins to flag, Clov uses the same words as Hamm has in order to revive it: "Keep going, can't you, keep going!" (*E*, p. 41). It is evident from this that Clov has allowed himself to be bullied into conversation originally because he prefers conversation to silence; he is anxious for Hamm to continue, despite his apparent initial unwillingness to speak. What at first sight appears to be bullying on Hamm's part is in fact, then, manipulation on Clov's: it is a matter of the ego's using the techniques of an intelligent rider to control a difficult horse.

When Freud says that the ego uses "borrowed forces" to control the id, he means that it makes use of the prohibitions of the super-ego, or conscience, to re-direct the id's energies. The super-ego, represented in *Endgame* by Nagg and Nell, is a constituent of the mind which arises out of the male child's early Oedipus complex—his infant erotic desire for his mother and jealous hatred of his father.[21] While harbouring these feelings toward his parents, the child at the same time identifies with each: with his mother, as the object of his father's affections; and with his father as his mother's lover. Consolidation of the child's masculine characteristics requires that the Oedipus complex be quashed. The boy must accordingly take some of his father's authority into himself: out of his father's prohibitions—"you must not do this or that"—arises the super-ego, a mental component that takes on the character of his father, and contributes to the boy's developing masculinity. Yet the super-ego also takes on, to a lesser extent, the authority of the mother, so that both parents influence the formation of the boy's conscience.

The fact that the super-ego derives from parental authority—and especially paternal authority—is the evidence for suggesting that Nagg and Nell represent the conscience in Freudian terms. The fact that Nagg is the more dominant of the two indicates that *Endgame* is concerned with the interior of a *masculine* mind. Moreover, it is arguable that Nagg and Nell appear in dustbins because they are authority figures Hamm no longer respects. As Freud tells us, the "course of childhood development leads to an ever-increasing detachment from parents, and their personal significance for the super-ego recedes into the background,"[22] to be replaced by the influence of teachers, self-chosen heroes, and so on.

It would be possible to elaborate further this Freudian reading of *Endgame*. Yet no amount of additional detail would disguise the fact that it embodies a number of shortcomings, some being the shortcomings of expressionist readings in general. The first of these is that the identification of characters with the various components of mind is inexact and ultimately unsatisfactory. To some extent, Hamm resembles the id; yet his composition of a story, his abstract reflections on the meaning of existence, and his teaching of language to Clov are all inconsistent with the wholly unintellectual workings of the id. Similarly, though as ego Clov should theoretically embody, as Freud says, "reason and common sense" (*EI*, p. 25), he is often given to angry, uncontrolled outbursts of passion; he ends the play, tellingly, with a bitter indictment of friendship, beauty and order. And, while in Freudian terms, Nagg and Nell ought to serve as Hamm's conscience, that role is more often assumed by Clov—as for example, in the following passage:

> Clov: (*harshly*). When old Mother Pegg asked you for oil for her lamp and you told her to get out to hell, you knew what was happening then, no?
> (*Pause*).

You know what she died of, Mother Pegg? Of darkness.

HAMM: (*feebly*). I hadn't any. (*E*, p. 48).

Here there are two inconsistencies with Freudian theory: not only does Clov act as conscience, independently of Nagg and Nell, but Hamm is seen to feel guilty—unlike the id, which is completely amoral, and merely redirects the discharge of its energies when subject to the super-ego's prohibitions.

One important difficulty with expressionistic interpretations of *Endgame* is that of trying to find a psychological theory to fit the play exactly. A Freudian interpretation, though attractive at first sight, does not hold up under scrutiny; nor do the Jungian or Cartesian interpretations other critics have offered. Another difficulty is that of finding mental equivalents for the various on-stage props: critics are quick to identify the *characters* with various elements of the mind, but neglect to assign expressionistic significance to the biscuits, wheel-chair, rat, flea and flea-powder that also appear in the play. It could be argued, of course, that these items are meant to be memories of an earlier life; but there are other problems as well. For example: if Hamm and Clov are meant to be two of the constituents of a mind, what significance are Hamm's confinement to a wheel-chair and Clov's limp meant to have? Or again: if *Endgame* is not altogether expressionistic, but is instead meant to portray two naturalistic characters, Hamm and Clov, and their shared projection of mind—Nagg and Nell—why is it that Hamm and Clov have this projection in common? Why should it be the case, in other words, that they suffer from exactly the same sort of madness?

Human ingenuity being what it is, answers to each of these questions can probably be found.[23] Beckett, however, pre-empts our critical efforts in one of Hamm's speeches. "Imagine," says Hamm, "if a rational being came back to earth, wouldn't he be liable to get ideas into his head if he observed us long enough. (*Voice of a rational being*). 'Ah, good, now I see what it is, yes, now I understand what they're at' " (*E*, p. 27). Here we are being teased: *Endgame* is clearly too complex to yield either to a straightforward naturalistic, expressionistic or symbolic interpretation on the one hand, or to some combination of such interpretations on the other. Its range of allusions and interpretive possibilities is simply too vast. In no matter what direction we move as audience, we are in check.

But what is the underlying purpose behind a play of this kind? We may feel that Beckett simply wants to perplex us, as he does in his novel *Watt*, which, though full of symbolic suggestiveness, ends with the teasing comment, "no symbols where none intended."[24] Another, more interesting possibility has been suggested, however, by Robert Wilcher, who argues that in *Endgame*, Beckett's aim is to make us "feel the inadequacy of approaching reality by trying to impose systems upon the minute-by-minute flux of sense impressions."[25] Wilcher is essentially right; but his argument needs to be further developed, because it proceeds from an insufficiently detailed reading of an important passage in *Murphy*, Beckett's first novel; and because it presents *Endgame* as a paradigm of the world of sense-data, without admitting that it might also be a paradigm of the human mind.

The passage in *Murphy* to which Wilcher refers us occurs in the opening chapter, where Murphy bids Neary farewell:

> Neary came out of one of his deep sleeps and said:
> "Murphy, all life is figure and ground."
> "But a wandering to find home," said Murphy.
> "The face," said Neary, "or system of faces, against the big blooming buzzing confusions."[26]

Wilcher does not point out that Neary's comments derive from the work of two famous experimental psychologists, Edgar Rubin and William James. In *The Principles of Psychology*, James argues that we experience sense-data initially as a "great blooming, buzzing confusion";[27] Rubin holds that we organise the data by assigning a greater prominence to some, which we form into a perceptual whole known as "figure"; and a lesser importance to the rest, which we resolve into a secondary configuration, "ground."[28]

Experiments performed by Rubin's contemporaries reveal that the figure-ground distinction makes for a simplification of what is perceived. "Experienced perceptual wholes," the experimenters found, "tend toward the greatest regularity, simplicity, and clarity possible under the given conditions."[29] To perceive and interpret *Endgame* is to simplify it, inevitably. The play invites interpretation in response to its allusions; but these are so many and varied as to require us to give greater prominence to some than to others—to treat some as figure and others as ground. If Beckett's allusions to Freud or Jung or Descartes strike us especially forcibly, we will interpret *Endgame* expressionistically, and treat other possibilities as secondary. But if, on the other hand, his allusions to the Bible or nineteenth-century history or fiction seem more important, we will tend to assume that the play is concerned with the world at large. Neither kind of interpretation is, however, definitive: to move decisively in one direction or another is, as we have seen, to move into check.

Wilcher is right to suggest that *Endgame* is a comment on the "inadequacy of approaching reality by trying to impose systems upon the minute-by-minute flux of sense impressions." Since our every experience of sense-data is a simplification, our overall view of the world, which is based on a series of simplifications of sense-data, is of necessity a mere approximation to the world's infinite complexity. But the term "reality" includes more than Wilcher seems prepared to admit it: it includes our experience not only of the world at large, but of the world within—the world of our minds. Unlike the world at large, the mind is not available for perceptual investigation; theories about what it is like must therefore be based partly on the investigator's own experience of introspection, and partly on his observation of the behaviour and inner experience of other people. Obviously, both sources of information are unsatisfactory, because they are not as direct as perception, and because in the process of interpreting the information, the investigator is obliged to assign some of it the prominence of "figure," while treating other material as "ground." Every theory of the nature of the mind will therefore be as inadequate to describe it as the metaphysical systems that have been advanced to describe the complexities of the world at large.[30] Only an omniscient God can appreciate fully what the world and the mind are like: no human theory about either (or about the final meaning of *Endgame*) will suffice.

It is because mankind is less than omniscient that Beckett wins his chess game against the audience; and it is because the play's characters are (ostensibly) mortal that they are fated to lose their game against death. If they could be certain of the existence of God, there would be consolation for their awareness of the inevitability of defeat: their hopeless struggle could then be seen to be part of His inscrutable (but to the faithful, ultimately beneficent) plan. But Hamm and Nagg both cast God's existence seriously into doubt—Nagg by questioning the traditional argument from design in his story of the tailor's botched pair of trousers; and Hamm by posing to God's disadvantage the equally traditional problem of evil in his story of the unfeeling feudal lord who turns from his preparations for Christmas to deny help to a supplicant. In the absence of God, and in the context of eternity, man's life is meaningless. As Pozzo remarks in *Waiting for Godot*, "They give birth astride of a grave, the light gleams an instant, then it's night once more":[31] the individual life is a mere glimmer in the eternal dark. Yet Vladimir points out shortly afterwards that the traditional three score years and ten is, paradoxically, a very long time: "Astride of a grave and a difficult birth. Down in the hole, lingeringly, the grave-digger puts on the forceps. We have time to grow old. The air is full of our cries. (He listens). But habit is a great deadener."[32]

This comment finds a parallel in *Endgame* in Beckett's reference to the paradox of the millet seed—the paradox of "that old Greek" (*E*, p. 45), Eubulides of Miletus.[33] Just as, in the paradox, a heap of millet seed can never be formed, so, as Hamm says, it would seem impossible for the millions of moments in a lifetime to amount to anything significant. For the individual unable to accept that there is a God-given meaning to life, "life protracted" is indeed "protracted woe." What Vladimir means by saying that "habit is a great deadener" is partly that we each have a Proustian mechanism for coping with the harshness of the experience of sense-data;[34] and partly that establishing a routine—a series of habits—can serve as a palliative to our painful awareness that life is meaningless and death inevitable.

The structural circularity of *Endgame* suggests that the play as a whole is a routine endlessly repeated by the four characters in order to pass the time. It is part of the routine for Hamm and Nagg to tell their stories over and over again; and it is significant that in *his* story, Hamm identifies with the narrator / feudal overlord, who has the power of life and death over other people. This is consistent with Hamm's repeated attempts outside the story to elevate himself to the level of tragic hero in his many echoes of Shakespeare, and to the level of Christ in his echo of the Passion.[35] But Hamm's aspirations to godhead are futile: aware of the brevity and meaninglessness of life, and of the need to palliate what Beckett has called "the suffering of being,"[36] Hamm assumes throughout his chess game with death a thinly-veiled pretence of power. He is joined in the game by the other characters, who are also aware of being fated to lose; and who, in pretending to a power they lack, resist Hamm's attempts to dominate them.

Martin Esslin has said that "*Endgame* . . . has a very deep and direct impact, which can spring only from its touching a chord in the minds of a very large number of human beings."[37] Surely it is the case that *Endgame* touches two chords: a deeply-felt sense that the characters' impotence in the face of death—the certainty that they will lose their chess game—is something all of us share; and a sense, too, that the game Beckett plays against us is the game we play against the world and our minds all our lives long—and are, again, inevitably fated to lose.

Notes

1. Deirdre Bair, *Samuel Beckett: A Biography* (London, 1978), p. 467.

2. All quotations from *Endgame* are from the Faber and Faber edition (London, 1968). Page numbers are given in the text, preceded by the abbreviation *E*.

3. David Hesla, *The Shape of Chaos* (Minneapolis, 1971), p. 151.

4. Francis Doherty, *Samuel Beckett* (London, 1971), p. 93. In her biography, p. 484, Bair points out, significantly, that in his own productions of *Endgame*, Beckett has given all four characters white faces.

5. See Ruby Cohn, "The Beginning of *Endgame*," *Modern Drama*, IX (1966), 319–23.

6. F.N. Lees, "Samuel Beckett," *Memoirs and Proceedings of the Manchester Library and Philosophical Society*, CIV (1961–2), 8–9.

7. See Basil Collier, *A Short History of the Second World War* (London, 1967), pp. 137–9.

8. See C.W. Hollister, *Medieval Europe: A Short History* (New York, 1974), pp. 24–5.

9. Again, how is it possible for a blind man to know, as Hamm does, that his eyes have gone "all white?" (*E*, p. 13).

10. Michael Robinson provides a convenient summary of *Endgame*'s echoes of Shakespeare in *The Long Sonata of the Dead* (London, 1969), pp. 264–70. The play's echoes of *King Lear* and the fact that the ageing Hamm has a young male attendant in Clov put one in mind of Charlus and Jupien. See the narrator's description of Charlus in *A la recherche du temps perdu* (Paris, 1954), III, p. 859, where the baron is said to have suffered temporary blindness; and where, though almost childlike in his dependence on Jupien, he is described as having "la majesté shakespearienne d'un roi Lear."

11. The suggestion that "Nell" is a variant on the English "nail", Nagg on the German "Nagel", and "Clov" on the French "clou" has been made so often as to have become a critical commonplace.

12. See Ross Chambers, "An Approach to *Endgame*," in *Twentieth Century Interpretations of "Endgame,"* ed. Bell Gale Chevigny (Englewood Cliffs, N.J., 1969), pp. 72–3.

13. *The Shape of Chaos*, p. 154.

14. Martin Esslin, *The Theatre of the Absurd* (Harmondsworth, 1968), pp. 64–5. Esslin suggests that Hamm is the emotional half, and Clov the rational.

15. Colin Duckworth, *Angels of Darkness* (London, 1972), p. 89.

16. See G.C. Barnard, *Samuel Beckett: A New Approach* (London, 1971), pp. 101–9.

17. Hesla's assertion that Clov, as body, is, in Cartesian terms, extended and unthinking, is inconsistent with the fact that he both speaks and reasons in the play. Esslin admits that Beckett may never have read Evreinov's play, and points out in any case that equating Hamm with the emotional, and Clov with the rational half of a personality raises as many problems as it solves. Duckworth overlooks Hamm's suggestion that Clov build a raft so they can drift with the currents, "far away, to other . . . mammals" (*E*, p. 28). Though the suggestion is never acted upon, Hamm seems less averse to going out than Duckworth says he is. Nor is there any conclusive evidence to support the view that *Endgame* presents us with the interior of a schizophrenic mind. Clov's reports of what exists outside may be those of the "madman" Hamm describes, who thought "the end of the world had come" (*E*, p. 32); but it may just as easily be that Clov's reports are an accurate description of the outer world.

18. All quotations from this essay are taken from *The Standard Edition of the Complete Psychological Works of Sigmund Freud*, trans. James Strachey *et al.* (London, 1961), XIX, pp. 12–66. Page numbers will be given in the text, preceded by the abbreviation *EI*. G.C. Barnard's approach to *Endgame* in *Samuel Beckett: A New Approach*, though Freudian, is not based on this essay. In *Samuel Beckett*, p. 96, Francis Doherty says that we can, "if we wish, see the Freudian principles of Ego, Id and Super Ego at work" in *Endgame*; however, he does not develop this comment further.

19. See *EI*, p. 24.

20. See for example, *E*, p. 32, where Clov says to Hamm: "I use the words you taught me. If they don't mean anything more, teach me others."

21. See *EI*, pp. 28–39.

22. "The Economic Problem of Masochism" (1924), in *The Standard Edition of the Complete Psychological Works of Sigmund Freud*, trans. James Strachey *et al.* (London, 1961), XIX, p. 168.

23. Kenneth Tynan, for example, has suggested that Hamm's inability to stand and Clov's to sit exists because Beckett wants to indicate that, in Schopenhauerian terms, Hamm represents the will to live and Clov the intellect. (See Tynan's review of *Fin de Partie* in *The Observer*, 7 April 1957, p. 15; reprinted in *Samuel Beckett: The Critical Heritage*, ed. Lawrence Graver and Raymond Federman (London, 1979), pp. 164–6. Tynan's argument is based on a passage in which Schopenhauer says that the will is, metaphorically, "the strong blind man who carries on his shoulders the lame man who can see" (*The World as Will and Idea*, trans. R. B. Haldane and J. Kemp [London, 1948], II, p. 421).

24. Samuel Beckett, *Watt* (London, 1970), p. 255.

25. Robert Wilcher, " 'What's It Meant to Mean?': An Approach to Beckett's Theatre," *Critical Quarterly* XVIII (1976), 21.

26. Samuel Beckett, *Murphy* (London, 1970), p. 7.

27. William James, *The Principles of Psychology* (London, 1902), I, p. 488.

28. For a discussion of Rubin's work, see Robert I. Watson, *The Great Philosophers from Aristotle to Freud* (Philadelphia, 1968), p. 439.

29. Solomon E. Asch, "Gestalt Theory," in *The International Encyclopedia of Social Sciences* (London, 1968), VI, p. 168.

30. In "*Murphy's* Metaphysics," *Journal of Beckett Studies* V (1976), 9–23, I have argued that in *Murphy*, Beckett is at pains to demonstrate that the world is too complex to admit of description by any metaphysical system. He continues the demonstration tacitly in *Endgame*.

31. Samuel Beckett, *Waiting for Godot* (London, 1967), p. 89.

32. *Ibid.*, pp. 90–1.

33. In her biography, p. 465, Bair points out that it is Eubulides to whom Hamm refers, and not Zeno, who for years has been incorrectly identified by critics as "that old Greek." Eubulides' paradox is given in Diogenes Laertius' *Lives of Eminent Philosophers*, trans. R. D. Hicks (London, 1950), II, p. 191, as follows: "It cannot be that if two is a few, three is not so likewise, nor that if two or three are few, four is not so; and so on up to ten. But two is few, therefore so also is ten." Obviously, the paradox may be extended beyond ten to infinity: a heap of millet seed can never be formed because whatever the number of seeds, there will always be only a few.

34. For a fuller discussion of the Proustian concept of habit, see my article, "Beckett, Proust, and Schopenhauer," *Contemporary Literature*, XIX (1978), 165–79.

35. For Hamm's echo of the Passion, see *E*, p. 52, where he calls out: "Father ! (*Pause. Louder.*) Father!"

36. Samuel Beckett, "Proust," in *Proust / Three Dialogues: Samuel Beckett and Georges Duthuit* (London, 1965), p. 19.

37. *The Theatre of the Absurd*, p. 68.

A Theatre of Stasis—Beckett's Late Plays

Martin Esslin*

Pozzo and Lucky are the only characters in Beckett's stage plays who move freely through the landscape. Vladimir and Estragon, with whom they are contrasted in *Waiting for Godot*, are waiting and, in that capacity, rooted to one spot. In the last two lines of the play they announce their intention to go away. But the final stage direction puts paid to that intention: "*They do not move.*" The man in *Act Without Words I*, who is flung backwards onto the stage at the start of that mime play, demonstrates one of the processes by which immobility of this kind is induced: all his attempts to reach his objective, the carafe of water with which he might quench his thirst, are frustrated; so that even when "the carafe descends from the flies and comes to rest a few feet from his body. *He does not move.*"

In *Endgame* Hamm is immobile in his chair. Clov can move, indeed he must, as he cannot sit. But he can move only within the narrow

*Reprinted from *Mediations: Essays on Brecht, Beckett, and the Media* (Baton Rouge: Louisiana State University Press, 1980) by permission of the publisher.

confines of the play's circular room. If he leaves, he dies. At the end of the play he is dressed to leave but does not, or cannot, go. "He halts by the door and stands there, *impassive and motionless* . . . till the end." And Nagg and Nell are confined in their bins.

Krapp moves freely within his room; but we know that he never ventures out. And he listens to his *own voice* on tapes from his past.

In *Happy Days* Winnie is rooted in the earth, like a tree and sinking deeper and deeper. The three characters of *Play* are stuck in urns, only their heads protrude from them. And the words they utter, fragments of memory and meditation, are, we gradually realize, rigidly patterned: when they have all been uttered, they are uttered again, and then, as the play closes, the whole sequence seems to start again; no doubt it will continue to be spoken in that order and in that pattern through all eternity.

Flo, Vi, and Ru, the three women in the dramaticule, *Come and Go*, seem to be able to move; each of them, in turn, leaves the stage for a moment, but the pattern of their going and coming is so rigid that there can be no doubt that it is, also, set for all time, an endless ritual permutation.

In Beckett's most recent plays, this movement to stricter and stricter patterns seems to have carried him towards a new and far more austere form of drama: not only have his plays become more and more concise, they have also shed the notion of *characters in action* which is so often regarded as the basic minimum definition of drama itself. In *Not I* our attention is focused on no more than a *mouth* from which words issue. Admittedly, there is an Auditor of indeterminate sex who listens to the mouth, and, four times, makes a "gesture of helpless compassion." But he seems almost a representative of the audience itself. In *That Time* we see no more than a face, that of a character termed by the author, "the Listener," suspended "about ten feet above stage level midstage off centre." It is the face of an old man with long white hair. Three voices—all of them the Listener's own—are heard from three distinct sources at both sides of the stage and directly above him.

A mouth without a face or body, then, on the one hand: a mouth, merely as the orifice from which a voice issues; and, on the other, a face without a body, motionless except for the eyes, listening to voices. So thoroughly has the world been reduced to the essentials of consciousness and the self. In Beckett's third recent play, *Footfalls*, the process of concentration on the minimal essentials is different, but on very similar lines. Here the audience's attention is focused on a narrow strip downstage, which allows exactly seven (in a later version, nine) steps to be taken. A woman, disheveled, gray-haired, wearing a worn gray wrap which hides her feet, is pacing up and down on this strip, making a right-about-face turn when she reaches the left extremity, a left-about-face at its right limit. The lighting is dim throughout, but relatively strongest at floor level, "less on body, least on head." So we are concentrating on the feet hidden behind the trailing wrap. The woman, May, occasionally speaks to her—unseen—mother, and finally delivers a long speech straight into the audience. The mother's voice is heard from the dark, upstage. The action of *Footfalls* is clearly divided by long pauses in total darkness into three distinct sections: first, a dialogue between May and her unseen Mother; second, the mother's voice while May is pacing up and down (In other words: May hears her mother's voice within herself. The voice clearly says: "My voice is in her mind"); third, May, facing the audience tells a fragment of a story concerning a mother and a daughter, called Amy (an anagram of May). When darkness descends for the third time and, after a pause, the lights very faintly come up on the strip, there is no trace of May. For fifteen seconds the dim light remains on the empty strip on the ground, then the curtain comes down.

All three plays are monodramas. In each of them we are inside the mind of one human being. All three focus the attention on a portion of that human being's body: mouth, eyes, feet. All three achieve total stasis (for even pacing up and down within the narrow range of seven or nine steps amounts to immobility). All three are concerned with memories of a past life, before the final state of stasis afflicted the central characters. All three are very short, which is another way of saying that they are densely concentrated images of human existence, whittled down to the barest essentials, the stream of consciousness that constitutes the self's only awareness of its own being, a stream that essentially is a sequence of words carried on an inner voice.

If we compare these to Beckett's earlier plays we can see how they condense and concentrate elements that have always been present, but in a more diffuse, more traditionally theatrical form. Nell, after all, is Hamm's mother, and he hears her voice (no doubt not literally) emerging from a dustbin. That bin is merely there as a picturesque illustrative detail. In *Footfalls* the mother's voice remains; the dustbin, and the mother's face protruding from it, have been dispensed with as inessentials. Likewise in *Krapp's Last Tape* the tape recorder merely serves as an almost naturalistic device to make us accept Krapp's experience of his former selves. In *That Time* the voices of memory are still there, but the tape recorder has been discarded, as have Krapp's clownish antics as he puts the tapes on and off, the old man's eyes, opening and closing from time to time, are sufficient to give us the full impact of his reactions to his memories.

The stasis of these plays, far from being an absence of action, can thus be seen as, on the contrary, a concentration, condensation, and therefore maximal intensification of the tensions that make conventional plays dramatic. The real world has been left behind by these characters; but having, as it were, *fallen out* of it (in the manner of the inmates of the Magdalen Mental Mercyseat who so greatly impressed and affected Murphy; or of Watt in his pavilion who so intriguingly discoursed with

Sam; or—indeed—in the manner of those victims of *encephalitis lethargica* and Parkinson's disease whom Dr. Oliver Sacks so movingly describes in his great book *Awakenings*, which often seems to be about characters from Beckett's plays and prose works), having fallen out of the world these characters carry within them the encapsulated essence of their life-experience, fused into a minimal number of key images. It is because these key images fully sum up the experiences of a complete life and because their number is a bare minimum, that they arrange themselves in rigidly structured patterns; they have become, as it were, the mathematical formulae which sum up a life; they have reached their briefest and most elegant formulation and can be retained, *must* be retained, by formalized repetition, in the way in which schoolboys remember rules of grammar by enshrining them in easily memorized rhymed patterns, mnemonic verses.

The immense dramatic tension in *Not I*, for instance, issues from the mouth's refusal, or inability, to acknowledge the experience it recounts as that of its own self. The words "Who? . . . no! . . . she!" are the recurring trigger that sets off the Auditor's gesture of helpless compassion. Highly concentrated and condensed though it is, the story the mouth tells contains the substance of a whole conventional full-length play or novel; it is the story of a life without love (hence, perhaps, so passively experienced that it was never felt to be a life lived by the self, but rather something which was passively endured like someone else's experience). The degree of concentration may be judged by just one example: what, in a conventional form, detailing all accidentals, might fill several chapters, here emerges as "out . . . into this world . . . this world . . . tiny little thing . . . before its time . . . in a god-for- . . . what? . . . girl? . . . Yes . . . tiny little girl . . . into this . . . out into this . . . before her time . . . godforsaken hole called . . . called . . . no matter . . . parents unknown . . . unheard of . . . he having vanished . . . thin air . . . no sooner buttoned up his breeches . . . she similarly . . . eight months later . . . almost to the tick . . . so no love . . . spared that." The supreme artistry behind this highly condensed form of writing lies in Beckett's ability to concentrate without ever becoming schematic or abstract. Note the way in which the place of birth is first mentioned as merely the beginning of the phrase about the "godforsaken hole," the way it is later fully uttered, only to be abandoned before the name of the place itself is pronounced. The minimalization of the actual storytelling is achieved by, as it were, deleting all but the most essentially visual portion of what might be a long descriptive paragraph ("no sooner buttoned up his trousers" is clearly the remnant of what in a more conventional genre would be a circumstantial description of the meeting, lovemaking and parting of the parents; but the six words which remain of it all clearly imply *all* the rest).

On closer examination the text of a short play like *Not I* thus unfolds like one of those Japanese paper flowers which gain form and color as they are immersed in water and soak up its expanding force. The person with whose story the mouth is concerned spent a long life, into her sixties, practically speechless, except for bouts of logorrhea in her childhood ("sudden urge to . . . tell . . . then rush out stop the first she saw . . . nearest lavatory . . . start pouring it out . . . steady stream.") Then, suddenly in her old age, words began pouring out of her. And it is this outpouring which constitutes the play.

The Listener in *That Time* hears three voices, all his own, in a steady flow, yet with each voice clearly distinguishable as slightly different: the first of these concentrates on the image of a memory of his return to a lonely ruin where he used to hide as a child; at a much later stage in his life he had returned there, from overseas ("straight off the ferry") and had almost immediately fled back to where he had come from: the second voice describes a series of flights from wandering the streets in the rain, to the National Portrait Gallery, or a public library, or a post office; the third one to be heard (B—hence, probably, the one which comes from above, center) dwells on a moment of love, the bodies of the lovers never touching, "on a stone together in the sun . . . at the edge of a little wood as far as the eye could see the wheat turning yellow." The three images intertwine like the strands of melody in a symphony, recur and are varied into a tapestry with a clearly perceptible pattern of tensions, emotional colors, and structures of a life's essential experience: the child avidly reading in the old ruin as seen by the white-haired old man just off the boat, still carrying his nightbag; the sadness and bliss of the lovers in their summer landscape; and the rain outside, contrasted with the dust enveloping the library and the post office, the dark portraits staring at the fugitive from the street as he sits in the Portrait Gallery.

Compared with these clear and poetic fragments of memory the matter of *Footfalls* must appear mysterious, its message more heavily coded. Is Amy, the daughter about whom May speaks in the third section of the play (and whose mother is called Mrs. Winter), in fact the same as May herself? The story May tells in that third section is clearly a passage from a book—perhaps one that she (like Hamm in *Endgame*) is in the act of composing. And the dialogue that passage relates—to a "reader" who is directly apostrophized—culminates in Amy denying that she was present at evensong, which, however, she seems definitely to have attended in her mother's company. "I was not there," she categorically states in the story May recounts to the audience. Perhaps the emphasis here lies not so much on the word "there" as on "I"? Perhaps the phrase should be stressed: *I* was not there. In which case the name Amy might refer to the question *Am I*? And Amy's answer to her mother might simply indicate that there might have been someone there, but *Not I*. And if the name Amy might be so interpreted, might the name May (its anagram) not also be seen as the auxiliary verb indicating potentiality or possibility of being? And then, in the second section of the play, when the mother's voice, which is in May's mind, speaks of her insistence that the carpet on the strip of floor on which she paces up and down be removed because she "must hear the feet, however faint they fall," might not that indicate that the daughter yearns for some proof of the existence of her merely potential self and can find its only concrete manifestation in hearing the rhythm of her steps on the bare floor? These are some questions the mysterious text raises; there are some deeper and more mysterious ones beneath and behind these. For something—*it*—*it all*—is occasionally referred to, which seems to have been the cause of all that pacing up and down. And in the first section the mother who is there said to be around ninety years old is clearly an invalid, requiring injections, the rearrangement of pillows, the administering of warming pans and bedpans, and the dressing of sores, sponging down and moistening of lips. For which the mother asks the daughter's forgiveness.

The key to the riddle probably lies in the recurring lines: "Will you never have done revolving it all. It? It all." It is the revolving, the incessant reliving of a traumatic key experience which clearly is the foundation of the insistent pattern of seven steps, turnabout, seven steps back, turnabout, seven steps . . . To revolve also means to turn about. The steps and turns are the expression of the event which is being turned about in May's (Amy's?) mind.

Economy—concentration upon essentials—is one of the hallmarks of supreme artistry. Throughout his life as a writer Beckett has striven to reach the utmost degree of economy and density. Dramatic forms of presentation tend to be more economical than mere narrative, for here the images, which need to be *described* in discursive prose, can be made concrete and instantly perceptible on the stage. Drama of the kind Beckett writes is poetry of concrete, three-dimensional stage images, complex metaphors communicable in a flash of visual intuitive understanding. For let there be no mistake about it: while Beckett's texts yield great insights to those who closely analyze them by repeated reading, that is not the manner in which they are meant to communicate to an audience. In plays like *Not I*, *That Time*, and *Footfalls*, it is by no means essential that the audience in the theatre should be able to decode the complex story lines and intellectual puzzles they enshrine. On the contrary, what the audience should experience and take home with them after their brief exposure to these dramatic metaphors is precisely the *overall impact* of a single overwhelmingly powerful image, composed of the startling visual element; the strange murmur of subdued voices in a dim half-light; the strange and powerful *rhythms* of both light and voices; the magical effect of the poetic phrasing and the richness of the images the language carries along on its relentless flow.

It is by making his images *unforgettable* through the startling novelty of their visual impact and the density of a multitude of linguistic, visual, and dramatic elements deployed at one and the same time at a multitude of levels, that Beckett reaches his audience. Many people who have seen *Not I* will never be able to forget the image of the mouth, a patch of light in the surrounding darkness, from which, as though it came from an unfathomable depth, the breathless hurried voice of Billie Whitelaw issued forth. Some of these may since have gone to the text and puzzled out the full story it contains. But far more important is the fact that the image of the mouth pouring out the contents of a mind has, for these spectators, crystallized and encapsulated one of the basic mysteries of human existence, the strange duality between body and mind of which the mouth is the manifest image: the mouth, which is the threshold between the material world and the immaterial world of consciousness; the mouth which thus becomes the symbol of the mystery of the self which *should* be the link between the body and its consciousness—but which, as the body is in constant change and the consciousness in constant flux, remains ever elusive.

Looked at from this point of view, Beckett's plays will appear as materializations, incarnations of some of the basic questions of our existence.

Play

James Knowlson*

Play is in several respects a key work in Beckett's dramatic canon. In spite of its many obvious affinities with earlier plays—*Endgame*, for instance, in which Nagg and Nell confined to their dustbins clearly anticipate the figures set in urns in *Play*, or *Happy Days*, in which Winnie's natural mode of expression, like that of the three speakers in *Play*, is the cliché—*Play* looks forward to some of the most important and more experimental features of the miniature dramas of the 1970s.

Earlier in Beckett's theatre, light had been a more or less constant factor, grey in *Endgame*, "blazing" in *Happy Days*, and used spatially in *Krapp's Last Tape* to create a zone of light separate from the darkness. But *Play* reveals the dramatic effectiveness of a rigorously and rhythmically controlled interplay of light and darkness, produced in this case by the spotlight switching rapidly from one head to another and so governing the dramatic tempo of the play. For, in principle at least, the actors take their cue from the light and not from the other actors. This sharp intercutting of speeches by means of light was never again used in exactly the same form by Beckett. But the principle of intercutting itself becomes a major structural device in *That Time*, and the idea of a single spotlight picking

*Reprinted from *Frescoes of the Skull: The Later Prose and Drama of Samuel Beckett*, by James Knowlson and John Pilling (London: John Calder, 1979), by permission of the publisher.

out a human head (or, as it was to become almost ten years later, a mouth) first arose soon after Beckett had finished writing *Play.*[1] *Play* also demonstrated how a rapidly delivered text could, despite its difficulties, rivet the attention.

Although Beckett had been involved on a number of occasions with productions of his plays in Paris and London, ever since Roger Blin's first production of *En attendant Godot* in 1953, it was only in the course of rehearsing *Play* in February to March 1963 with Jean-Marie Serreau in Paris and, immediately afterwards in March to April with George Devine in London, that Beckett came to be so intensely preoccupied with the effects that could be obtained by varying the intensity and the speed of both speech and lighting in the repeat of the play. George Devine was widely recognized as an expert on lighting techniques and Beckett worked very closely with him on this aspect of the production.[2] Later, a meticulous concern for the dramatic shapes as well as the effects that could be derived from variations in sound and lighting levels characterized *That Time* and, even more strikingly, *Footfalls*. As the production notebooks show, this same concern was to figure prominently in Beckett's own Berlin productions of *Endgame, Krapp's Last Tape, Happy Days* and *Waiting for Godot*, as well as *That Time* and *Footfalls*. It can therefore be said with some certainty that *Play* laid the foundations for Beckett's later emphasis on a subtle choreography of sound and silence, light and darkness, movement and stillness.

The title of *Waiting for Godot* describes a state and names its enigmatic, unseen cause; *Endgame* alludes to a game of chess; *Krapp's Last Tape* evokes excrement as a man's name and endows him with a tape-recorder; *Happy Days* recalls an ironic greeting. By comparison *Play*, like *Film*, seems to be Beckett's most explicit and plainly descriptive title. In one sense, this is exactly what it is. Three stock characters, a man, his wife, and his mistress are involved in an only too familiar triangular relationship. Clandestine meetings, domestic squabbles, partings and recriminations have long formed the staple diet of much domestic drama or light comedy. Once again here they are only too clearly the stuff of a "play." *Play* is also what it says it is in the sense that the three characters speak only when they are illuminated by that most theatrical of devices, the spotlight. And yet placing the figures in receptacles like funeral urns, situating them in a kind of purgatorial after-life, making the spotlight into an "inquirer" and the three figures into "victims," compelled to go over again and again the events of their previous relationship, clearly sets both the figures and the events into a very different perspective. *Play* seems then like "play" in another sense—concerned as it is with such a trivial, ludicrously squalid affair or "pastime"—that of a parody of both life and theatre. "I know now," says the man, "all that was just . . . play" (*Play and Two Short Pieces for Radio*, Faber and Faber, London, 1964, 16; all further references are to this edition), as he refers back to the incidents of his past life. One is reminded of Plato's words that "we should keep our seriousness for serious things and not waste it on trifles, and that, while God is the real goal of all beneficent serious endeavour, man . . . has been constructed as a toy for God . . . All of us then, men and women alike, must fall in with our role and spend life in making our *play* as perfect as possible."[3] And yet as M's subsequent question suggests ("And all this [their present plight] when will all this have been just play?," 16–17), if all is indeed regarded as "play," in limbo as in life, this will still not wipe out the pain as well as the absurdity from either. There is, in fact, not a scrap of comfort to be gained from the drastic change that has taken place. Even W2's apparently optimistic "At the same time I prefer this to . . . the other thing. Definitely. There are endurable moments" (15) is less optimism than a sour assessment of what has gone before. For this is, after all, only one small segment in a larger spectrum of emotional responses to their situation and is repeated in any case over and over again.

In his director's notes for the Old Vic production of *Play*, George Devine compared the inquisitorial light to a "dental drill."[4] And it is certainly far more of an "instrument of torture," to use Billie Whitelaw's picturesque phrase,[5] than an Opener like that which urges on Voice and Music in *Cascando* and takes an interest in what they reveal. But, as with the beam of light in *Not I*, the torture for the three figures caught up in this inquiry (as distinct perhaps from that of the actors playing the parts) comes not from the actual pain caused by the light as from its persistent piercing of the darkness and prevention of any possible peace. The light is both within the strange stage world to which the three figures are confined and outside the drama that it brings into existence, since, as spectators and listeners, we depend on it as on the conductor of an orchestra and, at the same time, recognize it for what it is, *viz*: a spotlight. Beckett seems to have been concerned in rehearsals with reducing this more objective, mechanical side of the light (which cannot, for obvious reasons, be entirely avoided) and playing up more the "human" side. For in writing to Devine about variations in speed and intensity, he suggested that "the inquirer (light) begins to emerge as no less a victim of his inquiry than they and as needing to be free, within narrow limits, literally to act the part, i.e. to vary if only slightly his speeds and intensities."[6] But the role of the light is even more ambiguous, for it has also been seen as "a metaphor for our attention (relentless, all-consuming, whimsical)"[7] and as a way of "switching on and switching off speech exactly as a playwright does when he moves on from one line of dialogue on his page to the next."[8] Neither of these analogies conflict, of course, with the more human qualities of Beckett's modified "inquirer."

In the stage directions relating to the voices in the opening Chorus, Beckett wrote that they should be "faint, largely unintelligible" (9). Although it is the rapid tempo of the play and audience laughter that prevents the remainder of the text from being understood in full the first time round. George Devine recognized that this play was treating language in a way that was significantly different from Beckett's earlier plays, except for Lucky's monologue in *Waiting for Godot*. For Devine made the following observations in his director's notes: "words not as conveying thought or ideas but as dramatic ammunition—cf. light . . . words have no significance or meaning whatsoever—just 'things' that come out of their mouths—the best dramatic use—the constant shock treatment . . . Tonelessness—speaking to themselves—no attitude to an audience—pointless to have tone on constant repetition."[9] There is, of course, nothing here or in the play itself (which does not entirely conform to Devine's commentary on it) that one would not already find in Artaud's *The Theatre and its Double*, which we know Beckett had read,[10] or in Ionesco's essay "Expérience du théâtre," printed in the *Nouvelle revue française* in 1958, which he may well have looked at. But what is striking about Beckett's theatricalism is that he adopts such distinctive devices only when they accord closely with his themes and when they can be integrated into a highly personal dramatic vision.

The "faint, largely unintelligible" voices of the Chorus provide a surprise and a shock at the opening of the curtain. If the words are to be followed at all, the spectator needs to bring the highest level of concentration to bear immediately on what he hears. The rest of the play is then able to capitalize on this heightened concentration. But the Chorus also manages in a matter of seconds to establish a sense of ritual, each voice intoning a statement which proceeds quite independently of the others. For, instead of choral unison, what we are offered is three separate monologues, which appear on first hearing to be related only rhythmically one to another, as Beckett's layout of the phrasing shows and the actors' delivery would make quite clear. In addition, the Chorus provides markers which separate the second part (or, as Beckett termed it, the "Narration")[11] from the third part (or the "Meditation"). It also indicates the end of the first and second runthroughs of the play.

As their lack of individual names suggests, the three figures in *Play* (M, W1, and W2) are not three-dimensional characters. Any attempt to analyze them as if they are would be absurd. The stereotype predominates: a virile male who wants the best of both worlds, domestic bliss and extra-marital spice; a possessive, shrewish wife; and a concerned, yet demanding "other woman." In fact, they have only enough individuality to be described, in Barbara Bray's words, as "people in all their funny, disgraceful, pitiable fragility and all the touchingness, in spite of everything, of their efforts to love one another, and endure."[12] The settings reek of deliberate cliché: the morning room of a large house set among lawns; a butler, Erskine by name; the mistress posed by an open window, indulging in the traditional pastime of idle mistresses, doing her nails or stitching; a private detective set on the adulterous trail; and a possible escape from it all to the Riviera or "our darling Grand Canary" (12). This all belongs, of course, to the artificial world of melodrama and romance embodied in romanticized fiction and echoed in a style of theatre parodied neatly by Tom Stoppard in *The Real Inspector Hound* (1968).

The parody extends from that of postures, actions and attitudes to finely etched parody of word, phrase and syntactical construction: "Judge then to my astoundment" (11), "as I was sitting stricken" (11), "Fearing she was about to offer me violence, I rang for Erskine" (11), "How could we be together in the way we are, if there were someone else" (11), "[I had] not much stomach for her leavings either" (13). These examples are borrowed from all three speakers, although it is the wife who is most extravagantly endowed with clichés.

Yet the humour of *Play* is not simply that of parodied romance and "finely enamelled cliché."[13] It has a much sharper edge than cliché is ever normally allowed. For among the stiffly genteel remarks, other more violent responses occur which, although they are almost as cliché-ridden, contrast sharply and incongruously with them. This conflict between two opposing sets of clichés not only provokes a sense of mixed amusement and shock but also brings one, however fleetingly, into closer touch with something approaching genuine emotional torment. The violence is expressed in animal or bird images, which, although lacking in freshness, still appear more vividly real than the glossy, novelettish world in which the adulterous affair took place. The mistress tells how the wife "burst in and flew at me" (10), "I smell you off him, she screamed, he stinks of bitch" (11); the man "slinks in" (11) like a dog to confess his guilt; and, according to the wife, his mistress "had means, I fancy, though she lived like a pig" (19). The description of the mistress by W1 is in terms more appropriate to a grotesque monster than a desirable woman, "Pudding face, puffy, spots, blubber mouth, jowls, no neck, dugs you could . . . calves like a flunkey" (13). The wife regularly uses verbs of smell and gutter level nouns when she speaks about her rival, "a bitch" (11), "a common tart" (13), "a slut" (14), "give up that whore . . . or I'll slit my throat" (10). The best example of humourous disparity of language is found in the man's "At home, all heart to heart, new leaf and bygones bygones. I ran into your ex-doxy, she said one night, on the pillow, you're well out of that. Rather uncalled for, I thought. I am indeed, sweetheart, I said, I am indeed. God what vermin women. Thanks to you, angel, I said" (14).

As George Devine pointed out in a dispute with Kenneth Tynan, *Play* cannot be understood in purely literary terms.[14] And the theatrical dimension means that these elements of parody, cliché, and verbal incongruity register rapidly, and only partially. For if the momentum of the production is to be maintained and there are to be no laughter pauses—as there were none in the British première or in the Royal Court 1976 revival—it will prove impossible to seize the whole of the text the first time round. Beckett was, however, clearly aware that, though much of the detail of this second part was missed or overlooked on first hearing, it would swim into focus during the *reprise*. As with the musical *reprise* that was included in some of Haydn's string quartets (which Beckett much admires), response to the "Narration" inevitably differs on the second run-through of the text. Themes already sound familiar, detailed variations are more easily recognized, and ordered patterns or more subtle echoes can be discerned in the composition. But also with *Play*, experience shows that reception changes from one of keen, but amused attention in the course of the first hearing to a more sombre appraisal of the tormented plight of the three figures during the second.

The median blackout, the simultaneous use of spots on all three heads and the lowered strength of both light and voice mark the opening of a third section of the play which already displays a torment arising partly out of the situation itself but also out of their imaginings of a life on earth of which they are not part. There is still humour, but it is in the form of irony rather than parody: "There is no future in this" (16), "things may disimprove, there is that danger" (16), "perhaps they have become friends" (17). Images and attitudes persist from the "Narration," but in a modified, muted, reduced form. They will now be "kissing their sour kisses" (18) speculates the mistress, while the wife pictures her rival still sitting by a window, gazing now at the olives, waiting for him to return; she tries hard to be precise in the most appropriate cliché selected for the occasion, "Shadow stealing over everything. Creeping. Yes" (20). Since individual statements are shorter in this part, the light cuts more rapidly from face to face and the impression is of a more frenzied pace. It is only in the "Meditation" that the inquisitorial light comes to be addressed directly by its victims. Attitudes liable to have been applied once to the man are now transferred to the light. The wife's "get off me" (16) and her "you will weary of me" (15) and the mistress's "go away and start poking and pecking at someone else" (16) echo tired or irritated reactions to a lover. This is part of a desperate need to anthropomorphize the light. For while it may be supposed capable of possessing human feelings of curiosity, pity, understanding, satisfaction or even weariness, there is some hope that unbroken darkness, silence and peace might be reached in the end. But while the motives and purpose of the light remain unknowable, release seems horrifyingly remote. M's last question "Am I as much as . . . being seen?" (22) assumes, then, an overriding importance.

The three figures retain a certain individuality of response to both the purgatorial situation and the "hellish half-light." W2 hopes that madness might provide her own form of release from torment, M seeks darkness and peace, and W1, more desperately, tries to discover what must be done or said to rid herself of the light. But more important than this is the fact that, rather like a fragmented musical round song, with each voice starting at a different point on the score, the three sets of statements follow the same basic patterns. The three voices can therefore be traced as they move through similar emotional responses to the light and imaginings of the other two left on earth, to speculations as to what is causing their torment and the possibilities of it ever ending. But these related statements do not coincide in time. Instead, they echo what another voice has recited earlier and, as in *That Time*, contrast or interrelate in more complex ways with the surrounding statements. Sometimes, since the range of their preoccupations is so limited, the lines of their statements converge briefly, only to move quickly apart again as they follow their own path. The impression is that of a clockwork mechanism, in which all the cogs are wound up so that they move inexorably on but coincide only momentarily one with another. Yet within the broader patterns of movement, there are intricate variations in tone, colour, intensity and pace, as the following series of responses will show:

> W1. Hellish half-light.
>
> *Spot from* W1 *to* M.
>
> M. Peace, yes, I suppose, a kind of peace, and all that pain as if . . . never been.
>
> *Spot from* M *to* W2.
>
> W2. Give me up as a bad job. Go away and start poking and pecking at someone else. On the other hand—
>
> *Spot from* W2 *to* W1.
>
> W1. Get off me! (*Vehement.*) Get off me! (16)

The identical repeat of the whole play reveals the three characters caught up for eternity it would seem in an endless repetition of story and inquisitorial ritual: the mechanism, in fact, never running down. However, in the course of rehearsing the French translation, *Comédie*, with Jean-Marie Serreau in Paris, an alternative version of the *da capo* which incorporated an important element of variation was adopted and developed further in the London Old Vic production. In brief, the changes consist of, first, a slight weakening of both the light and the voices in the first Repeat and even more so in the fragment of the second Repeat, the variation ranging in strength from A (the strongest) to strength E (the weakest). Secondly, an abridged Chorus is adopted for the opening fragment of the Second Repeat. Thirdly, there is a breathless quality in the voices from the beginning of Repeat 1, which increases to the end of the play. And fourthly, the actual order of the speeches at the opening of the Repeat is changed. In the letter to George Devine of 9 March, Beckett describes the new arrangements for the Repeat as "dramatically more effective."[15] But it is also clear that what is involved is a distinct evolution in his way of conceiving the replay. For he writes of "the impression of falling off which this would give, with suggestion of conceivable dark and silence in the end, or of an indefinite approximating towards it."[16] This view of the *da capo* brings the dramatic form of *Play* much closer to that of Beckett's earlier plays in which things are gradually running down and in which stasis, although it seems remote, nonetheless seems ultimately possible. Modifications to the order of the replies confers, of course, a degree of freedom on the inquirer-light. Variation in order seems, in fact, to have replaced Beckett's earlier idea of introducing into the Repeat "a quality of hesitancy, of both question and answer, perhaps not so much in a slowing down of actual débit as in a less confident movement of spot from one face to another and less immediate reaction of the voices."[17] A consequence of this change is that the light seems to be as much caught up in this unexplained ritual as the figures themselves are. It does not function, then, only by prompting them into speech, but is itself prompted like them to enact and reenact a role within this strange, purgatorial world.

A further effect of the repetition is to torment us, the spectators, as well as the victims of the light. For, as my co-author has pointed out elsewhere, "one feels that the light should have been able to unscramble the essentials more successfully the second time around. We are as much passive sufferers of the light as the heads are."[18] But if we did think we were there to unscramble what we hear, by the end of the second repeat we have come to recognize our mistake. We are there simply to observe and witness, as "they" were there to respond, and as the light is there to elicit these responses. There is no more question of understanding why this should be so than there is of supplying the "reasons unknown" that would account for man's "wasting and pining" in Lucky's monologue in *Waiting for Godot.*

If, as Deirdre Bair supposes,[19] biographical issues and tensions lie at the source of *Play*, they are soon transformed into a complex work which, while being rich in humour and humanity, still possesses its own special brand of repeated torment. If the later miniature dramas of the 1970s go back for inspiration to the world of *The Unnamable*, the technical dramatization of that world owes much to *Play.* The inheritance is clear enough: a rapidly delivered monologue, a head picked out by a spotlight from the surrounding darkness, fading lighting effects, and the intercutting of several voices. But there are deeper affinities too. *Play* brought together (without the help of a tape-recorder) different time states, as both *Not I* and *That Time* were to do, and treated them all as infernal. It also mapped out a world of apparently infinite time and space in which figures talk or wander restlessly, just as troubled there as they were in life. This world looks forward naturally enough to the various levels of ghostly existence that are found in *Footfalls* and in the television plays, *Ghost Trio* and . . . *but the clouds. . . .* In *Play*, visual and verbal elements function as one and are sufficiently vital to hold the attention, a virtue which, as we shall see, not all of the miniature dramas possess. More compelling than any of its progeny except *Not I*, and certainly more approachable than all of them, *Play* stays in the mind as much for its human as for its infernal characteristics. Perhaps for this reason alone it will survive the test of time as a piece of theatre worthy to figure alongside *Waiting for Godot, Endgame, Krapp's Last Tape,* and *Happy Days.*

Notes

1. In the "Kilcool" manuscript, dated Paris, Dec. 1963, Beckett envisaged a "woman's face alone in constant light." Trinity College, Dublin MS. 4664, p. 10. Rosemary Pountney first pointed out to me the connection between "Kilcool" and *Not I* and *That Time.*
2. As a letter from Beckett to George Devine, dated 9.3.64, shows; see J. Knowlson, ed., *Samuel Beckett: An Exhibition,* Turret Books, London, 1971, p. 92.
3. *The Collected Dialogues of Plato,* ed. E. Hamilton & H. Cairns, Pantheon Books, New York, 1961, *Laws,* VII, 803c, p. 1375.
4. *Samuel Beckett: An Exhibition,* p. 91.
5. *Journal of Beckett Studies,* no. 3, Summer 1978, p. 86.
6. *Samuel Beckett: An Exhibition,* p. 92.
7. H. Kenner, *Samuel Beckett: A Critical Study,* new edition, University of California Press, Berkeley and Los Angeles, 1968, pp. 210–11.
8. J. Fletcher and J. Spurling, *Beckett. A Study of his Plays,* p. 107.
9. *Samuel Beckett: An Exhibition,* p. 91.
10. Letter to J. Knowlson, 11.iv.72.
11. M. Esslin, "Samuel Beckett and the Art of Broadcasting," *Encounter,* Sept. 1975, p. 44.
12. B. Bray, "The New Beckett," *The Observer,* 16 June 1963.
13. H. Kenner, *Samuel Beckett,* p. 211.
14. I. Wardle, *The Theatres of George Devine,* Jonathan Cape, London, 1978, pp. 207–208.
15. *Samuel Beckett: An Exhibition,* p. 92.
16. *eo.loc.*
17. *eo.loc.*
18. J. Pilling, *Samuel Beckett,* Routledge and Kegan Paul, London, 1976, p. 90.
19. D. Bair, *Samuel Beckett: A Biography,* New York, Harcourt Brace Jovanovich, 1978, pp. 481–82.

Birth astride a Grave: Samuel Beckett's *Act without Words 1*

Stanley E. Gontarski*

Samuel Beckett's first mime, *Act without Words 1,* is one of the few slighted works in the Beckett canon. Often ignored, the play has generally not fared well even with those critics who do treat it. Ruby Cohn dismisses the work as "almost too explicit,"[1] and Ihab Hassan has noted that the first

*Reprinted from *Journal of Beckett Studies,* no. 1 (Winter 1976) by permission of Riverrun Press, Inc., New York.

mime seems "a little too obvious and pat."[2] John Spurling concurs: compared to *Godot, Act without Words 1* "is . . . over-explicit, over-emphasized and even, unless redeemed by its performer, so unparticularized as to verge on the banal."[3]

The play's directness is almost a source of embarrassment for critics and has prompted some forced interpretation. Martin Esslin, for one, has argued that the protagonist is "drawn to the pursuit of illusory objectives . . ."[4] Ruby Cohn echoes the view, suggesting that the "sustenance and tools are man's own invention, and his frustration the result of the impossibility of ever being able to reach what may be a mirage."[5] But the objects certainly seem substantial. The protagonist stands on the cubes and engages in a tug-of-war with a force outside himself, presumably the same force which threw him on stage. The scissors and rope may be man's own inventions, but they are nonetheless real; if they are not, the exterior force would have little reason to confiscate them. Rather than an obvious, unparticularized mime about illusion or mirage, Beckett has created here one of his most compact and concrete images of the birth of existential man, of the existential artist, with all the ironies implicit in the coincidence of birth and death.

Admittedly, the mime is obvious in many respects. It appears to be a behaviouristic psychological experiment within the framework of a classic myth. The protagonist (Adam, Tantalus, Everyman) is thrown, forced, born into a hostile environment where he can neither have nor succeed. What nature exists is apart from man and is alien, the curse of thistles and thorns. From the first the protagonist is a thinker, but inadequately made to deal with the hostile forces. He is pathetic, born, indeed created to fail, a caged rat frustrated by an inept or malicious handler. He examines his hands, his primary tool; his prehensile thumb opposes the fingers. Armed with two natural tools, mind and hands, those tools which separate him from lower orders of animals, he tries to survive, to secure some water in the desert. The mind works, at least in part: he learns—small cube on large; he invents, or is given inventions—scissors, cubes, rope. But when he learns to use his tools effectively, they are confiscated: the scissors, when he reasons that in addition to cutting his fingernails, he might cut his throat; the blocks and rope, when he discovers that they might make a gallows. So far, a rather obvious allegory: Tantalus punished, the offence uncertain. G. C. Barnard argues the prevalent interpretation of the ending; the protagonist does not move because he is simply crushed: ". . . the man remains, defeated, having opted out of the struggle, lying on the empty desert."[6]

The play, however, contains some anomalies which warrant investigation. This is not the usual Beckett world. No words, for one. Or more properly, one elemental word, water. While much has been made of the names of Beckett's characters, especially his M's, this protagonist is nameless. And he is, throughout most of the play, active and healthy, neither an avatar of Belacqua nor one of the cripples. Although his progress is toward immobility, he suffers no visible physical deterioration. Unlike *Godot* where we are never sure of Godot's existence,[7] here a force outside man certainly exists; the protagonist, like Jacob, wrestles with it to illustrate its substance. Finally, the action of the mime is linear, terminal, not the usual Beckettian circle.

In the end the superior force defeats the inferior, rather predictable, pathetic stuff. With this climax, the play appears more traditional and didactic than Beckett's other dramatic work. The mime seems to lack characteristic Beckettian innovation. But within this obvious, traditional ending, Beckett works his consummate skill, for the real play begins with its terminus. The climactic ending of the mime may signify not a pathetic defeat, but a conscious rebellion, man's deliberate refusal to obey. Lucky has finally turned on Pozzo. Ironically then, the protagonist is most active when inert, and his life acquires meaning at its end. In this refusal, this cutting of the umbilical rope, a second birth occurs, the birth of man. The protagonist has finally acquired, earned, a name, Man (another M). As he refuses the summons of the outside force, as he refuses to act predictably, in his own self-interest, as he refuses the struggle for the most elemental of man's needs, Man, in a frenzy of inactivity, is born. If at first we saw man created by another, we end with man creating himself. In his refusal to devote himself to physical existence, solely to survival and pleasure (shade, the off-stage womb), the protagonist has created a free man, a separate, individual self. He has said with Camus's rebel, so far and no further. Rebellion is, of course, dangerous business. The rebellious slave may indeed be physically destroyed by his master. In the final dramatic image of *Act without Words 1*, the moments of birth and death virtually coincide in an echo of blind Pozzo's insight. "They give birth astride of a grave." Tension here is produced by inaction, a corollary to the tension produced by silence in the wordplays.

In addition to an ending which is at least ambiguous, a series of brilliant visual allusions adds to the richness of the play. The protagonist's similarities to Tantalus, the patriarch of the troubled house of Atreus, and Jacob, the patriarch of Israel, have already been suggested. And the former myth provides most of the dramatic framework for the play, not unlike, on its own small scale, Joyce's use of the Odysseus myth to shape *Ulysses*. Moreover, the playlet contains several other Joycean echoes. The struggle between the protagonist and the more powerful outside force suggests not only Jaccob's wrestling with an angel, but Joyce's artistic quest for (at least in Beckett's eyes) omniscience and omnipotence. The protagonist of the mime, like Stephen Dedalus, finally says *non serviam*. The image of man paring his nails suggests (and perhaps parodies with Joyce) Stephen's aesthetic theories. Like Dedalus, the protagonist in *Act without Words 1* is an inventor and consequently an artist, a "fabulous artificer." If the inventions fail, that failure is inevitable and consistent with Beckett's attitude toward art. As Beckett suggested to Israel Shenker, Joyce is "tending toward omniscience and omnipotence as an artist. I'm working with impotence, ignorance."[8] The artistic associations of the protagonist are further reinforced with the reference to tailor's scissors. The tailor is himself a craftsman, a maker, and the scissors call to mind Nagg's story of the Englishman and the tailor from *Endgame*, the point of which is the imperfection of the world when compared to man's creations.

Act without Words 1 then is a not-so-banal dramatic image of rebellion, of artistic rebellion, of Sartre's man freeing himself from outside forces which may be god, instinct, tradition, mythology, human nature, and the struggle is punctuated with a series of visual images suggesting the artist's plight. As the mime closes, man is free of his instinct for survival, free of the limitation of acting according to his nature. The freedom may only be the spiteful freedom of Dostoevsky's Underground Man and the victory, as Thomas Barbour suggests, "may be hollow,"[9] but perhaps there are no meaningful victories. The ending is an existential and artistic triumph for whatever that is worth. *Act without Words 1* may finally be Beckett's portrait of the artist as a young (man, dog) rat.

Notes

1. Ruby Cohn, *Samuel Beckett: The Comic Gamut*, New Brunswick, NJ, Rutgers University Press, 1962, p. 247.

2. Ihab Hassan, *The Literature of Silence: Henry Miller and Samuel Beckett*, New York, Alfred A. Knopf, Inc., 1967, p. 192.

3. John Fletcher and John Spurling, *Beckett: A Study of His Plays*, New York, Hill and Wang, 1972, p. 118.

4. Martin Esslin, *The Theatre of the Absurd*, New York, Doubleday and Company, Inc., 1961, p. 38.

5. *The Comic Gamut*, p. 247.

6. *Samuel Beckett: A New Approach*, New York, Dodd, Mead & Company, Inc., 1970, p. 109.

7. In fact, in the early versions of *Godot*, the existence of Godot is more certain as Didi and Gogo have a note from him. In revision, the note is excised, the existence of Godot open to question.

8. Israel Shenker, "A portrait of Samuel Beckett, author of the puzzling *Waiting for Godot*," *New York Times*, 6 May 1956, Section 2, p. 1, p. 3.

9. "Beckett and Ionesco," *Hudson Review*, 11, Summer 1958, p. 273.

A Footnote to *Footfalls*: Footsteps of Infinity on Beckett's Narrow Space

Enoch Brater*

Footfalls, "a very small play" with "a lot of problems concerning precision,"[1] had its world premiere performance on May 20, 1976, as part of a triple bill with *Play* and *That Time* at the Samuel Beckett Festival celebrated at the Royal Court Theatre in London. Beckett, who directed the British production starring Billie Whitelaw as May, staged a new German version several months later at the Schiller-Theater Werkstatt in Berlin. The English version was performed again that same year at the Kreeger Theatre in Washington, D.C., and late in 1977 Alan Schneider re-interpreted his original American production for the Manhattan Theatre Club in New York. Even after four major productions of this thirty-minute work, *Footfalls* continues to affect its audiences as a theatricalized enigma. What are we to make of the seemingly endless pacing of a female protagonist wearing "the costume of a ghost"[2] on the narrow strip of space suddenly illuminated before our eyes?

Let us consider for a moment the pure value of the visual element in this play: Beckett projects an image, a moving, lyrical spectacle tracing the footsteps of a lonely human being. The lighting is a major feature in the visual impact; "dim," it is "strongest at floor level, less on body, least on head."[3] Beckett's emphasis, as his stage directions imply, is on the "clearly audible rhythmic pad" of a finite number of steps on a tiny strip downstage. The width is only "one metre, a little audience right," but growing shorter and narrower following each fadeout. Although footsteps can be heard, no feet are to be discerned: a "worn grey wrap" enshrouds May quite literally from top to toe. The curtain rises slowly; May fades-in before our eyes as "a faint tangle of pale grey tatters." It is her endless pacing and, above all, the sound of her footfalls, which interrupt the silence, stillness, and darkness of the "faint, though by no means invisible" substance of this play.

During rehearsals for the Berlin production, Beckett emphasized the importance of those footsteps: "The walking up and down is the central image." The script for the play, he continued, was "built up around this picture."[4] In the text Beckett puns, asking us to watch "how feat" (neat, dexterous) May "wheels" when she moves "rightabout at L, leftabout at R." Yet our perception of movement depends here on something even more basic than the coordinates Beckett specifies as relative right and relative left. For in Beckett's world movement is often a tricky business. "What ruined me at bottom was athletics," we read in one of the eight recent

*Reprinted from *Comparative Drama* 12 (Spring 1978) by permission of the editors of *Comparative Drama*.

prose "fizzles."[5] Long before this we have been literally overwhelmed by the variety of "funambulistic" staggers encountered in his work. In the unpublished *J. M. Mime*, sketched on two pages from a *Herakles* notebook, Beckett's two actors begin their progression at a central point on stage.[6] The entire action consists of the greatest number of permutations and combinations within the framework of a large square blocked on the same stage floor. "That's not moving," we read in "Whoroscope," "that's *moving*." Maddy Rooney in *All That Fall*, Winnie in *Happy Days*, and Hamm and Clov in *Endgame* have run (usually in slow motion or in no motion at all) into similar problems. For the direction of movement on Beckett's stage depends not necessarily on left and right, but on the particular vantage point from which it is being perceived. Maddy Rooney's heavy movement is, for example, not seen at all, merely heard: she is a figure in a radio-play "written to come out of the dark."[7]

In *Footfalls* Beckett introduces still another challenge to his audience's power of perception. Observed from our seats in the theater, May's pattern of movement is "parallel with front" and appears to be singularly linear. She moves back and forth, from right to left, "like one of Dante's damned." Metaphorically circular, May's movement, from where we sit, appears to be strictly limited to one horizontal plane.

But human perception, as Merleau-Ponty reminds us, cannot always be trusted. We cannot, to use one of his most graphic examples, see a cube: we can only imagine it.[8] We intuit the totality of its six surfaces from the three that show themselves to our restricted visual horizon. The rest we must take on blind faith or—for the less spiritually inclined—on epistemological evidence. So it goes with May's movement from right to left, from left to right. The movement we perceive along a horizontal plane will look quite different from above. From this lofty perspective we would see the tracing on the stage floor of a tremendously elongated variation of the figure 8 turned on its side.

Beckett's theater has long been interested in the significance of numbers. Clov romanticizes his off-stage kitchen for its "nice dimensions, nice proportions" of "ten feet by ten feet by ten feet," and Dan Rooney anxiously apostrophizes a threatened dismissal of arithmetic: "Not count! One of the few satisfactions in life?" The figure 8 in *Footfalls* similarly demands our consideration. Turned on its side, as Beckett renders it here, it is the mathematician's symbol for infinity.

One does not wish to be too clever. Nor does one wish to look for symbols which distract us from the essential impact of this piece in performance. We remember Beckett's stricture in the Addenda to *Watt*: "No symbols where none intended." But the moment one entertains the possibility of a configuration of infinity within the small scale of *Footfalls*, the notion is not quite so easy to dismiss. For Beckett has used the figure 8 turned on its side before. Commenting in 1938 on the poetic virtuosity of Denis Devlin's "Communication from the Eiffel Tower,"[9] Beckett wrote in the pages of *Transition*: "If only the 8 in the last line had been left on its side. So: ∞." The discovery of such a timeless, endless, boundless realm within the diminutive proportions of *Footfalls* becomes ever more tantalizing and seems to offer us important options in our response to this work. Although this narrow projection of infinity tempts us to search for the kind of symbolic texture Beckett has warned us not to look for, it makes us suspect that there is far more in his play than first meets the eye.

When we recognize that there is both a surface and a depth to this small piece, we try to focus on one or the other. When we consciously focus on the surface, the depth becomes apparent and gets in the way. When we try to focus on the depth, the surface becomes apparent and gets in the way.[10] "The insistence with which the ground invades the surface," Beckett writes in "Denis Devlin," "is quite extraordinary. Extraadenary."[11] Although this conflict brings dynamic vitality to the drama, it raises more problems than it solves. We seek to fix the surface and the depth, each in its last place, as Clov says in *Endgame*, "under the last dust," or else we try to ignore surface at the expense of depth, or depth at the expense of surface. But *Footfalls*, like so much in Beckett's recent "ends and odds," will not put itself to rest. In the miniaturized grandeur of this play the infinity we are tempted to uncover, the allusive content, and the emotional effect by no means coincide or even mutually support each other, "I am concerned with a thing's not being what it was," noted Beckett's recent collaborator Jasper Johns, "with its becoming something other than what it is, with any moment in which one identifies a thing precisely, and with the slipping away of that moment."[12]

The footsteps of infinity on Beckett's narrow space complicate rather than elucidate the meaning of *Footfalls*. The actual value of infinity threatens to slip through our fingertips once we try to define its significance in this play. Should we say that May is human and therefore finite? At the end of the play she disappears from the set, and all that remains is the faint trace of a small circle of light. Tangibility seems to have been merely provisional. Beckett makes absence become a hovering presence in a sudden unity-of-no-place. Staged darkness, staged silence, and staged emptiness mark the only infinity on Beckett's tiny plane. "Strange or otherwise," eternity is not for the likes of May and not for the likes of mankind. But *Footfalls* may not really be about this human finite as opposed to the eternal infinite. May may not really be human after all. Even her name, "May" rather than "Bea," implies potentiality of being rather than being itself. Beckett suggested to his German actors that May herself has not really been properly born. The voice of the off-stage mother interrupts herself in the sentence "In the old home, the same where she—(*pause*)" and then continues "The same where she began." Beckett explained the pause and the emendation in the following way: originally the mother's voice was going to say ". . . the same where she was born." But that would have been wrong. May is "ageless" because she has not been born. She just began. "It began," Beckett told his company. "There is a difference. She was never born."[13] The dramatic situation therefore concerns a life which didn't begin as a life, but which was just there, as a thing.

Beckett said that in the thirties he attended a lecture in London in which the psychologist Jung spoke about a young patient he was unable to help even after fifteen years of therapy. She existed, but she did not actually live. "But, of course," Jung expostulated, "she was never born."[14] Beckett transforms Jung's lecture into a concise dramatic image. *Footfalls* is a play about someone who is really "not there" at all. "I was not there," says May in the suspiciously autobiographical story she tells about Amy (anagram for May) and old Mrs. Winter near the end of her performance. Offering us a "semblance" of two-character dialogue in her fragment, May is in the process of creating a fictionalized language which simultaneously refers to the dramatic situation in which we see her taking part:

> What is it, Mother, are you not feeling yourself? (*Pause.*) Mrs. W. did not at once reply. But finally, raising her head and fixing Amy—the daughter's given name, as the reader will remember—fixing Amy full in the eye she said—(*pause*)—she murmured, fixing Amy full in the eye she murmured, Amy, did you observe anything . . . strange at Evensong? Amy: No Mother, I did not. Mrs. W: Perhaps it was just my fancy. Amy: Just what exactly, Mother, did you perhaps fancy it was? (*Pause.*) Just what exactly, Mother, did you perhaps fancy this . . . strange thing was you observed? (*Pause.*) Mrs. W: You yourself observed nothing . . . strange? Amy: No, Mother, I myself did not, to put it mildly. Mrs. W: What do you mean, Amy, to put it mildly, what can you possibly mean, Amy, to put it mildly? Amy: I mean, Mother, that to say I observed nothing . . . strange is indeed to put it mildly. For I observed nothing of any kind, strange or otherwise. I saw nothing, heard nothing, of any kind. I was not there. Mrs. W: Not there? Amy: Not there. Mrs. W: But I heard you respond. (*Pause.*) I heard you say Amen. (*Pause.*) How could you have responded if you were not there? (*Pause.*) How could you possibly have said Amen if, as you claim, you were not there? (*Pause.*) The love of God, and the fellowship of the Holy Ghost, be with us all, evermore. Amen. (*Pause.*) I heard you distinctly.

May is a presence, not a person—certainly not a person who has ever been properly born outside of the imagination. She is neither more nor less substantial than any other stage character. *Footfalls* cannot really sustain the "neat identification"[15] we have been so tempted to make between the human finite in contrast to the eternal infinite. As a theatricalized enigma, it cannot, to paraphrase Beckett's famous statement on *Finnegans Wake*, really be about something; it must, instead, be that something itself.[16]

Why should we consider the linear trail of infinity that May traces on the floor of Beckett's stage? Primarily to point out the possibilities, limitations, and relativities implicated in our perception of time and space in his theater. In *Footfalls*, perhaps more graphically than anywhere else in the Beckett canon, intellectual dilemma, emotional effect, and physical blocking coincide in an "absolute absence of the Absolute."[17] Our questions about this drama will prove to be as endless as the path May is fated to tread. The figure 8 turned on its side epitomizes our own experience as we confront this strange work. For *Footfalls* is a combination of its own completion and continuity, a drama that assaults us with its own uneasy presentness. As members of the audience we become obsessed with the materialization of Beckett's precise illusion, its menace, and its progressive validation. But what is central to the integrity of this illusion is not symbolism, but consistency. There is no authorization to make a subtext out of the text we read. The drama is primarily concerned with linking its own absolute qualities, its own inner vitality and definiteness, within the limits of its narrow space. Making no direct appeal to any reality outside of itself, *Footfalls* is, instead, a synthesis of those visual and verbal concretions Beckett makes us see and hear when we sit in his theater.

"The motion alone"—in any of its spatial configurations—is certainly "not enough." May's footsteps are, therefore, gigantic, for their singular compactness has already accumulated an enormous range of intention and suggestion. There is no real need to introduce an extraneous path of infinity into *Footfalls*, for infinity is already present in the continuous actuality of the continuous pacing that is this play. *Footfalls* is a constant becoming, a work which can never be abandoned through definition because the enigma of its being on stage is its only essence. Indexification is refined out of existence, a gratuitous intrusion. Objects, motivations, exposition, and even explanation, the paraphernalia of the realistic theater, have been cancelled and omitted. What remains is an immense—we are tempted to say infinite—landscape of potentiality. No two encounters with this play can ever be exactly alike, for the multiplicity and simultaneity of interpretations will forever compete for our attention. The adventure of experiencing this play is, then a continual temptation. The actuality of May's endless pacing and the haunting reverie of her footsteps therefore subject us to the most infinite of all dramatic options, spartan simplicity. "The forms are many," writes Beckett in *Malone Dies*, "in which the unchanging seeks relief from its formlessness."

Notes

1. Beckett quoted by Walter D. Asmus, "Rehearsal Notes for the German Premiere of Beckett's *That Time* and *Footfalls* at the Schiller-Theater Werkstatt, Berlin," trans. Helen Watanabe, *Journal of Beckett Studies*, 2 (Summer 1977), 88.

2. Asmus, p. 85.

3. Citations in my text from *Footfalls* are from the Faber edition (London, 1976).

4. Asmus, p. 83.

5. Samuel Beckett, *Fizzles* (New York: Grove, 1976), p. 22.

6. Sighle Kennedy, *Murphy's Bed* (Lewisburg, Pa.: Bucknell Univ. Press, 1971), pp. 64–65.

7. Alec Reid, *All I Can Manage, More Than I Could: An Approach to the Plays of Samuel Beckett* (Dublin: Dolmen, 1968), p. 68.

8. Maurice Merleau-Ponty, *Sense and Non-Sense*, trans. Herbert L. and Patricia Allen Dreyfus (Evanston: Northwestern Univ. Press, 1964), p. 50.

9. Samuel Beckett, "Denis Devlin," *Transition*, 27 (1938), 292.

10. In formulating this argument about *Footfalls*, I am indebted to the discussion by Lawrence D. Steefel, Jr., in "Dimension and Development in *The Passage from the Virgin to the Bride*," *Marcel Duchamp in Perspective*, ed. Joseph Masheck (Englewood Cliffs, N.J.: Prentice-Hall, 1975), pp. 90, 95.

11. "Denis Devlin," p. 293.

12. Quoted by Max Kozloff, "Johns and Duchamp" in *Marcel Duchamp in Perspective*, p. 144. Beckett collaborated with Jasper Johns in the *livre de peinture* called *Foirades / Fizzles* published by the Petersborough Press in 1976.

13. Asmus, pp. 84, 87.

14. Alan Schneider, "I Hope to Be Going On With Sam Beckett—And He With Me," *The New York Times*, December 18, 1977, sec. 2, p. 3.

15. Samuel Beckett, "Dante . . . Bruno. Vico. . Joyce," *Our Exagmination Round His Factification for Incamination of Work in Progress* (Paris: Shakespeare and Company, 1929), p. 3.

16. Beckett, *Our Exagmination*, p. 14.

17. Beckett, *Our Exagmination*, p. 22.

"My Shade Will Comfort You": Beckett's Rites of Theater

Susan D. Brienza*

Samuel Beckett's dramatic characters spend much of their stage time performing comforting rituals while waiting, ending, or having "happy" days. In fact, the entire drama *Krapp's Last Tape* enacts an annual birthday rite, playing back past tapes and recording a new one. Yet these daily rites describe only the most superficial ways in which ritual appears on Beckett's stage. Besides all the obsessive behavior of his characters—ceremonial, albeit mundane, gestures and words that compose profane ritual—Beckett's drama also captures ritual in the religious, mythical sense. Virtually a one-to-one correspondence maps the essential elements of sacred ritual onto the central qualities of Beckett's theater. His dramas, like rites, take place outside ordinary space and time, consist of ordered play, explore ancient themes infused with myth, and are transmitted through an initiated performer often in a trance-like state to an audience in a participatory frame of mind. Beckett merges the entertainment of theater with the efficacy of sacrament to create plays that make us not just

*This essay was prepared for this volume and is published here for the first time.

feel, laugh, think, but also urge us to realize our metaphysical position in the universe. Modern man, disconnected from nature, God, and even little gods, derives a sense of order from Beckett's simple yet highly patterned dramas. "My shade will comfort you," says Reader in the recent play *Ohio Impromptu* as he intones from a gigantic alchemical-looking volume. And there is something oddly comforting as well as profoundly disturbing in the experience of Beckett's theater.

It is not surprising that Beckett early on explored the possibilities of myth and ritual as undercurrents for his plays since modern writers were everywhere finding compatible motifs in classical and primitive sources: Yeats borrowing from the Noh drama, Joyce rewriting Homer for *Ulysses* and myths of the Creation and Fall for *Finnegans Wake*, T. S. Eliot sifting through the wastes of Frazer's *Golden Bough* and seeking Weston's holy grail, and Ezra Pound interweaving literary and cultural fragments from Italy, Greece, and China. In the visual arts Picasso was using primitive animal totems as models for his avant garde masks, while in the performing arts Artaud was adapting trance states from Balinese dances. By the time Beckett began to write, modern artists had demonstrated that in order to move forward to the new they had to travel backward to the ancient past. Beckett takes his place among this group since his plays, not just in substance but also in structure and in performance, are highly ritualistic.

Significantly, Beckett discusses drama in terms of movement within a limited area: "We are dealing with a definite space and with people in this space," he says.[1] Both play (as in games) and rite occur in a specially delineated place, whether a baseball diamond, tennis court, chess board, or a "consecrated spot"[2]; and although every stage is a restricted performance area akin to a sports field or a religious altar, Beckett's stages are always further demarcated and prescribed. The notion of a sacred center, and of a long, dangerous journey to that center—be it palace or lake or temple—is one of the axioms of ritual. And Beckett transposes this motif into an obsessive quest for a particular spot on his stage. The *Godot* tramps are anxiously driven to position themselves on a mound near the tree (in Eden or Golgotha?) as they return to the same location every day. Hamm decrees that he must be situated precisely in the center of his room, called "the Refuge," and Clov circles around his lapsed god with patterned movements. Krapp seems compelled to return to the middle of his table after each short sally away from it, and to maintain his "zone of light" over the table.

But with Beckett's rituals, the central location may be a purgatory or a hell, rather than a peaceful Nirvana—perhaps because heavens are hard to come by in the contemporary cosmos—and the protagonist is not always free to continue the quest. In a mime called *Quad*, four creatures walking quickly in semi-circular paths keep approaching the center of a quadrant and then avoiding that center—as if repelled by some magnetic force. In many plays after *Endgame*, several degrees of freedom are removed since characters are already stalemated chess pieces at the drama's start; rather than an obsessive regaining of a center, they experience a forced fixity, suffering a Dantesque punishment. Winnie is buried within the center of her magic hill (while Willie—ceremonially "dressed to kill"—advances toward his wife with deliberate slowness). In *Play* the three dead heads are imprisoned within funereal urns centered on stage; but the most fixed of all is Mouth in *Not I*, a disembodied fragment of a face pinned to a central spot at a particular height above the stage floor.

Beckett characters as well as their creator make a ritual of arithmetic and geometry, dividing spaces and calculating times until mathematics becomes their form of metaphysics. Although in a world where magic and myth truly operated the actual numbers would effect a desired change, in Beckett's world counting is valuable for its own sake, as escape, as solace. "We took flight in arithmetic," says the protagonist of the story *Enough* (also performed as a monologue). In his Director's Notebook for *Endgame*, Beckett stipulates two distinct motions for Clov, his " 'thinking' walk" and his " 'winding up' walk" and also a constant eight steps between the door and Hamm's chair.[3] Similarly, when the actor playing Krapp departs from the magic circle circumscribed by his light, Beckett as director—often beating the rhythm as for music—instructs him to take precisely seven steps to his table and thirteen to his alcove. Even more measured and dance-like is May's cadenced glide in *Footfalls*, testing the boundaries of the floor as she paces and whirls according to meticulous stage directions. The paths of the female trinity in *Come and Go* evoke a preparatory rite for death, as the three women in rotation separate into a duo to whisper about the illness of the third member, and re-combine into their trio to evade the fact of mortality. Most formally choreographed of all, indeed resembling dance more than drama, is his voiceless piece *Quad*, in which four creatures, in hooded, monk-like garb, walk in and around a quadrant design of four colors, moving in ceremonial configurations following elaborate stage directions.

Time as well as space is re-defined or skewed in both game and ritual; adopting the atemporal sense, the *in illo tempore* (once upon a time) atmosphere from myth, ritual creates its own closed universe outside of clock time. In Beckett's dramatic world we may be placed at a mythical beginning in *Waiting for Godot*, at an apocalyptic ending in *Endgame* or *Happy Days*, or within the purgatorial stasis of *Play*. Both characters and audience experience a timeless state as the day of the drama's events could be any day, days in endless succession. Even more self-consciously in the later plays Beckett situates the character (and the spectator) in no-time by allowing him three time frames at once, either superimposed as in *Krapp's Last Tape* or interwoven as in *That Time*. Krapp at age 69 can listen to a tape of Krapp at 39 discussing the stupid young Krapp of 21; but since the elderly speaker is just as foolish as his youthful self, time is frozen in futility as it circles endlessly on spools of memory.

The phrase "that time," in the later play of that title, actually refers to three widely separated times depicted by three modulations, A, B, and C, of the same voice interspliced. Although the play begins with an indication of specificity, the phrase "that time," it ends with an infinite abstraction, the phrase "no time." Since the voices represent one person at three different stages of life, they call up many of the same places (a flat stone, a train terminus) as the times shift, thus providing spatial continuity within temporal flux. Unimpeded by capitals, periods, or punctuation of any sort, the speeches of *That Time*[4] flow on sans beginning or end, highlighting discrete memories of "that time when" and "another time" but undercutting them with terms of continuity like "still," "always," and "year after year" and with phrases of finality like "never" and "nothing new." Use of the mystical eleven for the number of the train in the text suggests for Beckett (as it did for Yeats and Joyce) a rebeginning, a new cycle; and yet later in the play time seems to be frozen at one season of the earth: "always winter then / endless winter year after year / as if it couldn't end / the old year never end / like time could go no further . . ." (p. 233, slashes mine).

In the closing speeches time is confused and out of joint as the speakers lose their judgment about both chronology and duration, causing them to contradict themselves phrase by phrase: "when was that an earlier time a later time before she came after she went or both," "that time after you went back soon after long after." Finally voice A speculates that perhaps all moments are subsumed in one moment: "or was that another time all that another time was there ever any other time but that time" (p. 235). Indirectly as well as directly, human clock time is superseded towards the end of the piece, transcended by apocalyptic, Biblical time with the verbal "dust" falling heavily until "suddenly this dust whole place suddenly full of dust . . . floor to ceiling nothing only dust." Like the women in *Come and Go* circling around the subject of mortality, the voice in *That Time* pivots on the word "gone" as the protagonist ends alone and timeless with an incantatory lament: "come and gone / come and gone / no one / come and gone / in no time / gone in no time" (my slashes). This ambiguous phrasal structure also allows Beckett to indicate simultaneously the senselessness of man's fleeting life on earth; we are all gone in no time.

Many of Beckett's plays hang suspended in a state between ordinary and super-ordinary reality analogous to the transcendent "dreamtime" in the dance-dramas of the Australian Arunta (whose special time is reserved for initiation cycles.)[5] In general, cycles and repetition in Beckett's plays correspond to Mircea Eliade's depiction of mythical time: "The past is but a prefiguration of the future. No event is irreversible and no transformation is final. In a certain sense, it is even possible to say that nothing new happens in the world, for everything is but the repetition of the same primordial archetypes; this repetition, by actualizing the mythical moment when the archetypal gesture was revealed, constantly maintains the world in the same auroral instant of beginnings."[6] We feel this infinite cycling acutely in *Endgame* in which the self-reflexive drama metaphors throughout the play suggest its restart for every performance each night, and in the drama *Play* since Act 2 repeats Act 1 word for word. For other Beckett plays, within each scene or speech there are verbal and gestural rebeginnings that imply that "nothing new happens in the world" of the stage. Although Beckett's characters share a mythical time sense with, say, epic heroes, the contrasts are huge: his questers are usually goal-less, and their journeys (often only mental) are endless.

Play, which becomes ritual when obligatory and efficacious, winds to a conclusion within a limited time and always manifests repetition within time in two ways: its fixed form can be repeated in its entirety and its internal structure exploits recapitulation. *Godot*, with its recycling of language and gesture in doubles and triplets (as Ruby Cohn has wonderfully documented), offers the fullest example of this; but each of Beckett's plays achieves ritualistic patterning through symmetry, rhythm, and pure repetition. What Johan Huizinga observes about the effect of play succinctly explains the effects of Beckett's drama: "[play] creates order, *is* order. Into an imperfect world and into the confusion of life it brings a temporary, a limited perfection."[7] This is precisely the sense of calm generated by *Ohio Impromptu* in which the Reader recites a story about two men to Listener, a story concerning a Reader who reads nightly to a listener many long years ago, a story that is repeated every night. And since orderly reiteration can signify either a downward spiral or a renewal, can mean either "over" (as the return of a song's refrain indicates closure) or "over again," in microcosm repetition represents the oldest of ritual themes—death and rebirth.

Of course Man's life and death are celebrated in ritual festivals through imaginative reconstructions of deaths and rebirths in Nature—seasons, stars, crops—and Beckett's plays reflect this imitation of the natural cycle. The man in *A Piece of Monologue* begins his speech with the word "Birth" ("Birth was the death of him") and ends with a mortal signal, the term "gone" ("Alone gone"); in between he tells of a (strangely similar) man who moves from a westward window to an eastern wall while lighting a lamp. Like the creature in Beckett's story *Still*, this monologist is chronicling the sun's cycle—only in reverse—with the dying light representing his own fading life; yet, rejecting the actual sun, he exists in a "black vast," and "black beyond," in an infinite and eternally dwindling universe.[8] With his piece of monologue about the human cycle, this speaker appropriates the archetypal qualities of the mythic hero, come back to tell us all. As Joseph Campbell describes it, since the hero "is the man or woman who has been able to battle past his personal and local historical limitations to the generally valid, normally human forms[,] . . . [he is] eloquent, not of the present, disintegrating society and psyche, but of the unquenched source through which society is reborn. The hero has died as a modern man; but as eternal man—perfected, unspecific, universal man—he has been reborn. His solemn task and deed therefore . . . is to return then to us, transfigured, and teach the lesson he has learned of life renewed."[9] Beckett's born again heroes (Lucky and Pozzo also descend to a dark night of the soul and then return with a special knowledge) bring back no redemptive messages from the gods but do give us their insights of despair in lyrical language, supplying the Yeatsian comfort of art even when religious transcendence is impossible. It is through poetry that they create a new order in the shattered universe.

Rites concerning regression to Chaos, annihilation of the old world, and rebirth of the New Year include a return of spirits; besides *Monologue*, whose speaker keeps imagining a burial spot, *Endgame* provides another version of this religious cycle with the death of Mother Pegg and the reincarnation of the Buddha-like little boy. Hamm's shelter, the telluric womb, represents both skull and sepulchre; symbols of ritual death paradoxically suggest embryonic life (Clov's flea *will* repopulate the earth as he fears). In a deeper paradox, "joining the company of the dead and the Ancestors"[10] means that a new spiritual life can begin. This idea of transmigration of souls provides a fuller significance for the story within the story in *Ohio Impromptu*, with the current Reader on stage playing the metempsychosis of a voice out of the past: "In his dreams he had been warned against this change. Seen the dear face and heard the unspoken words, Stay where we were so long alone together, my shade will comfort you" (p. 30). In several cultures ritual provides a way of transmigrating back across generations of time in order to hear the shades of the past, to receive the wisdom of the Ancestors. It is an interesting parallel that in the story *Company* (1980), where voices in the darkness afford the main company and comfort, the narrator often conjures up his father's shade, and that Beckett has given permission for this fiction to be dramatized. Further, it is no coincidence that in two favorable reviews of the first English adaptation of *Company*, the writers liken the play to ritual.[11] In *Company* the son, the voice recalling the past, gradually becomes the father as he ages.

Within the paradigm of the son replacing the father or the new leader supplanting the old king-god is the tradition of the scapegoat—usually an innocent victim who can expiate the sins of the community and thereby restore order and fertility to the land. Although the ritual murder of a sacrificial victim is not as important to a Beckett play as it is, say, to an early Pinter work (where it often structures the entire drama[12]), the scapegoat does surface on Beckett's stage: with Lucky as Christ-like pseudo-savior, with the starving young son in *Endgame*, and more subtly with the little boy mysteriously killed, supposedly murdered, in the radio play *All That Fall*. This play is permeated with images of death, decay, and sterility: the aging protagonist Maddy Rooney with her diseases, infirmities, and her childless daughter, and even her archaic "dead language"; the motifs of shit, slowness, and termination; the song "Death and the Maiden" in the background—virtually every detail of the play. The only spark of life—besides Maddy's irrepressible yet ludicrous sexuality—is the little boy on the train, described by Mr. Rooney as a "young bud," and presumably pushed onto the tracks by this withered man. Is the sightless Mr. Rooney blind, then, to the ritualistic renewal such a bud of springtime offers? Is Mr. Rooney an old Oedipus punished in advance of his crime and bringing pestilence to the land? Or are all saviors and scapegoats impotent in the contemporary world? In any case, Beckett's play ends with the boy's enigmatic death, not with any resulting rebirth.

The general patterns of ritual and myth appear in Beckett's drama truncated (as in *All That Fall*), or disguised, or distorted, but always dimly visible. Even the tiny drama *Come and Go*, which seems too fragile to bear much mythic weight, has great allusive density. The bird-like characters, in their costume, dialogue, and gesture, simultaneously convey both Life and Death. In the first French production, the three women, wearing large hats decked with fruit, flowers, and feathers, suggested totems of vegetation;[13] in fact they actually become parodic fertility goddesses. And yet Flo (Flower), Ru(e), and Vi (Violet)—Ophelia's handmaidens in death—portray mortality as they feel the "rings" of growth and aging on their tree-like limbs.[14] In *Act Without Words I* we can perceive in crystallized, humorous yet poignant, form the myths of Sisyphus and Tantalus. One of the many ways of approaching *Waiting for Godot* is as an extended dialogue between the two thieves, Gogo and Didi, with Christ missing. Thus Beckett borrows ritual and mythic sources and condenses them, inverts them, or parodies them—always to suit the particular purposes of his short ceremonies of theatre.

Happy Days becomes, in this light, a comic version of *Prometheus Bound*: Jan Kott suspects that Winnie was the first dramatic character since Prometheus who was unable to move throughout an entire drama.[15] Just as myths are parodied in Beckett, rituals are reversed, usually with the surface of the rite intact but its aim subverted. Perhaps the best example of this—again comic yet painful—is Winnie's return to the womb of Mother Earth. In most cultures the *regressus ad uterum* is either an initiation rite achieving rebirth into adulthood or into a transcendental state, or a curative rite for the aged or infirm promising rebirth into health and vigor.[16] Poor Winnie, though, is being buried alive, swallowed up never to return—and simultaneously baked by a "hellish light." What is usually a positive symbol of mystical "going back" or "return to the origin" becomes a deadly regression. Spiritual embryo becomes a near corpse.

Often Beckett explicitly names a rite or myth only to undermine it within the play itself, as if he is warning his modern audience that the classical comforts alone no longer suffice. In *Endgame* the goddesses Flora, Pomona, and Ceres are specifically mocked; and Hamm jeers at the preposterous notion that his world might turn green and fresh come Spring. Ceres is an especially ironic figure for Hamm to call up since she is the Goddess of the Corn, symbol of harvest and new grain, while all Hamm can harvest is grains of sand. Demeter (another name for Ceres) with her only daughter Persephone, appears in several of Beckett's plays—including *All That Fall*, in the guise of Maddy with her only daughter who dies. Beckett no doubt avoided some other gods and goddesses because they were too powerful and optimistic for his infertile and melancholy creatures to be modeled on—however ironically. By contrast, Demeter is the only female immortal to suffer human grief and pain; she is "the divine sorrowing mother who saw her daughter die each year"[17] and thus serves as the perfect analog for creatures in various purgatories and hells. The sorrowful mother-daughter pair in *Footfalls* displays again Beckett's technique of inverting myth. While May's steps simply continue or express suffering as she revolves "it all" in her mind, Demeter's daughter rejuvenated the earth with her footsteps:

> Persephone was the radiant maiden of the spring and summertime, whose light step upon the dry, brown hillside was enough to make it fresh and blooming, as Sappho writes,
>
> I heard the footfall of the flower spring . . . —Persephone's footfall.[18]

Of course in Beckett's play where the title suggests this irony, footfalls accomplish nothing—certainly not renewal. In *Footfalls*, May's name is rendered as Amy in the story within the play as if her own name must be distorted, and Persephone—surrounded in classical literature by an atmosphere of death and strangeness—is referred to as "the maiden whose name may not be spoken." This added attribute of the mythological girl could have prompted Beckett to borrow her for yet another female character, one who refuses to admit her identity, who effaces herself behind "she," and "not I."

Thus an altered transposition of the Persephone story may be what is streaming from the Mouth in the monologue *Not I*. Once upon a time Persephone was picking flowers with her mother Demeter when she was stolen away to Hades where she was imprisoned for six months of the year, causing winter to spread over the land; during the six months when the young girl was allowed back on earth, springtime reigned. One day Mouth was "wandering in a field . . . looking aimlessly for cowslips. . . . when suddenly . . . gradually . . . all went out . . . all that early April morning light . . . and she . . . found herself in the dark"; then she regains her speech (her cultural life) "once or twice a year . . . always winter some strange reason." Showing a seasonal reversal of this myth but demonstrating the same harmony with earth's cycles, for many societies winter is the Sacred Time when the spirits return to the living: in the Christian liturgical calendar, All Souls Day is November 2. In the Judaic tradition the days of atonement and the remembrances of the dead occur during autumn. And in some non-Christian tribes there is a time when the men relinquish their summer names and reclaim their sacred winter titles. During this period, the whole community celebrates its mythical origins while the novice, caught up in dances and the sounds of hallowed instruments, drifts into a trance which indicates his death to the profane life and his rebirth as a Spirit.[19] These rites conjure up (next to *Not I*) *Footfalls* once again with May's trance-like walk, her alter ego "Amy," her mother's fictional name of Mrs. Winter, and finally May's vanishing at the end of the play. (Analogously, at the climax of the Winter rite in some religions, the novice was either "carried off" into the forest, or "ravished" to Heaven.) May's disappearance from the audience's vision at the last instant of the play affirms her non-existence as corporeal being.

The prayers and trance states of initiands and ritual performers are echoed by many of Beckett's characters. Besides the deliberate, rhyming words of May in *Footfalls* and the frenetic phrases of Mouth in *Not I*, we hear the incantatory, almost hypnotic litany of V (Voice) in *Rockaby*:

> so in the end
> close of a long day
> went down
> in the end went down
> down the steep stair
> let down the blind and down
> right down
> into the old rocker
> mother rocker
> where mother sat
> all the years
> all in black
> best black
> sat and rocked
> rocked
> till her end came
> in the end came (pp. 17–18)

Beckett's tradition of trance-like performers on stage started early on with *Godot*'s Lucky spewing out his fragmented and inverted soteriology in a fit of repetition, irrationality, and despair. More recently Beckett directed an actress playing Winnie to read her classical quotation passages in a chant,[20] distinguishing literary language from everyday speech, and suggesting that fractured poetry becomes prayer for the hopeless woman trying desperately to find solace if not happiness. Beckett's stage directions for *Endgame* ask Hamm to adopt a special tone and intonation for his Chronicle—a cumulative, repetitive story that has become a daily rite for speaker and witness alike, another ritual game that will not end. In a calmer, more level voice than these and with a fairy tale quality, the Reader in *Ohio Impromptu* comforts himself and us with the ritualized recitation of his beginnings from a tome appearing to contain the secrets of the ages.

Myth in ancient times literally provided explanations for how the universe worked, and also created the rites—for birth, initiation, marriage, and burial—that showed man how to conduct his life. It was enough for him that "this is the way the Ancestors did it" and that rites guaranteed certain cures. Contemporary man, lacking the catharsis of religious redemption and the stability of cultural ritual, places heavier burdens on ritualistic drama. From Beckett's dramatic characters the modern theater-goer can at least learn how *not* to conduct his life: not by repudiating the past as does Krapp, not by revising the present as does the self-deluding Winnie; but perhaps like Gogo, Didi, and Clov he can maintain calm with stoicism, a little humor, and dashes of brutal hope, or like Hamm and the nameless protagonist in *Company* (and like Mr. Beckett himself), with the ancient practice of storytelling. Folktales and myths were not just stories told around a primitive campfire to keep the wind and wolves at bay, but more importantly were the sacred accounts that gave a tribe a sense of its unique identity. Beckett's voices in *That Time* offer similar reasons for their recollections and fictions:

> B: . . . just one of those things you kept making up to keep the void out just another of those old tales to keep the void from pouring in on top of you . . . (p. 230)
>
> A: making it all up on the doorstep as you went along making yourself all up again for the millionth time . . . (p. 234)

The act of storytelling provides comfort for nearly all of Beckett's characters—in the fiction even more so than in the drama—but something in addition seems necessary for their creator. To satisfy a need for order the spatial alignment of a finite stage becomes essential, which returns us to the notion of ritual theater as ordered play. During rehearsals for a production of *Endgame* Beckett stressed this drama as a self-contained game, as "simply a basis for acting," and implied that it created its own system:

> the link between individuals and things no longer exists. . . . There are so many things. The eye is as unable to grasp them as the intelligence to understand them. Therefore one creates one's own world, *un univers à part* in order to withdraw . . . to escape from chaos into an ever simpler world. . . . The value of theatre lies for me in this. One can set up a small world with its own rules, order the game as if on a chessboard—Indeed, even the game of chess is too complicated.[21]

Of course one way to simplify further is to eliminate words completely and to restrict stage space and gesture entirely—that is, to create a theatrical dance, which is exactly what Beckett has done recently with *Quad*. A similar goal was achieved through fusion of modern dance and expressionist theater during the 1920's in Mary Wigman's experiments with dramatic ballet. Beckett's four dancers avoiding a mid-point, walking mechanically and with bowed heads to steady drum beats, look very much like Mary Wigman's performers as described by Christopher Innes: ". . . the dancers created their own expressive patterns of sound from the rhythms beaten out by their feet or drum beats, which were regulated by the tempo of the dance and (as in O'Neill's *Emperor Jones*) not only echoed the heartbeat of the performers, but helped to excite a corresponding pulse rate in the audience. . . . Observers were struck by the trance-like or somnambulistic impression given by Wigman's troupe—an impression given as much by the frenzied 'nervous energy verging on hallucination' as by the fixed eyes and mask-like rigidity of their faces—and described what they were watching as the 'visions and spectral obsessions of a nightmare'."[22] Considering that these dance-dramas, early twentieth-century attempts to produce intense rites of theatre, exploited archetypal movements within atavistic, universal shapes, we can now interpret Beckett's performers in *Quad* as painters of a large mandala on the stage floor—a symbol of the Cosmos, yet a contemporary cosmos that will not permit of a center. Similarly, Beckett's dramas appear as quasi-religious rites centered by no god; all those creatures can do is circle around, never reaching a point of integration, comforted by the rhythm of their own footsteps.

As audience, our acknowledging and then our yielding to the ritual sensibility of performance in Beckett's theater allies us with audiences of the past whose belief and participation in rites were necessary for social and cultural survival. When, in answer to Clov's question "What is there to keep me here?" Hamm responds "The dialogue," this reply, amplified and intensified, serves for us as well. With the line in *Footfalls* "as the reader will remember" we have ceased to be mere spectators, if indeed we ever were. Starting with *Godot*, Beckett's self-conscious and self-referential performers drew us into our active roles in the drama, and increasingly, as Ruby Cohn puts it, "the late plays fuse the actual audience experience into the dramatic fiction"[23]; thus we all play Auditor in *Not I* and Listener in *Ohio Impromptu*. In our most challenging role, we must play detective, finding order and meaning as we listen to the murder mystery of *All That Fall*; and while there is no spiritual rebirth for Mr. or Mrs. Rooney, the audience becomes the mythical hero who must return to the world with new knowledge. Like ancient shamanistic ritual, Beckett's ritualistic theater appeals to both the smaller group that is privy to a hermetic language and to the larger group that shares a general culture. Like ancient man, we encounter a simple yet allusive, primitive yet sophisticated ceremony that brings the order of rhythm, repetition, and pattern to an uncertain, confusing world. Beckett unites his audience not with Nature or with nature's gods (except in parody) but with artificial fabrications, yet in such a structured, ritualistic manner that it reassures, it comforts.

Notes

1. Quoted in Ruby Cohn, *Just Play: Beckett's Theater* (Princeton: Princeton University Press, 1980), p. 231.

2. Johan Huizinga, "Nature and Significance of Play as a Cultural Phenomenon," in Richard Schechner and Mady Schuman, eds. *Ritual, Play, and Performance: Readings in the Social Sciences / Theater* (N.Y.: The Seabury Press, 1976), p. 53.

3. Cohn, *Just Play*, pp. 238, 243.

4. Pages refer to the text in *The Collected Shorter Plays of Samuel Beckett* (New York: Grove Press, 1984), pp. 225–36.

5. Richard Schechner, "From Ritual to Theatre and Back," in *Ritual, Play, and Performance*, pp. 199–200.

6. Mircea Eliade, *The Myth of the Eternal Return*, trans. by Willard R. Trask (New York: Pantheon Books, 1954), pp. 89–90.

7. Huizinga in Schechner, p. 53.

8. Ruby Cohn, "Beckett's Theatre Resonance," in Morris Beja, et al., eds., *Samuel Beckett: Humanistic Perspectives* (Columbus: Ohio State University Press, 1983). p. 12.

9. Joseph Campbell, *The Hero With a Thousand Faces* (1949; Princeton: Princeton University Press, 1973), pp. 19–20.

10. Mircea Eliade, *Rites and Symbols of Initiation: The Mysteries of Birth and Rebirth* (New York: Harper & Row, 1958), p. xiv.

11. Michael Lassell says of the Figure's communing with himself, "His dialogue is that of ritualized philosophic inquiry" (*L.A. Weekly*, Feb. 22–28, 1985, p. 100). T. H. McCulloh mentions the timelessness of ritual in this unstructured monologue: "The beginning, middle and ending may not be easily discernible to an unwary mind but a second glance will locate the beginning in insight, the middle in language, and the ending in pure, reassuringly theatrical ritual; . . . the theatrical ritual is of its beginnings and its future" (*Drama-Logue*, Feb. 21–27, 1985, p. 4). In this production at the L.A. Actors' Theater Stan Gontarski directs Alan Mandell.

12. Katherine H. Burkman, *The Dramatic World of Harold Pinter: Its Basis in Ritual* (Ohio State University Press, 1971), pp. 19–47.

13. Cohn, *Just Play*, p. 235.

14. Hersh Zeifman, "*Come and Go*: A Criticule," in *Humanistic Perspectives*, pp. 140–41.

15. Jan Kott, *The Eating of the Gods* (London: Methuen, 1974), p. 41.

16. Mircea Eliade, *Myth and Reality* (New York: Harper & Row, 1963), pp. 79–83.

17. Edith Hamilton, *Mythology: Timeless Tales of Gods and Heroes* (1940; New York: New American Library, 1963), pp. 49 and 53.

18. Hamilton, pp. 53–54.

19. Eliade, *Initiation*, pp. 68–69.

20. Cohn, *Just Play*, p. 254.

21. Quoted in Christopher Innes, *Holy Theatre: Ritual and the Avant Garde* (New York: Cambridge University Press, 1981), pp. 214–15.

22. In *Holy Theatre*, p. 53.

23. Cohn, "Beckett's Theatre Resonance," p. 12.

Appendix

Three Dialogues

Samuel Beckett and Georges Duthuit*

I
Tal Coat

B.—Total object, complete with missing parts, instead of partial object. Question of degree.

D.—More. The tyranny of the discreet overthrown. The world a flux of movements partaking of living time, that of effort, creation, liberation, the painting, the painter. The fleeting instant of sensation given back, given forth, with context of the continuum it nourished.

B.—In any case a thrusting towards a more adequate expression of natural experience, as revealed to the vigilant coenaesthesia. Whether achieved through submission or through mastery, the result is a gain in nature.

D.—But that which the painter discovers, orders, transmits, is not in nature. What relation between one of these paintings and a landscape seen at a certain age, a certain season, a certain hour? Are we not on a quite different plane?

B.—By nature I mean here, like the naivest realist, a composite of perceiver and perceived, not a datum, an experience. All I wish to suggest is that the tendency and accomplishment of this painting are fundamentally those of previous painting, straining to enlarge the statement of a compromise.

D.—You neglect the immense difference between the significance of perception for Tal Coat and its significance for the great majority of his predecessors, apprehending as artists with the same utilitarian servility as in a traffic jam and improving the result with a lick of Euclidian geometry. The global perception of Tal Coat is disinterested, committed neither to truth nor to beauty, twin tyrannies of nature. I can see the compromise of past painting, but not that which you deplore in the Matisse of a certain period and in the Tal Coat of today.

*Reprinted from *Disjecta: Miscellaneous Writings and a Dramatic Fragment*, ed. Ruby Cohn (New York: Grove Press, 1984) by permission of the publisher and Samuel Beckett. The essay originally appeared in *Transition*, no. 5 (December 1949).

B.—I do not deplore. I agree that the Matisse in question, as well as the Franciscan orgies of Tal Coat, have prodigious value, but a value cognate with those already accumulated. What we have to consider in the case of Italian painters is not that they surveyed the world with the eyes of building contractors, a mere means like any other, but that they never stirred from the field of the possible, however much they may have enlarged it. The only thing disturbed by the revolutionaries Matisse and Tal Coat is a certain order on the plane of the feasible.

D.—What other plane can there be for the maker?

B.—Logically none. Yet I speak of an art turning from it in disgust, weary of its puny exploits, weary of pretending to be able, of being able, of doing a little better the same old thing, of going a little further along a dreary road.

D.—And preferring what?

B.—The expression that there is nothing to express, nothing with which to express, nothing from which to express, no power to express, no desire to express, together with the obligation to express.

D.—But that is a violently extreme and personal point of view, of no help to us in the matter of Tal Coat.

B.—

D.—Perhaps that is enough for today.

II
Masson

B.—In search of the difficulty rather than in its clutch. The disquiet of him who lacks an adversary.

D.—That is perhaps why he speaks so often nowadays of painting the void, "in fear and trembling." His concern was at one time with the creation of a mythology; then with man, not simply in the universe, but in society; and now . . . "inner emptiness, the prime condition, according to Chinese esthetics, of the act of painting." It would thus seem, in effect, that Masson suffers more keenly than any living partner from the need to come to rest, i.e. to establish the data of the problem to be solved, the Problem at last.

B.—Though little familiar with the problems he has set himself in the past and which, by the mere fact of their solubility or for any other reason, have lost for him their legitimacy, I feel their presence not far behind these canvases veiled in consternation, and the scars of a competence that must be most painful to him. Two old maladies that should no doubt be considered separately: the malady of wanting to know what to do and the malady of wanting to be able to do it.

D.—But Masson's declared purpose is now to reduce these maladies, as you call them, to nothing. He aspires to be rid of the servitude of space, that his eye may "frolic among the focusless fields, tumultuous with incessant creation." At the same time he demands the rehabilitation of the "vaporous." This may seem strange in one more fitted by temperament for fire than for damp. You of course will reply that it is the same thing as before, the same reaching towards succour from without. Opaque or transparent, the object remains sovereign. But how can Masson be expected to paint the void?

B.—He is not. What is the good of passing from one untenable position to another, of seeking justification always on the same plane? Here is an artist who seems literally skewered on the ferocious dilemma of expression. Yet he continues to wriggle. The void he speaks of is perhaps simply the obliteration of an unbearable presence, unbearable because neither to be wooed nor to be stormed. If this anguish of helplessness is never stated as such, on its own merits and for its own sake, though perhaps very occasionally admitted as spice to the "exploit" it jeopardized, the reason is doubtless, among others, that it seems to contain in itself the impossibility of statement. Again an exquisitely logical attitude. In any case, it is hardly to be confused with the void.

D.—Masson speaks much of transparency—"openings, circulations, communications, unknown penetrations"—where he may frolic at his ease, in freedom. Without renouncing the objects, loathsome or delicious, that are our daily bread and wine and poison, he seeks to break through their partitions to that continuity of being which is absent from the ordinary experience of living. In this he approaches Matisse (of the first period needless to say) and Tal Coat, but with this notable difference, that Masson has to contend with his own technical gifts, which have the richness, the precision, the density and balance of the high classical manner. Or perhaps I should say rather its spirit, for he has shown himself capable, as occasion required, of great technical variety.

B.—What you say certainly throws light on the dramatic predicament of this artist. Allow me to note his concern with the amenities of ease and freedom. *The stars are undoubtedly superb*, as Freud remarked on reading Kant's cosmological proof of the existence of God. With such preoccupations it seems to me impossible that he should ever do anything different from that which the best, including himself, have done already. It is perhaps an impertinence to suggest that he wishes to. His so extremely intelligent remarks on space breathe the same possessiveness as the notebooks of Leonardo who, when he speaks of *disfazione*, knows that for him not one fragment will be lost. So forgive me if I relapse, as when we spoke of the so different Tal Coat, into my dream of an art unresentful of its insuperable indigence and too proud for the farce of giving and receiving.

D.—Masson himself, having remarked that western perspective is no more than a series of traps for the capture of objects, declares that their possession does not interest him. He congratulates Bonnard for having, in his last works, "gone beyond possessive space in every shape and form, far from surveys and bounds, to the point where all possession is dissolved." I agree that there is a long cry from Bonnard to that impoverished painting, "authentically fruitless, incapable of any image whatsoever," to which you aspire, and towards which too, who knows, unconsciously perhaps, Masson tends. But must we really deplore the painting that admits "the things and creatures of spring, resplendent with desire and affirmation, ephemeral no doubt, but immortally reiterant," not in order to benefit by them, not in order to enjoy them, but in order that what is tolerable and radiant in the world may continue? Are we really to deplore the painting that is a rallying, among the things of time that pass and hurry us away, towards a time that endures and gives increase?

B.—(*Exit weeping.*)

III
Bram van Velde

B.—Frenchman, fire first.

D.—Speaking of Tal Coat and Masson you invoked an art of a different order, not only from theirs, but from any achieved up to date. Am I right in thinking that you had van Velde in mind when making this sweeping distinction?

B.—Yes. I think he is the first to accept a certain situation and to consent to a certain act.

D.—Would it be too much to ask you to state again, as simply as possible, the situation and act that you conceive to be his?

B.—The situation is that of him who is helpless, cannot act, in the event cannot paint, since he is obliged to paint. The act is of him who, helpless, unable to act, acts, in the event paints, since he is obliged to paint.

D.—Why is he obliged to paint?

B.—I don't know.

D.—Why is he helpless to paint?

B.—Because there is nothing to paint and nothing to paint with.

D.—And the result, you say, is art of a new order?

B.—Among those whom we call great artists, I can think of none whose concern was not predominantly with his expressive possibilities, those of his vehicle, those of humanity. The assumption underlying all painting is that the domain of the maker is the domain of the feasible. The much to express, the little to express, the ability to express much, the ability to express little, merge in the common anxiety to express as much as possible, or as truly as possible, or as finely as possible, to the best of one's ability. What—

D.—One moment. Are you suggesting that the painting of van Velde is inexpressive?

B.—(*A fortnight later*) Yes.

D.—You realize the absurdity of what you advance?

B.—I hope I do.

D.—What you say amounts to this: the form of expression known as painting, since for obscure reasons we are obliged to speak of painting, has had to wait for van Velde to be rid of the misapprehension under which it had laboured so long and so bravely, namely, that its function was to express, by means of paint.

B.—Others have felt that art is not necessarily expression. But the numerous attempts made to make painting independent of its occasion have only succeeded in enlarging its repertory. I suggest that van Velde is the first whose painting is bereft, rid if you prefer, of occasion in every shape and form, ideal as well as material, and the first whose hands have not been tied by the certitude that expression is an impossible act.

D.—But might it not be suggested, even by one tolerant of this fantastic theory, that the occasion of his painting is his predicament, and that it is expressive of the impossibility to express?

B.—No more ingenious method could be devised for restoring him, safe and sound, to the bosom of Saint Luke. But let us for once, be foolish enough not to turn tail. All have turned wisely tail, before the ultimate penury, back to the mere misery where destitute virtuous mothers may steal stale bread for their starving brats. There is more than a difference of degree between being short, short of the world, short of self, and being without these esteemed commodities. The one is a predicament, the other not.

D.—But you have already spoken of the predicament of van Velde.

B.—I should not have done so.

D.—You prefer the purer view that here at last is a painter who does not paint, does not pretend to paint. Come, come, my dear fellow, make some kind of connected statement and then go away.

B.—Would it not be enough if I simply went away?

D.—No. You have begun. Finish. Begin again and go on until you have finished. Then go away. Try and bear in mind that the subject under discussion is not yourself, not the Sufist Al-Haqq, but a particular Dutchman by name van Velde, hitherto erroneously referred to as an *artiste peintre*.

B.—How would it be if I first said what I am pleased to fancy he is, fancy he does, and then that it is more than likely that he is and does quite otherwise? Would not that be an excellent issue out of all our afflictions? He happy, you happy, I happy, all three bubbling over with happiness.

D.—Do as you please. But get it over.

B.—There are many ways in which the thing I am trying in vain to say may be tried in vain to be said. I have experimented, as you know, both in public and in private, under duress, through faintness of heart, through weakness of mind, with two or three hundred. The pathetic antithesis possession-poverty was perhaps not the most tedious. But we begin to weary of it, do we not? The realization that art has always been bourgeois, though it may dull our pain before the achievements of the socially progressive, is finally of scant interest. The analysis of the relation between the artist and his occasion, a relation always regarded as indispensable, does not seem to have been very productive either, the reason being perhaps that it lost its way in disquisitions on the nature of occasion. It is obvious that for the artist obsessed with his expressive vocation, anything and everything is doomed to become occasion, including, as is apparently to some extent the case with Masson, the pursuit of occasion, and the every man his own wife experiments of the spiritual Kandinsky. No painting is more replete than Mondrian's. But if the occasion appears as an unstable term of relation, the artist, who is the other term, is hardly less so, thanks to his warren of modes and attitudes. The objections to this dualist view of the creative process are unconvincing. Two things are established, however precariously: the aliment, from fruits on plates to low mathematics and self-commiseration, and its manner of dispatch. All that should concern us is the acute and increasing anxiety of the relation itself, as though shadowed more and more darkly by a sense of invalidity, of inadequacy, of existence at the expense of all that it excludes, all that it blinds to. The history of painting, here we go again, is the history of its attempts to escape from this sense of failure, by means of more authentic, more ample, less exclusive relations between representer and representee, in a kind of tropism towards a light as to the nature of which the best opinions continue to vary, and with a kind of Pythagorean terror, as though the irrationality of pi were an offence against the deity, not to mention his creature. My case, since I am in the dock, is that van Velde is the first to desist from this estheticized automatism, the first to admit that to be an artist is to fail, as no other dare fail, that failure is his world and the shrink from its desertion, art and craft, good housekeeping, living. No, no, allow me to expire. I know that all that is required now, in order to bring even this horrible matter to an acceptable conclusion, is to make of this submission, this admission, this fidelity to failure, a new occasion, a new term of relation, and of the act which, unable to act, obliged to act, he makes, an expressive act, even if only of itself, of its impossibility, of its obligation. I know that my inability to do so places myself, and perhaps an innocent, in what I think is still called an unenviable situation, familiar to psychiatrists. For what is this coloured plane, that was not there before. I don't know what it is, having never seen anything like it before. It seems to have nothing to do with art, in any case, if my memories of art are correct. (*Prepares to go.*)

D.—Are you not forgetting something?

B.—Surely that is enough?

D.—I understood your number was to have two parts. The first was to consist in your saying what you—er—thought. This I am prepared to believe you have done. The second—

B.—(*Remembering, warmly*) Yes, yes, I am mistaken, I am mistaken.

INDEX